Listening To

The Beatles

Reference Series
Tom Schultheiss, Series Editor

1. **ALL TOGETHER NOW**
The First Complete Beatles Discography, 1961-1975
by Harry Castleman & Walter J. Podrazik

2. **THE BEATLES AGAIN**
Sequel to All Together Now
by Harry Castleman & Walter J. Podrazik

3. **A DAY IN THE LIFE**
The Beatles Day-By-Day, 1960-1970
by Tom Schultheiss

4. **THINGS WE SAID TODAY**
The Complete Lyrics and a Concordance to The Beatles' Songs, 1962-1970
by Colin Campbell & Allan Murphy

5. **YOU CAN'T DO THAT!**
Beatles Bootlegs & Novelty Records, 1963-1980
by Charles Reinhart

6. **SURF'S UP!**
The Beach Boys On Record, 1961-1981
by Brad Elliott

7. **COLLECTING THE BEATLES**
An Introduction & Price Guide to Fab Four Collectibles, Records & Memorabilia
by Barbara Fenick

8. **JAILHOUSE ROCK**
The Bootleg Records of Elvis Presley, 1970-1983
by Lee Cotten & Howard A. DeWitt

9. **THE LITERARY LENNON**
A Comedy of Letters
The First Study of All the Major and Minor Writings of John Lennon
by Dr. James Sauceda

10. **THE END OF THE BEATLES?**
Sequel to The Beatles Again and All Together Now
by Harry Castleman & Walter J. Podrazik

11. **HERE, THERE & EVERYWHERE**
The First International Beatles Bibliography, 1962-1982
by Carol D. Terry

12. **CHUCK BERRY**
Rock 'N' Roll Music
Second Edition, Revised
by Howard A. DeWitt

13. **ALL SHOOK UP**
Elvis Day-By-Day, 1954-1977
by Lee Cotten

14. **WHO'S NEW WAVE IN MUSIC**
An Illustrated Encyclopedia, 1976-1982
by David Bianco

15. **THE ILLUSTRATED DISCOGRAPHY OF SURF MUSIC, 1961-1965**
Second Edition, Revised
by John Blair

16. **COLLECTING THE BEATLES**
Volume 2
An Introduction & Price Guide to Fab Four Collectibles, Records & Memorabilia
by Barbara Fenick

17. **HEART OF STONE**
The Definitive Rolling Stones Discography, 1962-1983
by Felix Aeppli

18. **BEATLEFAN**
The Authoritative Publication of Record For Fans of the Beatles, Volumes 1 & 2
Reprint Edition, With Additions

19. **YESTERDAY'S PAPERS**
The Rolling Stones In Print, 1963-1984
by Jessica MacPhail

20. **EVERY LITTLE THING**
The Definitive Guide To Beatles Recording Variations, Rare Mixes & Other Musical Oddities, 1958-1986
by William McCoy & Mitchell McGeary

21. **STRANGE DAYS**
The Music of John, Paul, George & Ringo Twenty Years On
by Walter J. Podrazik

22. **SEQUINS & SHADES**
The Michael Jackson Reference Guide
by Carol D. Terry

23. **WILD & INNOCENT**
The Recordings of Bruce Springsteen, 1972-1985
by Brad Elliott

24. **TIME IS ON MY SIDE**
The Rolling Stones Day-By-Day, 1962-1986
by Alan Stewart & Cathy Sanford

Available only through Popular Culture, Ink., P.O. Box 1839, Ann Arbor, Michigan 48106
Phone 1(800) 678-8828 or (313) 973-1460.

25	**HEAT WAVE** The Motown Fact Book by David Bianco			

Remembrances Series
Tom Schultheiss, Series Editor

25 **HEAT WAVE**
The Motown Fact Book
by David Bianco

26 **BEATLEFAN**
The Authoritative Publication of Record
For Fans of the Beatles,
Volumes 3 & 4
Reprint Edition, With Additions

27 **RECONSIDER BABY**
The Definitive Elvis
Sessionography, 1954-1977
Reprint Edition, With Additions
by Ernst Jorgensen, Erik Rasmussen &
Johnny Mikkelsen

28 **THE MONKEES**
A Manufactured Image
The Ultimate Reference Guide To
Monkee Memories & Memorabilia
by Ed Reilly, Maggie McManus &
Bill Chadwick

29 **RETURN TO SENDER**
The First Complete Discography Of Elvis
Tribute & Novelty Records, 1956-1986
by Howard Banney

30 **THE CHILDREN OF NUGGETS**
The Definitive Guide To
"Psychedelic Sixties" Punk Rock
On Compilation Albums
by David Walters

31 **SHAKE, RATTLE & ROLL**
The Golden Age of American Rock 'N' Roll,
Volume 1: 1952-1955
by Lee Cotten

32 **THE ILLUSTRATED DISCOGRAPHY
OF HOT ROD MUSIC, 1961-1965**
by John Blair & Stephen McParland

33 **POSITIVELY BOB DYLAN**
A Thirty-Year Discography, Concert &
Recording Session Guide, 1960-1989
by Michael Krogsgaard

34 **OFF THE RECORD**
Motown By Master Number, 1959-1989
Volume I: Singles
by Reginald J. Bartlette

35 **LISTENING TO THE BEATLES**
An Audiophile's Guide to
The Sound of the Fab Four,
Volume I: Singles
by David Schwartz

Remembrances Series
Tom Schultheiss, Series Editor

1 **AS I WRITE THIS LETTER**
An American Generation
Remembers The Beatles
by Marc A. Catone

2 **THE LONGEST COCKTAIL PARTY**
An Insider's Diary of The Beatles,
Their Million-Dollar Apple Empire
and Its Wild Rise and Fall
Reprint Edition, With Additions
by Richard DiLello

3 **AS TIME GOES BY**
Living In The Sixties
Reprint Edition, With Additions
by Derek Taylor

4 **A CELLARFUL OF NOISE**
Reprint Edition, With Additions
by Brian Epstein

5 **THE BEATLES AT THE BEEB**
The Story of Their Radio Career,
1962-1965
Reprint Edition, With Additions
by Kevin Howlett

6 **THE BEATLES READER**
A Selection of Contemporary Views, News
& Reviews of The Beatles In Their Heyday
by Charles P. Neises

7 **THE BEATLES DOWN UNDER**
The 1964 Australia & New Zealand Tour
Reprint Edition, With Additions
by Glenn A. Baker

8 **LONG LONELY HIGHWAY**
A 1950's Elvis Scrapbook
Reprint Edition, With Additions
by Ger Rijff

9 **IKE'S BOYS**
The Story Of The Everly Brothers
by Phyllis Karpp

Trivia Series
Tom Schultheiss, Series Editor

1 **NOTHING IS BEATLEPROOF**
Advanced Beatles Trivia
for Fab Four Fanciers
by Michael J. Hockinson

Available only through Popular Culture, Ink., P.O. Box 1839, Ann Arbor, Michigan 48106
Phone 1(800) 678-8828 or (313) 973-1460.

Listening To The Beatles

An Audiophile's Guide To
The Sound Of The Fab Four

Volume I:
Bootlegs & Singles

by
David Schwartz

Popular Culture, Ink.
1990

COPYRIGHT © 1990
BY DAVID SCHWARTZ
ALL RIGHTS RESERVED

No part of this data may be reproduced, stored in a retrieval system, or transmitted in any form or by any means, electronic, mechanical, photocopying, recording, or otherwise, without prior written permission of the copyright proprietor thereof.

The inclusion of photographs of bootleg or counterfeit recordings and/or the associated jackets of such recordings in this volume should not be construed or interpreted as an endorsement of the practice of record piracy on the part of the author or the publisher.

Book design and layout by Tom Schultheiss.
Computer programs by Alex Przebienda.
Cover design by Diane Bareis.
All cover art is copyright © 1990 by Popular Culture, Ink.
Back cover photo of the author by Sandra Schwartz.
Photos of record jackets and sleeves are copyright
© 1990 by Richard's Photography.
All Rights Reserved.

ISBN 1-56075-005-7
LC 89-92316

Published by Popular Culture, Ink., P.O. Box 1839,
Ann Arbor, MI 48106 U.S.A.

"The best rock-and-roll books in the world!"

Dedication

This book is dedicated, with all my love, to my wife Sandy. Words cannot adequately express all I'd like to say. You have made my life! You're my daily inspiration and guiding light, my treasured friend, companion, lover, confidant, wife. You are my happiness and joy. *I LOVE YOU.*

And Then I Think Of You!

In Memoriam

To the memory of my mother-in-law, Rhea C. Kane, with thanks and love. Your love and encouragement was always appreciated and is still felt by Sandy and me. As the most voracious reader I knew, I'm sorry you didn't get to see this book, but more importantly, I'm sorry you missed our darling Sarah.

Sandy and I miss you very much.

Contents

Preface	xv
Acknowledgements	xvii
List of Illustrations	xi
Introduction	xix

SECTION ONE: BOOTLEG RECORDS

Bootlegs: What and Why?	3
7-inch Bootlegs	7
12-inch Bootlegs	37
Ratings Summaries	165
Table 1: 7-inch Ratings in Review Order	166
Table 2: 7-inch Ratings in Numerical Order	167
Table 3: 12-inch Ratings in Review Order	168
Table 4: 12-inch Ratings in Numerical Order	170

SECTION TWO: COMMERCIAL SINGLES

The Mass Market	175
Getting to Know Your Discs	175
Reading the Records	176
Singles	179
Reading These Reviews	181
Ratings Summaries	303
Single Package Comparisons	304
Individual Singles Comparisons	306
Summary of Individual Comparisons	308

GLOSSARY	309
INDEXES	
Song & Record Title Index	315
People, Places & Things Index	327

List of Illustrations

BOOTLEG SINGLES

Crying, Waiting, Hoping/Till There Was You	17
Have You Heard The Word/Futting Around	31
How Do You Do It/Revolution (live)	8
Love Of The Loved/Love Of The Loved	33
Memphis/Love Of The Loved	12
Searchin'/Like Dreamers Do	14
Sheik Of Araby/September In The Rain	11
Strawberry Fields Forever/Penny Lane	29
Sure To Fall/Money	16
Three Cool Cats/Hello Little Girl	9
To Know Him Is To Love Him/Besame Mucho	19

BOOTLEG EPs

By Royal Command	20, 22
Exclusive! Beatles Interviews 1966	25
From Us To You	35
The Really Big Shew	33
Souvenir Of Their Visit To America	29
Television Outtakes	27
Top Of The Pops	23
Twickenham Jams	31

BOOTLEG LPs

The Beatles At Shea	104
The Beatles At The BEEB Volume 1	122
The Beatles At The BEEB Volume 2	122
The Beatles At The BEEB Volume 3	127
The Beatles At The BEEB Volume 4	127
The Beatles At The BEEB Volume 5	131
The Beatles At The BEEB Volume 6	131
The Beatles At The BEEB Volume 7	136
The Beatles At The BEEB Volume 8	136
The Beatles At The BEEB Volume 9	140
The Beatles At The BEEB Volume 10	140
The Beatles At The BEEB Volume 11	144

Title	Page
The Beatles At The BEEB Volume 12	144
The Beatles At The BEEB Volume 13	148
The Beatles Broadcasts	53
The Beatles Budokan 1966	86
The Beatles Collector's Items	56
The Beatles Conquer America	82
The Beatles Live At Abbey Road Studios (2 LPs)	38
The Beatles Mach Shau!	90
The Beatles On Stage In Japan, The 1966 Tour	63
The Beatles Stockholm & Blackpool	86
Beautiful Dreamer	48
Casualties (Picture disc)	44
The Decca Tapes (Picture disc)	72
Dig It!	105
Don't Pass Me By (2 LPs)	56
EMI Outtakes	46
The Get Back Journals (12 LPs)	90
Hahst Az Sun (Two Weeks In January, 1969) (2 LPs)	38
Have You Heard The Word	66
Johnny & The Moondogs: Silver Days Air Time	42
Judy	66
The Lost BEEBs	118
Meet The BEEB	115
1967	115
No. 3 Abbey Road	52
Not For Sale	76
Not Guilty: The Beatles	78
Nothing Is Real	98
Original Audition Tape - Circa 1962	60
The Original Greatest Hits	60
Outtakes Vol. 1	69
Outtakes Vol. 2	70
Quarrymen Rehearse With Stu Sutcliffe Spring 1960	162
Return To Abbey Road	110
Sessions	100
Top Of The Pops	63
Ultra Rare Trax Vol. 1 & Vol. 2 (2 LPs)	148
Ultra Rare Trax Vol. 3 & Vol. 4 (2 LPs)	155
Ultra Rare Trax Vol. 5 & Vol. 6 (2 LPs)	155

An Audiophile's Guide to the Sound of the Fab Four

COMMERCIALLY AVAILABLE SINGLES

Act Naturally	293
All You Need Is Love	244
Baby, You're A Rich Man	247
Back In The U.S.S.R	278
The Ballad Of John And Yoko	266
The Beatles' Movie Medley	287
Can't Buy Me Love	204
Come Together	271
A Day In The Life	284
Day Tripper	230
Eleanor Rigby	238
For You Blue	291
From Me To You	192
Get Back	263
A Hard Day's Night	210
Hello Goodbye	247, 250
Help!	222
Hey Jude	258
I Am The Walrus	250
I Feel Fine	213
I Want To Hold Your Hand	200, 201
I Saw Her Standing There	293
I'm Down	226
Lady Madonna	254
Let It Be	275
Love Me Do	182, 184
Nowhere Man	296
Old Brown Shoe	268
Paperback Writer	230
Penny Lane	241
Please Please Me	189
P.S. I Love You	186
Revolution	260
Sgt. Pepper's Lonely Hearts Club Band	282
She's A Woman	216
She Loves You	196
Something	271
Strawberry Fields Forever	241
Thank You Girl	194
This Boy	204
Ticket To Ride	218

xiii

Twist And Shout	**279**
We Can Work It Out	**226**
Yellow Submarine	**234**
Yes It Is	**220**
Yesterday	**298, 299**
You Can't Do That	**207**
You Know My Name (Look Up The Number)	**275**

Preface

If you enjoy listening to the Beatles, this book is for you. Certainly the Beatles changed the world in the areas of style and fashion, but their music was (and still is) their main contribution. This book focuses on two of the most significant areas of listening to the Beatles -- songs on singles and bootlegs.

While there have been artists with more and/or better-selling record albums than the Beatles, there has never been, and never will be, anyone more successful as singles artists. Think of a successful singles artist -- Michael Jackson, for example. He's had a string of hits from his **Off The Wall**, **Thriller**, and **Bad** albums. A great track record, you say; check out the *Billboard* magazine from April 1964 and you'll know instantly why Michael bought the Lennon/McCartney song publishing catalogue!

Part of the thrill of reliving the Beatles' era via their timeless music is the consideration and discussion of their vinyl singles heritage. While the legacy of vinyl is dying in America, it is nonetheless an essential part of the Beatles' story. Feeling the rush of a two-and-a-half minute gem like *Can't Buy Me Love*, flipping the small record with your hands in a moment of silence and anticipation, and enjoying the renewed thrill of listening to *You Can't Do That* is an experience that is unattainable with LPs, cassettes, or CDs. After seven stirring minutes of *Hey Jude*, the time needed to turn the record over gives you a chance to recharge your batteries before being bombarded by *Revolution*.

While first generation Beatles fans probably all started out enjoying the group's music on inexpensive sound systems or little transistor radios, as we've grown up so has our collective investment in audio equipment. We now desire good quality software (records, tapes, CDs) to play on our stereo hardware. Is it possible to still enjoy the Beatles' singles and get good sound at the same time? You bet it is, and that is what this book will help you to do. You'll be able to find the very best-sounding singles from among those available in America, England, Australia, and Japan, and hear them as they were meant to be heard -- as close as possible to a live performance.

Why are bootlegs important? It is EMI, Paul, George, and Ringo that make them so. By trying to perpetuate a perfect image, the lore (and value) of unreleased Beatles material has grown substantially over the two decades since the group's breakup. Paul McCartney has stated on numerous occasions that the Beatles released all the music that they wanted to release. Anything left unreleased was not up to their standards of quality, and should never see the light of day. He speaks as if the image and place in history of the Beatles will be tarnished if the EMI vaults are opened, but he could not be more wrong! From the fan's point of view, access to unreleased material serves only to explain the genius behind the Beatles' music, and to enhance our appreciation of their artistry. Has release by Rykodisc Records of many David Bowie rarities tarnished his image? No. It has only served to delight his fans. Would Paul McCartney really turn down an opportunity to obtain a copy of a bootleg featuring ten never-before-released Buddy Holly recordings? Think about that one.

The Beatles love of Chuck Berry can only be appreciated by hearing their BBC performances of his material. The development of George's guitar solo on *I Saw Her Standing There* through the many takes leading up to the "keeper" is quite interesting, as are the differences between Take 1 and the officially released versions of both *Can't Buy Me Love* and *While My Guitar Gently Weeps*.

As long as EMI refuses to officially open its vaults, bootlegs will continue to be historically and musically important. The question is, how do you know what to expect from a particular bootleg in terms of content and sound quality? The bootleg section of this book will give you the answer, with track-by-track sound quality evaluations of the best of the older and the more recent bootlegs.

If you love listening to the Beatles, and want to hear the cream of the sonic crop in singles and bootlegs, read on. You'll be guided to many auditory delights. Isn't it only fitting to listen to the best sounding records by the very best band in rock music history?

D.S.

Acknowledgements

To Sarah,
    Although you're now too young to read this, I want to tell you that Mom and I love you very much. You've truly made us into a family. You're our pride and joy!

To Mom and Dad,
    It is with much love that I thank you for everything! I could never imagine anyone growing up in better circumstances than I did. Your constant support, friendship, help, and love for Sandy and me are greatly treasured. Your interest and support in Jake's and my Beatle-ing has always been great!
    P.S. - Sarah loves you, too!

To Jake,
    You're the best brother anyone could ever wish to have! May we always stay friends and share in the Beatles collection - there are Japanese red vinyls yet to get. If someday our children can be as close as we are, they will have nothing but blue skies and red roses before them.

To Sue,
    You're the nicest and finest person I could ever have for a sister-in-law. Stay happy and share nothing but good things and times with Jake forever.

To My Family,
    Thanks for all the good times and feelings throughout the years. I wish health and happiness to all. I love you.

To my co-workers at Man-Machine Systems at RCA (oops, GE),
    The spirit of camaraderie and good will that exists in our group is something to behold. May each of you have continued professional success and personal happiness.

To My Friend the Beatlefest Sound-Alike Performer,
    Get rid of that tape and get a music stand!

To Steve Rabeler,
Thanks for being the first person I knew who ordered a book. I wish you success in all you do (remember, send me a promo copy of your first record).

To Todd Beck,
Thanks for the A above middle C!

A special hello to my friend Jeff Kleinbaum! Our correspondence over the past years has been wonderful; when will you next come visit? It's your turn to send a tape!

Thanks to Joel Glazier for all of the wonderful work on behalf of the John Lennon Peace Forest in Israel for the JNF. Thanks also for keeping the "Paul Is Dead" saga alive; when is the book coming out?

Thanks to John Gallant for getting Jake and me the French Box and all of the other discs. Be and stay well!

Thanks to Charles Rosenay!!! for the great fanzine *Good Day Sunshine*, and for giving me a continuing outlet for my Beatle thoughts and opinions.

Thanks to Joe Pope for *Strawberry Fields Forever*. Glad you're back!

To Mark and Carol Lapidos for staging Beatlefests; please never stop. When will you make the John Lennon Peace Forest the official charity? How about having Joel Glazier give his "Paul Is Dead" presentation at the next NYC 'fest?

To Richard of Richard's Photography in Edgewater Park, NJ; thanks for doing such an outstanding job of photographing the record covers, and for being so enthusiastic about the project in general.

Thanks to Castleman and Podrazik for the great discographies.

Special thanks to Tom Schultheiss for being receptive to my unsolicited idea of doing this book! Your advice throughout the project has been greatly appreciated. This book has been a long time coming, but it's finally out!

And, of course, to John, Paul, George, and Ringo for the best music this planet has ever heard!

Introduction

WHY THIS BOOK WAS WRITTEN

With the mindless event of December 8, 1980, the Beatles as a group became a permanent piece of history. Their music, as with all great art, nonetheless continues to play a significant role in the social and cultural evolution of our planet. This fact is borne out by the acceptance and appreciation of the Beatles' music by a generation of fans as yet unborn when EMI's Abbey Road Studies echoed to the sound of the four lads from Liverpool.

It has been nearly three decades since the appearance of *Love Me Do/P.S. I Love You*, EMI's first Beatles release on the Parlophone label in England on October 5, 1962. In those decades the Beatles' recordings have sold in countless numbers throughout the world. Estimates place the actual figure somewhere in the hundreds of millions, although it is long past the time when an exact total can be known.

The Beatles' music has been the most universally accepted of all the popular recording artists of the twentieth century. Their records have been published by EMI in more than forty-five countries around the world - from the Americas to South Africa to Iceland to Malaysia to India to almost every country in between. This fact alone shows the creative and artistic magnitude of the Beatles' achievement. Not only has it withstood the test of time, but it has transcended the barriers of language and culture as well.

The impact of the Beatles' music continues to spread with every passing day. The works of the Beatles form the best selling catalogue of any group in the history of popular music, with the number of units sold growing by millions every year. That fact was the primary impetus behind the writing of this book.

Many works have been written detailing the lives of John, Paul, George, and Ringo - from their childhood years through their careers as solo recording artists. Discographies have been published, most notably the three-volume set by Castleman and Podrazik, as well as books reviewing and commenting on their music and its impact upon the world.

What this book is intended to do is comment upon the physical recordings, and on how the Beatles' music sounds when you unwrap that new record and place it on your turntable. Evaluative judgments will generally be made about sonics, not content, for it is safe to say that by reading this book you've already shown your appreciation for the Beatles' music.

The need for this book is twofold. First of all, in the almost thirty years since the Beatles started recording for EMI, the art and science of music reproduction have made tremendous advances. Even modest home audio systems of today have broken the bounds of early sixties state-of-the-art equipment. The majority of today's homes have audio systems that offer a degree of musical realism that was all but unachievable two decades ago.

Advances in both software (records and tapes) and hardware (audio equipment) have made it possible to capture and present a listening experience in the home that comes surprisingly close to perfect reproduction of an artist's original performance. Because of these advances the scrutiny and potential enjoyment of the best music available (certainly the Beatles fall into this category) have been heightened. It is important, however, to remember that a chain is only as strong as its weakest link. A poorly recorded or manufactured record or tape will not be transformed into heavenly art by a quality audio system. Garbage in, garbage out, as computer buffs say.

The second need for this book stems from the proliferation of records by the Beatles in the marketplace. Throughout the world, EMI is continually repackaging and reissuing older material. Do these repackages offer improved sonics in comparison to the 1960's originals? The answer to this question alone could save fans and collectors millions of dollars every year.

Repackages and reissues from EMI are not the only source of this proliferation, however. Two other areas are very important: import/export, and audiophile pressings. In this day and age it is possible to go into a record store and find Beatles records from England, Germany, Japan, Australia, France, and other countries side by side with domestic American releases. The import/export phenomenon has narrowed the price gap between domestic and foreign pressings, and in so doing has created a dilemma for the Beatles fan and collector. Is an extra few dollars for an imported record a wise investment? If so, which pressing is the best? When even an American pressing costs $8 - $10, these questions become very important.

To the uninitiated, an audiophile pressing found at at a record store can be almost indistinguishable, visually speaking, from a regular domestic pressing. Other than a small note on the jacket, the album cover is usually identical. The price, however, is quite a different matter. What makes the **Abbey Road** album manufactured by Mobile Fidelity Sound Lab command an $18.99 price, and is it worth it? How about **Sgt. Pepper's Lonely Hearts Club Band** for $50, or **The Beatles/The Collection** for $325? What can a Beatles collector expect for these prices? In the days when an LP was available for $3.99 not much was lost on a bad purchase, but at $50 great caution must be exercised.

It is hoped that this book will serve as a shoppers' guide to the Beatles' recordings. When it becomes time to replace or upgrade your tired and worn Beatles records, this book will direct you to the Sonic Heroes available among the many Vinyl Villains hiding in the record marketplace.

How To Use This Book

This work consists of two physical volumes, the first of which you are reading. In order to cover the subject in its entirety and not overwhelm the Beatles fan and collector with an encyclopedia-sized work, the subject has been divided into equal parts. "How To Use This Book" deals with the contents of both volumes. It is intended to give the reader an overview of the entire subject: Listening To The Beatles. This volume contains sections covering bootlegs and singles, while the second volume covers EPs and LPs (including audiophile discs), and compact discs.

The main portion of this two-volume work, "THE MUSIC," is itself divided into three sections, each dealing with a different portion of the Beatles' record marketplace: "SECTION ONE: BOOTLEGS," "SECTION TWO: THE MASS MARKET" (singles, EPs, LPs, and compact discs treated separately), and "SECTION THREE: FOR AUDIOPHILES ONLY."

"SECTION ONE: BOOTLEGS" (contained in the volume you are reading), deals with a very important, but very illegal portion of the Beatles' recorded output. The major appeal of bootlegs lies in the opportunity they afford to hear otherwise unreleased or unrecorded (commercially, that is) performances. Very few bootlegs can be considered sonically outstanding; in fact, many are only fair at best.

Given these facts, this section is offered as an accompanying piece to three previously published books about Beatles bootlegs: *You Can't Do That* by Charles Reinhart (Popular Culture, Ink., originally published by Pierian Press in 1980), *Do You Want To Know A Secret* by

L. R. E. King (Storyteller Productions, 1988), and *Fixing A Hole* by L. R. E. King (Storyteller Productions, 1989).

Reinhart's "Beatles bootleg bible," as it has been affectionately called, is a discography including nearly 900 entries. Discographic and related information (date of recording, location of performance, source, songs included, etc.) is therein provided for the majority of Beatles bootlegs known to be in existence at that time.

Both of L. R. E. King's books pick up where Reinhart concluded, and provide similar information for the more recently released Beatles bootlegs. King does include comments about sound quality, but always in one-line general statements like "Good to excellent mono."

As risky as it may ahve been to spend eight or ten dollars on a new Beatles album from Capitol Records, buying bootlegs is an entire order of magnitude more dangerous (from a sound quality standpoint). The search for that 1963 live Beatles performance in Sweden, for example, may involve the expenditure of a great deal of money for discs that are mostly hum, hiss, or snap, crackle, and pop.

The bootlegs section includes track-by-track reviews of about seventy Beatles bootlegs - LPs, EPs, and singles. It is intended to provide information and guidance (although not encouragement and facilitation of purchase, due both to legal and ethical constraints) for the bootleg collector. Every review is cross-referenced to *You Can't Do That* or to L. R. E. King's books, so that more information is easily found when needed or desired. A sonic grading system of "A" through "E" has been devised (and is explained in the bootlegs section) to rate every track on each disc.

"SECTION TWO: THE MASS MARKET" addresses the commercial releases of the Beatles' music. The major focus is upon LPs, although singles, EPs, and CDs are included as well. The English releases by EMI serve as the organizational foundation for this second section. Reviews of every Beatles album released in England are included, along with reviews, comments, and comparisons to pressings from Japan, the United States, and other countries. England serves as the foundation because these LPs are arranged in the track sequence chosen by the Beatles, except for "after that fact" repackagings that were generally created independently of John, Paul, George, and Ringo. Since many countries altered the original LP track sequences (most notably Capitol Records in the U.S.), albums are frequently cross-referenced within this section. (LPs are reviewed in *Listening To The Beatles, Volume 2.*)

Because the Beatles were such a singles-oriented group in their early days (they did have *Billboard*'s "Top Five" all in the same week in April of 1964), reviews are included of many 45s. Throughout the world,

EMI has repackaged the singles in various boxed sets (many still in print); in England, the 20th anniversary reissue series was launched - each single appearing as a picture disc on its special day (*Love Me Do/ P.S. I Love You* was first on October 5, 1982); and Capitol in the U.S. has always kept the Beatles' singles in print in one form or another (although at the time of this writing, reports have Capitol deleting all but ten of them). Reviews are arranged by song rather than record, since most countries chose to issue their own couplings. (Singles are covered in this volume.)

Although the U.S. was not very active in issuing Beatles EPs - Vee Jay's **Souvenir Of Their Visit To America** and Capitol's **4 By The Beatles** and **Four By The Beatles** were the only such releases - imported EPs have long been a favorite of collectors. Reviews are included of EPs from England, Japan, Germany, and other countries. As with the reviews of singles, these are arranged by song rather than by disc. (EPs are reviewed in *Listening To The Beatles, Volume 2.*)

Because "SECTION TWO" focuses on the mass market, emphasis is placed upon currently available pressings. Original pressings are generally sought for their value as collectibles, not as sonic gems. Besides, the chances of finding an original pressing that is still sealed or in pristine mint condition are very remote. If you were so lucky as to locate one, you would be very wise to leave it intact and never let it touch your turntable. Its value as a collectable would most definitely surpass any sonic distinctions it might posses.

"SECTION THREE: FOR AUDIOPHILES ONLY" (contained in *Listening To The Beatles, Volume 2*), focuses on the high-priced, limited edition world of audiophile records. By measure of number of units sold this is a trivial portion of the Beatles marketplace, but by measure of sonic quality and value this is a most prominent area. No discussion of the sonic merits of the Beatles' recordings would be complete without it.

The number of audiophile releases to date has been very small, and almost all have been from one U.S. company, Mobile Fidelity Sound Lab of Chatsworth, California. EMI has not yet entered this field directly in any country other than Japan, where Toshiba-EMI has issued a half-speed mastered version of the **Abbey Road** album. Many of the items reviewed in this section have reached or are approaching sold-out status. It is therefore wise to be aware of the collectable value of these recordings when considering a purchase.

The audiophile record industry is currently in a declining period. Although technically far advanced, audiophile software (records and tapes) has not made a major dent in the marketplace. The majority of consumers are in need of an education in this field, so this section presents the "hows and whys" of audiophile software by way of introduction to the reviews themselves.

SECTION ONE

Bootleg Records

SECTION ONE

Bootlegs: What and Why?

Although highly illegal, bootleg recordings by the Beatles are extremely popular. In these days when EMI continually recycles and reissues familiar material, the chance to possess something new, different and out of the ordinary has become quite an alluring attraction. A 1982 reader survey conducted by the author in *Beatlefan* (one of the most popular Beatles fanzines) revealed that seventy-two percent of its readers collected bootlegs. The enormous popularity and widespread availability (despite recent FBI crackdowns) of Beatles bootlegs are the primary reasons for doing this section.

Bootleg recordings (discs or tapes) generally fall into three categories: counterfeits, pirates, and bootlegs. Counterfeit records are analogous to counterfeit money - designed to be indistinguishable from the real thing although actually worthless. These discs serve two purposes: to allow unscrupulous dealers to rip off unsuspecting customers, and to allow collectors to purchase "almost the real thing" for a reasonable price. One counterfeit record can serve to illustrate both purposes.

The Beatles Christmas Album (Apple SBC 100) has long been a favorite of collectors. This is a special case where both the rarity of the item and its contents, those wonderful Christmas messages, are attractive to collectors. Needless to say, this album, currently exchanging hands for somewhere over $100 (in mint condition), has attracted counterfeiters en masse. Originally (and still occasionally) dealers tried to pass counterfeits off as the real thing to unwary customers. Lately, however, dealers generally acknowledge copies as counterfeits and offer them for $10 - $15. This gives collectors a chance to acquire an otherwise unavailable (except on those astronomically valuable flexi-discs) piece of the Beatles legacy for a reasonable price.

Pirate recordings, although similar in origin to counterfeits, are different in execution. Whereas a counterfeit tries to pass as the real thing, a pirate does not. Although the recorded material in a pirate is a direct copy (or "dub") of a legitimate commercial release, the album cover and packaging is not. Some pirate recordings have elaborate and well-designed full-

3

color covers, while others are the simple "white cardboard with paper insert" style of most early bootlegs. **The Beatles Collectors Items** is an excellent example of a pirate collection of previously released commercial material. Consisting of rare mono and stereo versions of songs either long out of print or heretofore unavailable in America, it is packaged in a gorgeous color cover and has become quite a favorite of Beatles collectors. (More about this disc in the reviews to follow.)

Bootleg recordings can take on many forms, such as recordings of live concerts, radio or TV specials originally made for broadcast only and not for sale, and outtakes from studio sessions. Beatles bootlegs are available in all of these categories, mostly due to the unique history of the Beatles as a group.

Recordings of radio shows by the Beatles abound in the bootleg market. This is due to the fact that early in their career the Beatles were a fixture on BBC radio. American fans, not having access to the BBC, naturally are attracted to these recordings. The nationwide airing of "The Beatles At The Beeb" radio special, once thought as possibly signaling an end to the creation of this type of Beatles bootleg, has actually been bootlegged itself!

Although the Beatles toured extensively until August 1966, most of their concerts could have been billed as "The Beatles and a Cast of Thousands." The opportunity to hear a live performance unblemished by screaming fans was impossible in America, except on bootleg recordings, which provide documentaries of such concerts as Tokyo 1966 or Sweden 1963.

Being as valuable to EMI as they were, the Beatles were allowed, later in their career, almost free reign in the studio. Unlike today, where a band rehearses for weeks before entering a $200-per-hour recording studio, the Beatles did almost all of their rehearsing in the studio, much of it with the tape recorder running. This created a mass of studio outtake material for bootleggers to peddle. And peddle it they do, especially in the case of the "Let It Be" tapes (on such bootleg albums as **Sweet Apple Trax**, **Kum Back** and others).

As previously mentioned in the introduction, *You Can't Do That* by Charles Reinhart (Popular Culture, Ink.) still stands as the first, basic authoritative guide to Beatles bootlegs. By providing such information as track-by-track title listings, performance location, recording date, and performance type (live concert, radio or TV broadcast, studio outtake, etc.), this book has taken most of the mystique (and risk, speaking financially rather than legally, of course) from the prospect of purchasing Beatles bootleg recordings. Apart from some errors, part of the heritage of any classic, groundbreaking work, and the fact that it is obviously now dated in its coveraage, the main shortcoming of the book for this writer lies in its lack of "sound quality" gradings. The same shortcoming also holds for L. R. E. King's *Do*

An Audiophile's Guide to the Sound of the Fab Four

You Want To Know A Secret and *Fixing A Hole*, for even though these mention sound quality, it is in a sketchy, one-sentence-per-album manner. I realize, of course, that still others faulted these books because they did not contain bootleg price information, establishing yet another task for the author (a price guide!) beyond the bounds of the goals they originally set for himself. But even if you know what material is on a bootleg record, the risk of getting a totally unlistenable record is quite great. To put this matter in perspective, the least sonically desirable of the commercial discs reviewed in "SECTION TWO" of this book is probably better than seventy percent of all available bootlegs. It therefore seemed very important to me, without diminishing Reinhart's and King's achievements, to augment their work with a volume of this type.

In the following reviews, whenever possible, a cross reference to *You Can't Do That, Do You Want To Know A Secret*, and/or *Fixing A Hole* are provided in order to make background information easy to locate. In addition to providing detailed comments in some cases, the following grading system will be used:

A	**Excellent**	- Could possibly pass for a legitimate commercial release.
B	**Very Good**	- Some limiting of frequency range (such as loss of bass or treble) or a slight amount of extraneous noise.
C	**Fair**	- Some limiting of frequency range (such as loss of bass or treble) and a slight amount of extraneous noise.
D	**Poor**	- Significant limiting of frequency range and large amount of extraneous noise.
E	**Unlistenable**	- Unlistenable due to severe limiting of frequency range and/or tremendous amounts of extraneous noise.
N/R	No Rating	

Before reading the following reviews it must be understood that an "A" rating and glowing comments about a bootleg disc are not meant as a recommendation for purchase. Due to the illegal nature of every disc in this section, the decision to purchase must be a personal one. An in-depth essay on the legal status of bootlegs, "Everything You Always Wanted To Know About Bootlegs, But Were Too Busy Collecting Them To Ask," by Tom Schultheiss, is available as an appendix in *You Can't Do That*.

7-INCH BOOTLEGS

The following are reviews of 7-inch bootlegs. These may be singles, extended plays, 45 rpm, 33 1/3 rpm, large hole, small hole, etc. They are grouped by one common element: all are 7-inch records, except that...

The final review in this section is of a 10-inch bootleg. It is included here because it was felt that creating a section for only one disc was unnecessary.

How Do You Do It/Revolution (Live)

You Can't Do That #292

Ratings:
How Do You Do It	A-
Revolution (Live)	A

A-side recorded for George Martin on November 26, 1962; B-side recorded for David Frost TV Show in September 1968. (Large hole 45 rpm mono)

Comments:
This disc was originally pressed in four different colors of vinyl and distributed to fans attending Mystery Tour '76, the third Beatles fan convention in Boston, July/August 1976. Presented by *Strawberry Fields Forever* (*SFF*), the disc was also offered for sale to readers of that fanzine. Many generations of copies have since been issued by many bootleggers; comments here pertain only to the original record from *Strawberry Fields Forever*.

Sonically, this disc is excellent! *How Do you Do It* suffers only from a lack of very deep bass and a very slightly strained sound (as if distortion is trying to break through) on some of the vocals. These minor failings are the only things separating this from an A rating. *Revolution* earns an A rating, its only deviation from perfection being an ever-so-slightly ill-defined bass end.

Both songs show good midrange and treble definition and very little (if any) hiss. This is an outstanding record, certainly sonically worthy of a legitimate commerical release.

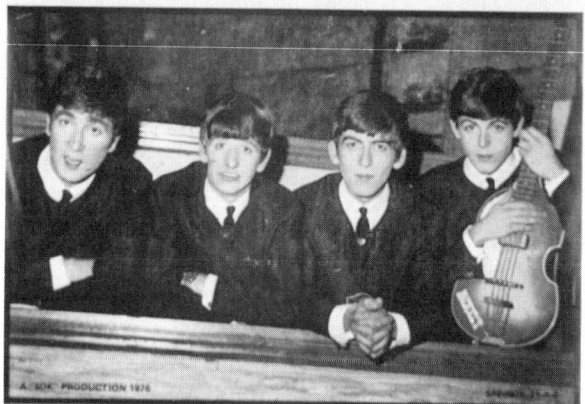
How Do You Do It/Revolution (Live) (front)

How Do You Do It/Revolution (Live) (back)

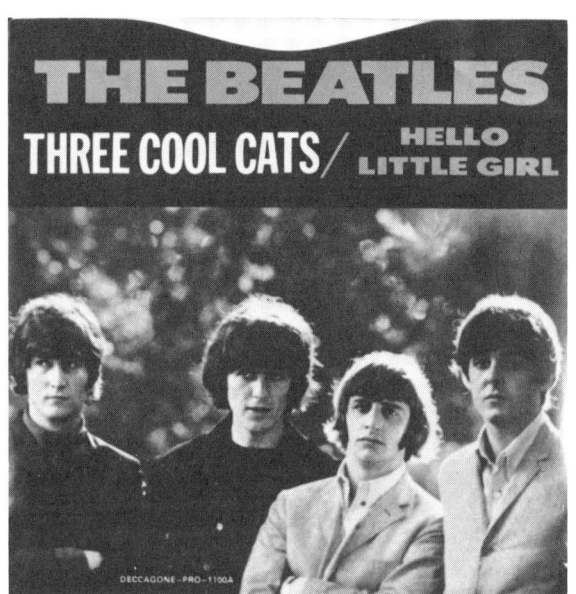

Three Cool Cats/Hello Little Girl (front)

Three Cool Cats/Hello Little Girl (back)

Three Cool Cats/Hello Little Girl Deccagone PRO-1100

You Can't Do That **#266**

Ratings:
Three Cool Cats   A
Hello Little Girl   A

From the Decca audition January 1, 1962, this is the original release from the *SFF* Beatles fan club in Boston. This came on blue vinyl with a purple label and silver printing, and has been counterfeited several times since its original release. (Large hole 45 rpm mono)

Comments:
This was the first release by *SFF* from the "Deccagone" series. As with all of the other records in this series, it has been copied by other bootleggers many times since its original release. One major clue to the identification of the original pressing is the colors of the vinyl/label/printing combination. Only the colors listed here (and this goes for every record in the series) are original. All Deccagone reviews presented in this work are of the original pressings.

Sonically this disc is a solid A, definitely the equal of most mono commerical 45s. Only a very slightly ill-defined bass end on both sides and a very slight depression in bass output on *Hello Little Girl* keep it from absolute perfection.

Sheik Of Araby/September In The Rain Deccagone PRO-1101

You Can't Do That **#478**

Ratings:
Sheik Of Araby   A-
September In The Rain   A

From the Decca audition January 1, 1962, this is the original release from the *SFF* Beatles fan club in Boston. This came on yellow vinyl with a yellow label and black printing, and has been counterfeited several times since its original release. (Large hole 45 rpm mono)

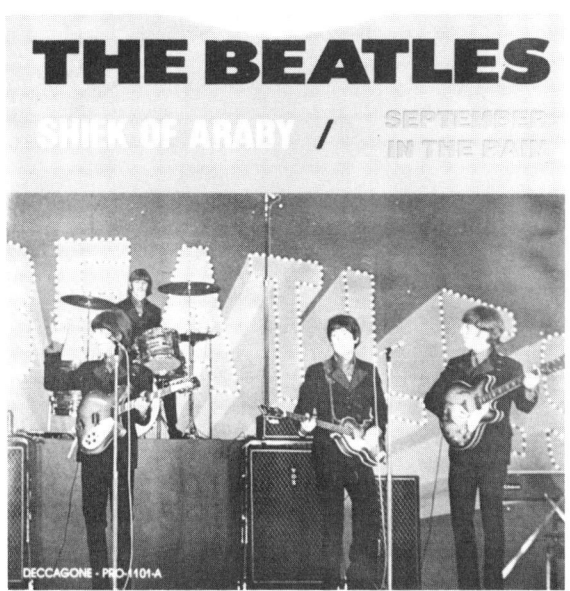

Sheik Of Araby/September In The Rain (front)

Sheik Of Araby/September In The Rain (back)

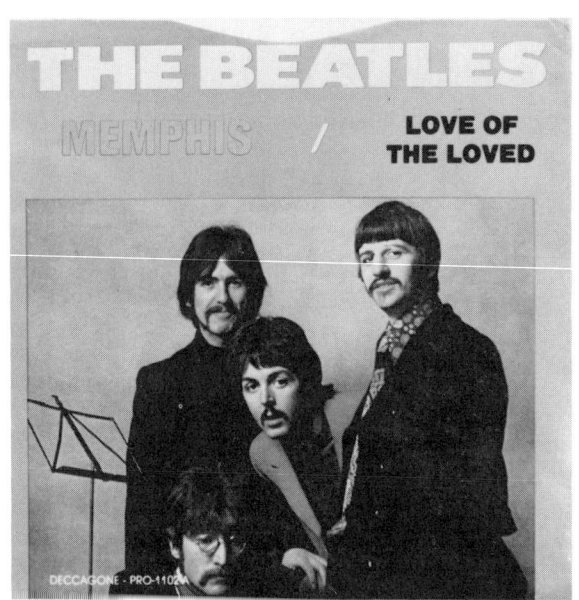

Memphis/Love Of The Loved (front)

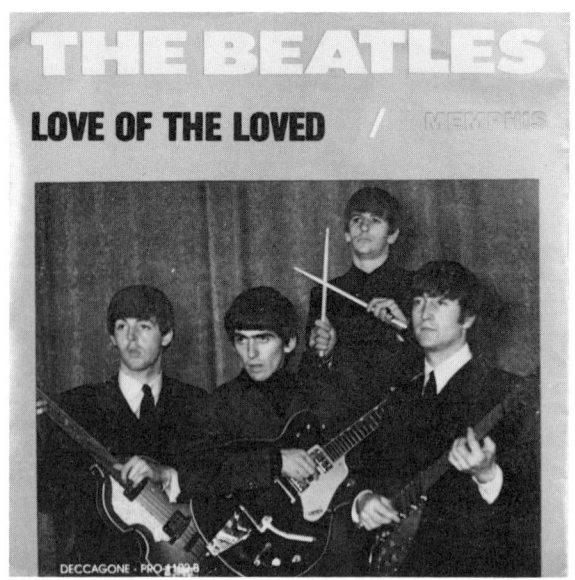

Memphis/Love Of The Loved (back)

An Audiophile's Guide to the Sound of the Fab Four

Comments:
Another sonically excellent disc from the "Deccagone" series. Both sides show very good treble extension, especially on Pete Best's cymbals. *Sheik Of Araby* only earns an A- due to the lack of much of the lower frequencies.

Memphis/Love Of The Loved Deccagone PRO-1102

You Can't Do That **#404**

Ratings:
Memphis	A
Love Of The Loved	A-

From the Decca audition January 1, 1962, this is the original release from the *SFF* Beatles fan club in Boston. This came on green vinyl with a blue label and black printing, and has been counterfeited several times since its original release. (Large hole 45 rpm mono)

Comments:
This third release from the "Deccagone" series is another fine-sounding disc. *Memphis* earns a solid A rating, with John's lead vocals clearly floating above the music - quite an achievement for a mono recording. One strange thing, however, is the lack of Pete Best's cymbals. No cymbals are present until the closing note of the song, which is a rarity for a Beatles performance.
Love Of The Loved, one of the few Lennon-McCartney compositions not officially released on record by the Beatles, is also a fine-sounding song. Its A- rating is due to a slight amount of distortion present on Paul's lead vocals, most noticeable on sibilants.

Searchin'/Like Dreamers Do Deccagone PRO-1103

You Can't Do That **#330**

Ratings:
Searchin'	A-
Like Dreamers Do	A-

Searchin'/Like Dreamers Do (front)

Searchin'/Like Dreamers Do (back)

An Audiophile's Guide to the Sound of the Fab Four

From the Decca audition January 1, 1962, this is the original release from the *SFF* Beatles fan club in Boston. This came on red vinyl with an orange label and black printing, and has been counterfeited several times since its original release. (Large hole 45 rpm mono)

Comments:
Record number four from the "Deccagone" series is another disc that is almost up to commericial standards. Both sides just miss the mark, earning A- ratings. *Searchin'* shows a slight depression of the bass frequencies, making the song sound "lightweight" in spots. *Like Dreamers Do*, although having a satisfying bottom end, only earns an A- due to some treble distortion of Paul's lead vocals, similar in sound to that found on *Love Of The Loved*.

Sure To Fall/Money Deccagone PRO-1104

You Can't Do That **#409**

Ratings:
Sure To Fall	A
Money	A-

From the Decca audition January 1, 1962, this is the original release from the *SFF* Beatles fan club in Boston. This came on clear vinyl with a white label and black printing, and has been counterfeited several times since its original release. (Large hole 45 rpm mono)

Comments:
On this fifth disc from the "Deccagone series," *Sure To Fall* earns an A rating based on its good frequency balance: bass, midrange, and treble are all presented in fine fashion. The uppermost treble is very slightly depressed, although the missing "air" or "sheen" on the cymbals is hardly noticeable. This is definitely a commercial quality recording.

Money shows a distinct lack of treble in that the cymbals and guitar harmonics are depressed. Also, John's voice is plagued by some distortion. Although these problems exist, they are only evident in comparison with a commercial record, hence an A-rating.

15

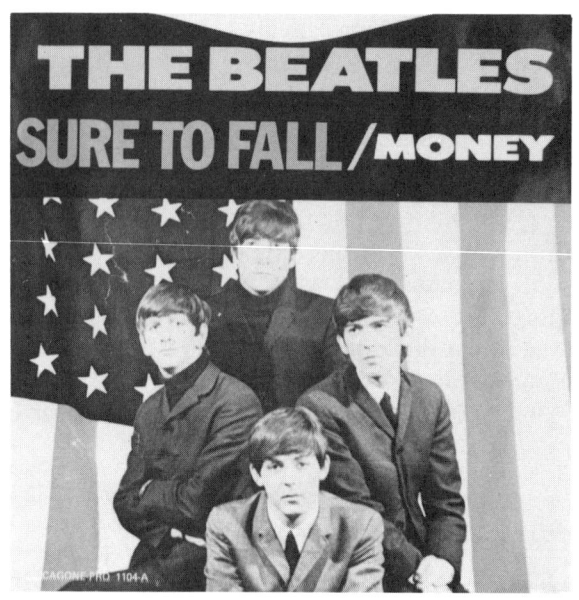

Sure To Fall/Money (front)

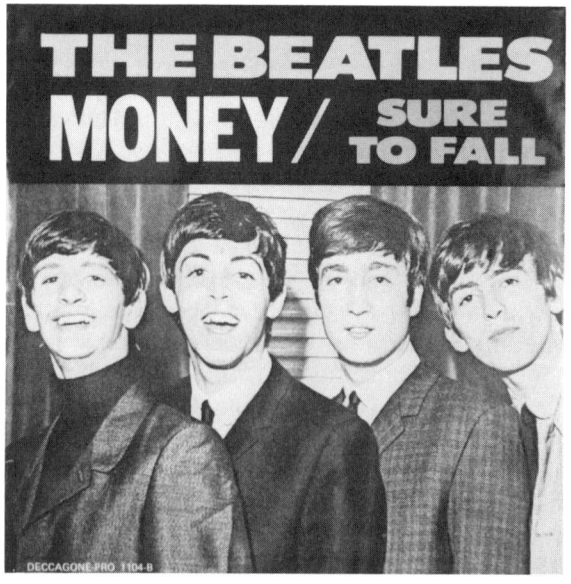

Sure To Fall/Money (back)

Crying, Waiting, Hoping/Till There Was You (front)

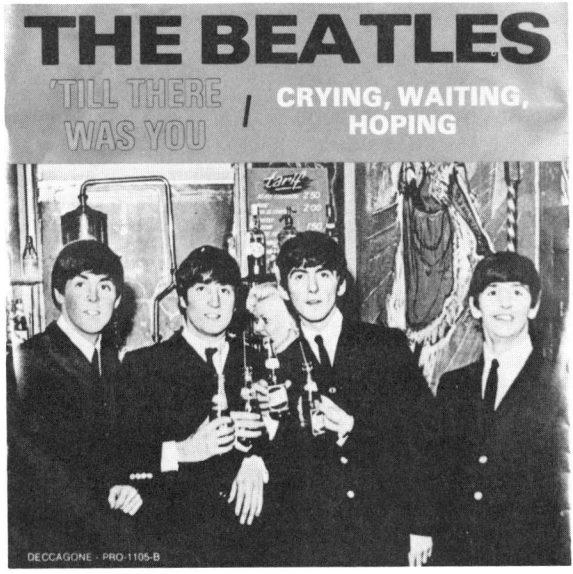

Crying, Waiting, Hoping/Till There Was You (back)

Crying, Waiting, Hoping/Till There Was You   Deccagone PRO-1105

You Can't Do That #179

Ratings:
Crying, Waiting, Hoping	A-
Till There Was You	A-

From the Decca audition January 1, 1962, this is the original release from the *SFF* Beatles fan club in Boston. This came on green vinyl with a green label and black printing, and has been counterfeited several times since its original release. (Large hole 45 rpm mono)

Comments:
One more fine-sounding disc, the sixth, from the "Deccagone" series. Both sides earn A- ratings due to the lack of any real bass. *Crying, Waiting, Hoping* sounds especially bass-shy: its frequency balance is heavily tilted upward. *Till There Was You* has some bass, but not enough to balance out the top end.

The bass problem encountered on both sides of this record is not a major one; it is only readily apparent because the disc is quite good in all other areas.

To Know Him Is To Love Him/Besame Mucho   Deccagone PRO-1106

You Can't Do That #140

Ratings:
To Know Him Is To Love Him	A
Besame Mucho	A

From the Decca audition January 1, 1962, this is the original release from the *SFF* Beatles fan club in Boston. This came on blue vinyl with a white label and black printing, and has been counterfeited several times since its original release. (Large hole 45 rpm mono)

Comments:
As fine as the first six "Deccagone" singles are, this is the best one of the entire series. Both *To Know Him Is To Love Him* and *Besame Mucho*

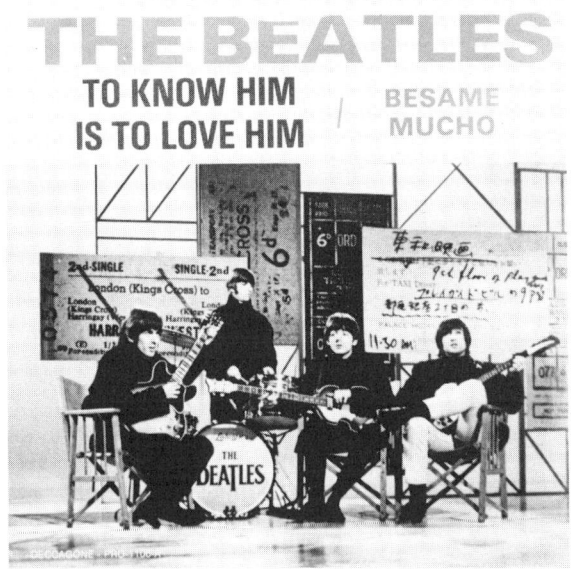

To Know Him Is To Love Him/Besame Mucho (front)

To Know Him Is To Love Him/Besame Mucho (back)

By Royal Command (EP) (front)

By Royal Command (EP) (back)

are strictly up to commercial standards and earn A ratings. This is a Beatles collector's ideal, combining outstanding sonics with two songs never officially released by the group.

The Beatles By Royal Command (EP) Vewy Queen Weccods PRO-1108

You Can't Do That #054
Do You Want To Know A Secret, page 99

Ratings:
Side One
From Me To You	C
She Loves You	C+
Till There Was You	C+

Side Two
Twist And Shout	C+

Recorded at the Prince of Wales Theatre during the Royal Command Variety Show, November 4, 1963, this is the original release from the *SFF* Beatles fan club in Boston. It was pressed in several colors, including blue and white marbled and orange and black marbled. It has an orange label with black printing. (Small hole 33 1/3 rpm mono)

Comments:
This is the last of the 7-inch records issued by *SFF*, and sonically it just doesn't measure up to the high standards set by the seven "Deccagone" singles. While it is a listenable EP, it suffers from a problem familiar to live recordings: limiting of frequency response at both the top and bottom ends of the sonic spectrum. It is believed that this disc originated from the BBC TV soundtrack of the 1963 Royal Command Performance, although the exact source is questionable.

This record provides a fair-sounding opportunity to hear the Beatles as they sounded live before they (or their music) made a big impact in America. *From Me To You*, which curiously fades in after the song has already started, suffers the most - even the vocals are slightly muffled (rating C). The other three songs have clear vocals, but the strong limiting of frequency range keeps the ratings at C+.

This record is noteworthy because it contains John's famous "Rattle your jewelry" remark.

By Royal Command (EP) (Side 1)

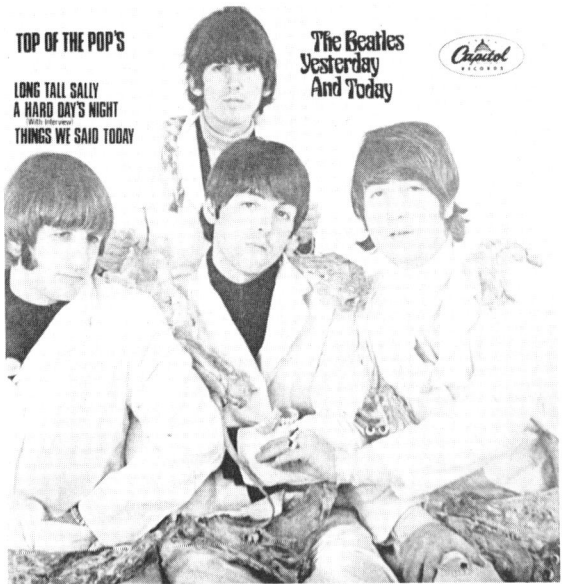

Top Of The Pops (EP) (front)

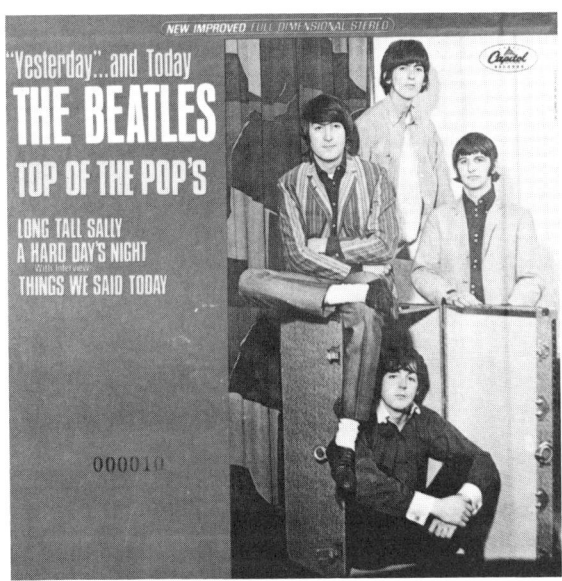

Top Of The Pops (EP) (back)

Top Of The Pops (EP) Capitol P9431

You Can't Do That #561
Do You Want To Know A Secret, page 242

Ratings:
Side One
Long Tall Sally	A-
A Hard Day's Night	A-

Side Two
Things We Said Today	A-

Comments:
This excellent off-the-air recording only gets an A- because of limiting of the extreme bass. Ringo's bass drum and Paul's bass guitar are almost non-existent; the disc's frequency balance is slanted towards the high end.

It is believed that this bootleg was pressed in two different 7-inch configurations: large hole 45 rpm, and small hole 33 1/3 rpm. The 33 1/3 rpm version was reviewed here; this is a possible explanation for the apparent reversal of sides 1 and 2 in comparison with *You Can't Do That* entry #561. In either case, the label was made to look like a Capitol Records promotional issue in both printing style and color.

Exclusive! Beatles Interviews 1966   Exclusive Beatles Interview
66x35A/66x35B

You Can't Do That #474

Ratings:
Side One	A-
Side Two	A-

Interviews recorded in Seattle, Washington during the Beatles' final American Tour in 1966. (Large hole 45 rpm mono)

Comments:
This disc contains slightly more than fifteen minutes of interviews and commentary from and about the Beatles. Although the interviews with Paul, George, and Ringo are not very informative or revealing, side two of this disc, focusing on John, is quite good.

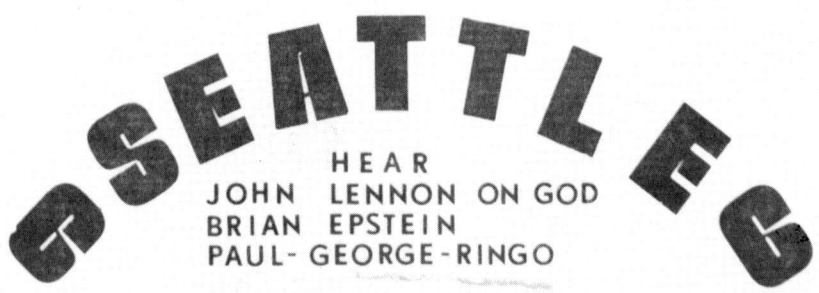

Exclusive! Beatles Interviews 1966 (EP) (front)

The subject of John's "Christ" comment is covered through interviews with John and tapes from various sources, including Tommy James, a disc jockey from Birmingham, Alabama credited with starting the "Ban The Beatles" movement in the South. Comments from Maureen Cleave (to whom John originally made the "Christ" remark) and Brian Epstein are also included. This capsule look captures the feeling of the incident and shows how shortsighted ignorance, when allowed to run unchecked, can be devastatingly dangerous.

Containing no music to speak of, the sound quality is very good for an interview disc. Rating: A-.

Television Outtakes (EP) Tobe-Milo STMLP-4Q3/4

You Can't Do That #648

Ratings:
Side One
Ringo On Smothers Brothers
Jokes, *No No Song*, Jokes   B-
Slippin And Slidin (John)   B-
And The House Came Down When
  ("Ed Sullivan Show")   C+
Side Two
George With Paul Simon On "Saturday
  Night Live"
Here Comes The Sun   B-
Homeward Bound   B-
Interview (from **The Beatles Second
  Album** Open End Interview)   B-

This disc features recordings of various solo television appearances by the Beatles. (Small hole 33 1/3 rpm mono)

Comments:
Recorded from various television soundtracks, the sonic quality of this disc is generally good. Some limiting of frequency range is evident in both bass and treble, however. The short snippets from "The Ed Sullivan Show" suffer the most, as the screaming crowd sounds almost totally obliterate the music. The inclusion on this disc of an interview from **The Beatles Second Album** Open End Interview promotional disc is problematic: what

Television Outtakes (EP) (front)

good are the answers without the questions?
Although the record cover indicates stereo, this is a mono recording.

Souvenir Of Their Visit To America (EP)   Vee Jay VJEP-1-903

You Can't Do That #503

Ratings:
Side One
Misery	B-
Ask Me Why	B-

Side Two
A Taste Of Honey	B-
Anna	B-

This is a 7-inch picture disc that reproduces the original picture sleeve in the vinyl. (Small hole 45 rpm mono)

Comments:
The sound on this picture disc is generally good, although it shares the major failing of almost all picture discs: surface noise. Hiss is slightly noticeable throughout the record, undoubtedly stemming from both the tape used to cut the master and the picture disc process itself. Also apparent is a greater than average helping of snap, crackle, and pop. But for a bootleg that contributes nothing to the overall pool of available Beatles material, what can you expect?

The only real potential value in this disc lies in its use as a wall hanging, and it makes a rather nice one at that!

Strawberry Fields Forever/Penny Lane   Capitol P5810

You Can't Do That #451

Ratings:
Strawberry Fields Forever	A-
Penny Lane	A-

This is a reproduction of the American promotional single from Capitol Records, including the trumpet ending of *Penny Lane*.

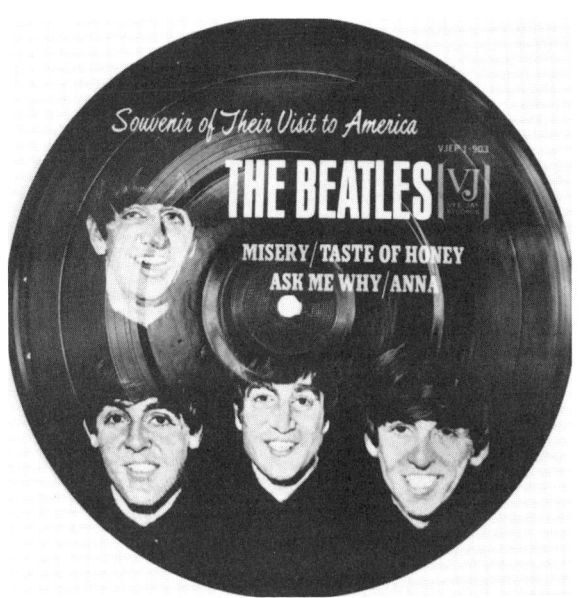

Souvenir Of Their Visit To America (EP) (Side 1)

Strawberry Fields Forever/Penny Lane (Side 1)

(Large hole 45 rpm mono)

Comments:
This is a counterfeit of the original U.S. promotional single featuring the trumpet ending of *Penny Lane*. Sonic quality of both sides is quite good (rating A-), although the commercial release of **The Beatles Rarities** LP (Capitol SHAL 12060) makes the uselessness of this disc quite obvious.

Have You Heard The Word/Futting Around Fut 160

You Can't Do That **#264**

Ratings:
Have You Heard The Word	B-
Futting Around	B-

It can finally be said that *Have You Heard The Word* has nothing to do with the Beatles, despite almost a decade of rumors claiming that John Lennon was performing on the disc. Pages XXIV and XXV of *You Can't Do That* present the facts about this tune, as uncovered by Harry Castleman and Wally Podrazik. Since many bootlegs exist in spite of the facts, it is included here for those fans who still insist they hear John Lennon on this record. (Large hole 45 rpm mono)

Comments:
Most of Side One of the disc suffers from a depressed high end and very slightly muffled vocals. The bass end is also fat and ill-defined - individual bass notes are sometimes hard to distinguish. The instrumental on Side Two suffers from similar sonic problems.

Twickenham Jams (EP)   PRO-909

You Can't Do That **#573**

Ratings:
Side One
Early In The Morning-Hi Ho Silver	C
Stand By Me	C+
Hare Krishna Mantra	C-

Have You Heard The Word/Futting Around (Side 1)

Twickenham Jams (EP) (front)

Side Two	
All Things Must Pass	D+
A Fool Like Me	D
You Win Again	D

These selections were recorded in January 1969 during the "Let It Be" sessions. (Small hole 33 1/3 rpm mono, pressed on green vinyl)

Comments:
This EP contains practice sessions and general horsing around from the "Let It Be" sessions of January 1969. Sound quality is barely fair, with varying amounts of hiss present and general unevenness of recording. Studio talking is muffled, as are some sounds when the Beatles move around the studio in relation to the microphones.

An early version of *All Things Must Pass*, although sonically disappointing, is the highlight of this disc. Despite George's muffled vocals (leading to the D+ rating), the musical treatment and harmony background given this song by the Beatles are quite interesting to hear.

In general, Side Two of the disc is lacking in bass and treble, presenting only midrange (ear-piercingly at times) amidst a background of hiss.

Love Of The Loved/Love Of The Loved PR-100

You Can't Do That #389

Ratings:	
Love Of The Loved	C-
Love Of The Loved	C-

Two versions of the same song are featured. (Large hole 45 rpm mono)

Comments:
This disc, having the same song on both sides, is a sonic mess. Vocals are muffled, frequency range is limited at both extremes, and some distortion is present. The C- rating is probably a bit generous, especially in comparison to the version available on Deccagone PRO-1102 (rated A). The original pressing, as reviewed here, has curiously become a collectors item, since it came with a black and white picture sleeve and predated the Deccagone issue.

Love Of The Loved/Love Of The Loved (front)

The Really Big Shew (EP) (front)

LISTENING TO THE BEATLES

The Really Big Shew (EP) CBS SP190

Do You Want To Know A Secret, page 205

Ratings:
Side One
1.	*All My Loving*	D+
2.	*Till There Was You*	D+
3.	*She Loves You*	D+

Side Two
4.	*I Saw Her Standing There*	C-
5.	*I Want To Hold Your Hand*	D+

This 1982 release is a 7-inch 33 1/3 rpm extended-play mono disc. It contains the five songs performed by the Beatles on their premier appearance on "Ed Sullivan Show," February 9, 1964.

Comments:
This is not a good-sounding disc. It has absolutely no bass, and very little treble. In fact, throughout most of the disc it is almost impossible to hear any of the Beatles' instruments. The vocals are so forward as to almost make this sound as if each song were performed a cappella. Audience screams get rather loud at times, almost obscuring the music in a few instances. Only *I Saw Her Standing There* is fairly well balanced between words and music. *I Want To Hold Your Hand* is somewhat plagued by distortion on the vocals, and is curiously performed at a very slow tempo.

From the sound of this disc it is hard to imagine what all the fuss was about that Sunday night in 1964.

From Us To You, A Parlophone Rehearsal Session (10-inch EP)
Ruthles Rhymes LMW-281F

You Can't Do That **#225**

Ratings:
Side One
1.	*From Us To You (Version 1)*	B-
2.	*Kansas City*	B-
3.	*Long Tall Sally*	C/B-/C

From Us To You, A Parlophone Rehearsal Session
(10-inch EP) (front)

From Us To You, A Parlophone Rehearsal Session
(10-inch EP) (back)

4.	*If I Fell*	D+
5.	*Boys*	C-
6.	*I'm Happy Just To Dance With You (Instrumental)*	D+
7.	*I'm Happy Just To Dance With You (Vocal)*	C

Side Two

8.	*I Should Have Known Better (False start)*	C-
9.	*I Should Have Known Better (Without harmonica)*	C-
10.	*I Should Have Known Better (With harmonica)*	C-
11.	*Things We Said Today*	C
12.	*A Hard Day's Night*	C
13.	*From Us To You (Version 2)*	B-

This 10-inch disc contains various studio recordings, its title comes from the name of a Beatles radio program aired on the BBC. Original pressings of this disc were on various colors of vinyl; later pressings are black.

Comments:

The sound of this record can be summed up as fair at best. The better sounding cuts (1, 2, and 13) are prone to hiss and have no real bass. The majority of the remaining cuts are plagued with distortion in the upper registers, absolutely no bass or very fat overblown midbass, and recessed vocals. The worst-sounding cuts (4 and 6) have all of the previously mentioned problems plus speed variations, sounding as if the master tape slowed down at times during the recording session.

12-INCH BOOTLEGS

Hahst Az Sun (Two Weeks In January, 1969) TAKRL 2950 (2 LPs)

You Can't Do That #254

Ratings:
Side One
1.	Two Of Us	A-
2.	Don't Let Me Down	A-
3.	When You Get To Suzy Parker Everybody Gets Well Done	A-
4.	I've Got A Feeling	A-
5.	No Pakistanis	B+
6.	Get Back	A-
7.	Don't Let Me Down (Reprise)	A-

Side Two
8.	Practice And Sound Check	B+
9.	Be Bop A Lula	B+
10.	She Came In Through The Bathroom Window	B+
11.	High Heeled Sneakers	B
12.	I Me Mine	B+
13.	I've Got A Feeling	B+
14.	One After 909	B+
15.	Norwegian Wood	N/R
16.	She Came In Through The Bathroom Window	B+

Side Three
17.	Let It Be (By The Numbers)	A-
18.	Shakin In The Sixties	A-
19.	Good Rockin' Tonight	B+
20.	Across The Universe	A-
21.	Two Of Us	A-
22.	Momma, You've Been On My Mind	A-

Hahst Az Sun (Two Weeks In January, 1969)
(2 LPs) (front)

The Beatles Live At Abbey Road Studios
(2 LPs) (front)

An Audiophile's Guide to the Sound of the Fab Four

    Side Four
23. *Tennessee* — A-
24. *House Of The Rising Sun* — A-
25. *Back To Commonwealth* — A-
26. *White Power Promenade* — A-
27. *Hi Ho Silver* — B+
28. *For You Blue* — A-
29. *Let It Be* — A-

This album, although two discs worth, is only a small piece of the Let It Be studio tapes from early January 1969. Recorded at Twickenham Film Studios in London, it includes a rare George Harrison performance of a Bob Dylan song that was never subsequently recorded for commercial release, *Momma, You've Been On My Mind*.

Comments:

This is a fine-sounding LP, taken directly from the many hours of studio tapes compiled during the Let It Be filming. Slight amounts of hiss are present throughout the album, as well as small extraneous noises, distortion, etc. None of these problems are severe, however, and all songs earn B or better ratings. This disc is a case where sonic rating and musical performance are not necessarily related, as the Beatles' performance is generally very sloppy even though the sound quality is good.

It is interesting to hear the development of many songs, such as *Let It Be* and *Get Back*, and to listen as the boys enjoy themselves horsing around in the studio. Harrison's performance of *Momma, You've Been On My Mind* is a beautiful six-minute solo acoustic piece. The guitar is beautifully recorded, although George's vocals are all but inaudible in many instances throughout the song.

The Beatles Live At Abbey Road Studios ARS 2-9083

Not included in *You Can't Do That*
Do You Want To Know A Secret, page 85

Ratings:
    Side One
1. *Love Me Do* — B-
2. *How Do You Do It* — B
3. *I Saw Her Standing There* — B

4.	Twist & Shout	B+

Side Two
5.	One After 909	B
6.	Don't Bother Me	B
7.	A Hard Day's Night	B+
8.	Leave My Kitten Alone	B+
9.	I'm A Loser	B+
10.	She's A Woman	B+
11.	Ticket To Ride	B+
12.	Help (Instrumental)	B+

Side Three
13.	Norwegian Wood	C
14.	I'm Looking Through You	B-
15.	Paperback Writer	B-
16.	Rain	B
17.	Penny Lane	B
18.	Strawberry Fields Forever	B/B+/B+

Side Four
19.	A Day In The Life	B
20.	Hello Goodbye	B+
21.	Lady Madonna	B
22.	Hey Jude	B+
23.	While My Guitar Gently Weeps	B-
24.	Because	B-
25.	No. 9 Dream	B

This two-recod set was recorded during the presentation of "The Beatles At Abbey Road Studios" multimedia show presented by EMI at Abbey Road Studios during the summer of 1983. It is packaged in an open-out laminated cover intended to look like a record from Mobile Fidelity Sound Lab's **The Beatles/The Collection** box set.

Comments:
    This album was recorded with a tape machine in the audience, and based on the security at Abbey Road Studios during the presentation, it must have been a small one at that. Bearing this in mind, the sound of this set is rather good. Sonic grading ranges from C to B+, with only one song, *Norwegian Wood* (cut 13), earning a C.

In general, this album suffers from a lack of very low bass. Ringo's bass drum and Paul's bass guitar are always audible, but at a somewhat depressed level. High frequency response and vocal presentation are the determining factors in grading the songs on this album. *Love Me Do* (cut 1) is an example of a depressed high end, while *Norwegian Wood* (cut 13) is an example of very distant and recessed vocals. The only other problem evident is speed variation, with cuts 17, 19, 20, and 21 all being presented noticeabley too fast. This is easily corrected, however, with a variable pitch turntable.

This album definitely shines based on its unique material, much of it having never been played before the general public prior to this multimedia show. Although the song titles are familiar, almost all are early working versions or unreleased takes. *Strawberry Fields Forever* (cut 18) is actually parts of three takes, including Take 7 (the fast one) and Take 26 (the slow one) that George Martin spliced together to make the finished verison. A short version of the original 1963 recording of *One After 909* (cut 5) and a partial version of the officially unreleased *Leave My Kitten Alone* (cut 8) are highlights. The most special song on this album is cut 23, *While My Guitar Gently Weeps* (Take 1), which features George Harrison playing unaccompanied acoustic guitar. As well as including an additional verse, the acoustic treatment totally changes the feel of the song, and can best be described as hauntingly beautiful. This is quite a change from the officially released version, which is, believe it or not, Take 44.

NOTE: This album has been released on compact disc as **Abbey Road Show 1983** (NML ARS 83-2)

Johnny & The Moondogs: Silver Days Air Time Warwick M16051 MX729A-B

Do You Want To Know A Secret, page 158

Ratings:
Side One
1.	*I Saw Her Standing There*	B+
2.	*From Me To You*	B+
3.	*Money*	B+
4.	*Roll Over Beethoven*	B+
5.	*You Really Got A Hold On Me*	B+
6.	*She Loves You*	B+
7.	*Twist & Shout*	B

Johnny & The Moondogs: Silver Days Air Time (LP) (front)

8.	*Nothin' Shakin' (But The Leaves On The Tree)*	A-
9.	*Lonesome Tears In My Eyes*	A-
10.	*So How Come No One Loves Me*	A-

Side Two

11.	*Please Mr. Postman*	B
12.	*Crying, Waiting, Hoping*	B+
13.	*Ticket To Ride*	B+
14.	*Rock And Roll Music*	B+
15.	*Kansas City/Hey-Hey-Hey-Hey*	A-
16.	*This Boy*	B+
17.	*Can't Buy Me Love*	B+

Here is a rundown of the recording dates for the songs included:

Cuts 1-7 - Recorded October 24, 1963 in Stockholm, Sweden
Cuts 8-11 - Recorded July 10, 1963 in England
Cut 12 - Recorded July 16, 1963 in England
Cut 13 - Recorded May 26, 1965 in England
Cut 14 - Recorded November 25, 1964 in England
Cuts 15-17 - Recorded February 28, 1964 in England

A brown-and-white photo of the Fab Four (including Pete Best) adorns the front of the laminated cover, with song information presented on Side Two.

Comments:
The accuracy of the information about these songs (copied from the album's back cover) is unknown. One incident present doubts about cuts 1-7. Paul introduces *Money* (cut 3) as being "... from our new album, released in November." Are these cuts really from Sweden, October 24, 1963?

Sonically this disc is very good. The concert songs (cuts 1-7) earn solid B+ gardes, with only very slight treble depression and bass over-emphasis. The remaining songs are all B to A-, with good frequency balance and very little distortion. The telling factor in grading is generally high frequency content: those with well-presented highs earn A- while those with depressed highs earn B or B+.

Casualties (Picture disc) (front)

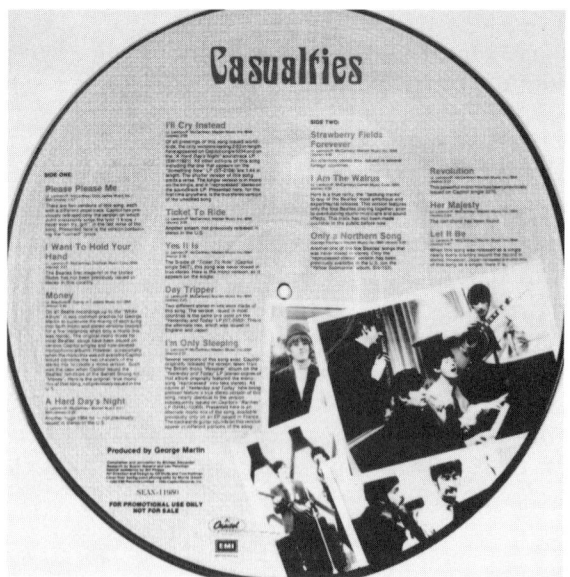

Casualties (Picture disc) (back)

An Audiophile's Guide to the Sound of the Fab Four

Casualties   Capitol SEAX-11950

Ratings:
Side One
1. Please Please Me   B+
2. I Want To Hold Your Hand   A-
3. Money   A-
4. A Hard Day's Night   A
5. I'll Cry Instead   A
6. Ticket To Ride   A
7. Yes It Is   A
8. Day Tripper   A
9. I'm Only Sleeping   A

Side Two
10. Strawberry Fields Forever   A
11. I Am The Walrus   A-
12. Only A Northern Song   A
13. Revolution   A
14. Her Majesty   A
15. Let It Be   A

The following is a rundown of information on songs included:

Cut 1 - Alternate mono version without lyric mistake by John
Cut 2 - Stereo version (claimed as first U.S. appearance)
Cut 3 - Original "true mono" version as released in England
Cut 4 - Stereo version (claimed as first U.S. appearance)
Cut 5 - True stereo version of unedited edition (claimed as "first time anywhere")
Cut 6 - Stereo version (claimed as first U.S. appearance)
Cut 7 - Mono version as on U.S. single
Cut 8 - Alternate stereo version as released in England and Japan
Cut 9 - Alternate mono mix previously released on an EP in France
Cut 10 - Alternate stero mix (claimed as issued "in several foreign countries")
Cut 11 - Mono, without overdubs
Cut 12 - "True mono" version
Cut 13 - Mono version as on U.S. single
Cut 14 - Mono version including the so-called "lost" chord
Cut 15 - Mono version as on Japanese single

EMI Outtakes (LP) (front)

This LP is another collection of rare versions of Beatles songs dubbed from various legitimate releases. Its one true rarity is *I Am The Walrus* (cut 11), which presents only the four Beatles playing in the studio, sans overdubs and sound effects.

This was first released as a picture disc with the "butcher cover" photo on Side One and liner notes and snapshots (similar in style to **The Beatles Rarities** - U.S. Capitol SHAL 12060) on Side Two. It is presented as a promotional disc, although its serial number is similar to that of the legitimate Capitol picture discs of **Sgt. Pepper, Abbey Road,** and **Band On The Run** (SEAX series). Later pressings of this disc were conventional issues on black vinyl.

Comments:

Other than treble distortion on *Please Please Me* (cut 1), this album earns top ratings on all other cuts. The differentiating factor between A and A- ratings is either a lack of extreme bass (cut 2) or slight high-end problems (cuts 3 and 11). This disc also suffers from occasional ticks and pops - probably a symptom of it being a picture disc. The later pressings on black vinyl would most likely be free of these noises.

EMI Outtakes   TAKRL 1374

You Can't Do That **#207**
Fixing A Hole, page 117

Ratings:
Side One
1.	*What A Shame Mary Jane Had A Pain At The Party*	B-
2.	*Penny Lane*	C
3.	*Blue Jay Way*	B+
4.	*All My Loving*	C
5.	*Sie Liebt Dich*	B+

Side Two
6.	*Twist And Shout*	C-
7.	*Roll Over Beethoven*	C-
8.	*I Wanna Be Your Man*	C-
9.	*Long Tall Sally*	C-

Beautiful Dreamer (LP) (front)

An Audiophile's Guide to the Sound of the Fab Four

    10.   *Medley (Love Me Do, Please Please Me, From Me To You, She Loves You, I Want To Hold Your Hand)*   C-
    11.   *Can't Buy Me Love*   C-

    This album is a collection of material from various sources including original recordings (cuts 2, 4, and 5) an outtake (cut 3), a song that was never officially released (cut 1), and the soundtrack of the "Around The Beatles" TV show aired in England May 6, 1964 (cuts 6-11).

Comments:
    Cuts 1 through 6 of this disc are preceded by short (about 30 seconds) snippets of interviews, including John talking about his "Jesus" remark, Paul about songwriting, "fan on the concert scene" interviews, and others. Grading on this disc ranges from C- to B+ with the average being about C. The live cuts (6 through 11) are the worst, suffering from an overabundance of screaming from the audience, no real bass, distortion on vocals, and poor instrumental/vocal balance. *All My Loving* (cut 4) is the "hi hat" intro version, but sounds as if the treble control had been turned all the way down. This song sounds very dark and closed in. *Sie Liebt Dich* (cut 5) earns the highest rating, B+, and although it is well-presented sonically, it is recorded entirely too fast.
    This is an older bootleg, of the "white cardboard jacket with an attached photocopied sheet on the front" style. It is somewhat typical of the older bootlegs: hastily put together and only fair-sounding at best.

Beautiful Dreamer   NEM 61842 Dream Records DH-9561

Do You Want To Know A Secret, page 89

Ratings:
    Side One
    1.   *Some Other Guy*   B-
    2.   *I'm Talkin' About You*   C
    3.   *Youngblood*   C
    4.   *Too Much Monkey Business*   C+
    5.   *I Got To Find My Baby*   C+
    6.   *Johnny B. Goode*   C
    7.   *Keep Your Hands Off My Baby*   C

8.	Beautiful Dreamer	C
9.	Glad All Over	C+
	Side Two	
10.	That's All Right Mama	C+
11.	I'm Gonna Sit Right Down And Cry Over You	C+
12.	To Know Her Is To Love Her	B/C-
13.	Sweet Little Sixteen	C+
14.	Ooh! My Soul	C-
15.	There's A Place	B-
16.	I'll Get You	C+
17.	Words Of Love	D+
18.	The Honeymoon Song	C

This album contains BBC radio performances by the Beatles from 1963, many of which were used in the "Beatles At The Beeb" radio special. It comes in a full-color laminated cover (with color photos on both sides), but strangely enough, although the performances on the record are from 1963, the photos appear to be from the 1965-66 time period.

Comments:

Although the gradings of all the songs on this album average in the "fair" range, this is a difficult disc to listen to in its unadulterated form. Every song is plagued by hiss and high frequency distortion, the extent of which determines the grade (range is B- to D+). The second half of *To Know Her Is To Love Her* (cut 12) and all of *Ooh! My Soul* (cut 14) contain a high-pitched whistle that is extremely irritating. *Words Of Love* (cut 17) has so much distortion as to be almost unlistenable.

The song selection and performances on this disc should make it quite attractive; unfortunately the sound quality is such that listening is a real chore, almost a headache. It is recommended that this album be experienced with the treble control on your preamplifier or receiver turned down. It is also suggested that the use of headphones be avoided with this disc.

An Audiophile's Guide to the Sound of the Fab Four

No. 3 Abbey Road   Horweite Stereophile NW8 AR8-69

You Can't Do That #423
Do You Want To Know A Secret, page 172

Ratings:
Side One
1. *Golden Slumbers* — B+
2. *Carry That Weight* — A-
3. *Her Majesty* — A
4. *You Never Give Me Your Money* — A-
5. *Octopus's Garden* — B+
6. *Maxwell's Silver Hammer* — A-
7. *Oh! Darling* — A
8. *Something* — A

Side Two
9. *How Do You Do* — N/R
10. *Blackbird* — N/R
11. *The Unicorn* — N/R
12. *Lalena* — N/R
13. *Heather* — N/R
14. *Mr. Wind* — N/R
15. *The Walrus And The Carpenter* — N/R
16. *Land Of Gisch* — N/R

Side One of this LP was recorded during the **Abbey Road** sessions. Unlike the many **Let It Be** bootlegs, where it is possible to hear the development of a song from beginning to end, these **Abbey Road** cuts are generally almost finished products. The highlight of this recording is the lack of studio production and overdubbing of instruments. This is the four Beatles playing live in the studio. The closing cut of Side One, *Something*, finishes with a 2 1/2-minute instrumental with grooves cut so close to the record label that many automatic record changers won't play them. Side Two features recordings of in-the-studio playing by Paul and Donovan.

Comments:
Golden Slumbers (cut 1) and *Octopus's Garden* (cut 5) both suffer from tape problems in spots, marring the almost perfect first side of this album. A very slight lack of high frequency response is evident on cuts 2, 4,

No. 3 Abbey Road (LP) (front)

No. 3 Abbey Road (LP) (back)

The Beatles Broadcasts (LP) (front)

The Beatles Broadcasts (LP) (back)

and 6, hence the A- ratings. *Her Majesty* (cut 3) contains the so-called "lost" chord at the song's conclusion.

Since Side Two does not contain any Beatles material it has not been reviewed.

The Beatles Broadcasts   Circuit Records LK4450

You Can't Do That **#053**
Do You Want To Know A Secret, page 96

Ratings:
  Side One
  1. Opening Theme: Pop Go The Beatles   A
  2. Long Tall Sally   A
  3. Carol   A-
  4. Soldier Of Love   A
  5. Lend Me Your Comb   A
  6. Clarabella   A-
  7. Memphis   A
  8. I Got A Woman   A-
  9. Sure To Fall   A-
  10. Do You Want To Know A Secret   A-

  Side Two
  11. Hippy Hippy Shake   A-
  12. Till There Was You   A-
  13. Matchbox   A
  14. I'm A Loser   A
  15. She's A Woman   A
  16. I Feel Fine   A
  17. Everybody's Trying To Be My Baby   A
  18. I'll Follow The Sun   A

This LP contains various performances by the Beatles broadcast on BBC radio. It was the first bootleg to offer high quality editions of *Carol, Soldier Of Love,* and *Clarabella*. Packaged in a full-color album sleeve, this is an excellent package. A small run of picture discs was printed almost a year after this LP first appeared. These songs were featured in the radio special "The Beatles At The Beeb," broadcast in England and the U.S. in 1982.

An Audiophile's Guide to the Sound of the Fab Four

Comments:
Sonically, this album is so good as to almost need no description. Everything is first-rate, with only minor problems in a few places. *Carol* (cut 3) gets only an A- due to a lack of low frequency content, as does *Clarabella* (cut 6). Very slight amounts of hiss or distortion bring the grades of cuts 8-12 down to A-, with all others earning A. The excellent sonic quality of this disc matches the commercial quality of the package to create an album that very few non-Beatles collectors would even recognize as a bootleg.

The Beatles Collector's Items Capitol SPRO-9462

You Can't Do That #057
Do You Want To Know A Secret, page 105

Ratings:
Side One
1.	Love Me Do	C+
2.	From Me To You	A-
3.	Thank You Girl	A-
4.	All My Loving	B
5.	This Boy	A-
6.	Sie Liebt Dich	A-
7.	I Feel Fine	A-
8.	She's A Woman	A-
9.	Help	A-
10.	I'm Down	A-

Side Two
11.	Penny Lane	A
12.	Baby, You're A Rich Man	A
13.	I Am The Walrus	A
14.	The Inner Light	A-
15.	Across The Universe	A
16.	You Know My Name (Look Up The Number)	A
17.	Sgt. Pepper Inner Groove	N/R

This LP contains rare versions of songs dubbed from various legitimate releases. It was rumored that this bootleg actually influenced Capitol Records in its ultimate release of **The Beatles Rari-**

The Beatles Collector's Items (LP) (front)

Don't Pass Me By (2 LPs) (front)

ties (SHAL 12060). This album is made to look like a Capitol promotional album, with promo serial number and purple label. The wonderful color cover shows various pieces of memorabilia against a background of Beatle wallpaper. The disc is out of print; its second pressing, also out of print had *Paperback Writer* in place of *I'm Down*.

Comments:
This album is a fine-sounding collection of rare and/or unusual Beatles songs. Although the titles are very familiar, the versions presented here are hard to find and/or unique. Some of these appear on the U.S. Capitol release of **The Beatles Rarities** (SHAL 12060), most notably *Penny Lane* (cut 11). This is a stereo version with the trumpet ending (from the U.S. promotional single) spliced on. Interestingly enough, the **Rarities** LP (released after this bootleg) claims that this version of *Penny Lane* was created especially for the legitimate release, yet it appeared first on this bootleg LP.

All cuts earn A or A- with the exception of *Love Me Do* (cut 1) and *All My Loving* (cut 4). The LP's liner notes state that the master tape for *Love Me Do* was unavailable, and it sounds like it! This cut has a depressed high end and distortion in many places. *All My Loving* is generally well recorded but sounds as if everything below 100 Hz was filtered out of the song. There is absolutely no bass end, hence only a B rating.

This LP, especially the first pressing (as reviewed here), is a valuable collector's item. Since it consists entirely of legitimate recordings, however, it offers nothing new in the way of Beatles material.

Don't Pass Me By CBM 3316 (2 LPs)

You Can't Do That #196
Fixing A Hole, page 113

Ratings:
Side One
1.	*Nothing Is Easy* - Jethro Tull	
2.	*Dig It*	
3.	*Christmas Record 1963*	B-
4.	*Christmas Record 1964*	B-
5.	*Christmas Record 1965*	B-
6.	*Christmas Record 1966*	B-

Side Two
7.	Christmas Record 1967	B-
8.	Christmas Record 1968	B-
9.	Christmas Record 1969	B-

Side Three
10.	The Saints	C+
11.	Glad All Over	C+
12.	I Just Don't Understand	C+/D
13.	Slow Down	C+
14.	Please Don't Ever Change	C
15.	A Shot Of Rhythm & Blues	C
16.	I'm Sure To Fall	C

Side Four
17.	My Bonnie	C+
18.	I Got A Woman	C
19.	Nothin' Shakin' But The Leaves On The Tree	C
20.	Lonesome Tears In My Eyes	C
21.	Everyone Loves Someone	C
22.	I'm Gonna Sit Right Down And Cry Over You	C
23.	Crying, Waiting, Hoping	C
24.	To Know Her Is To Love Her	C
25.	Bound By Love	C

This double-LP set features all of the Christmas messages dubbed from legitimate releases and an assortment of BBC radio performances. Two cuts (10 and 17) are dubs from legitimate releases. Many of the live BBC performances are the same as those on **Original Audition Tape - Circa 1962** on Wizardo Records.

Comments:
Potentially, this album is a good-sounding disc, but it is so plagued by surface noise as to be quite annoying. Although *Nothing Is Easy* and *Dig It* are listed as part of this two-record set in Reinhart's *You Can't Do That*, they are not included on Side One as mentioned.

The Christmas messages are the sonic highlights of this set, yet they only earn a B- at best due to the surface noise. Sides Three and Four are relatively constant in sonic character, exhibiting no bass at all. Only the amount of surface noise present differentiates the cuts, with the exception of

I Just Don't Understand (cut 12), which sounds as if the tape machine had troubles midway through the song.

If you can tolerate the constant surface noise present throughout, this is a nice album - especially for those wonderfully zany Christmas messages.

Original Audition Tape - Circa 1962 Wizardo WRMB 308

You Can't Do That #436

Ratings:
Side One
1. I Got A Woman — C
2. I Got A Woman — C-
3. Glad All Over — B-
4. I Just Don't Understand — B/C-
5. Hippy Hippy Shake — C
6. I'm Sure To Fall — C
7. Please Don't Ever Change — C
8. A Shot Of Rhythm And Blues — C-
9. A Shot Of Rhythm And Blues (Live) — E+
10. There's Nothin' Shakin' — B-
11. I Forgot To Remember — C+

Side Two
12. Bound By Love — B-
13. Lonesome Tears In My Eyes — B-
14. Everyone Wants Someone — B-
15. Love Of The Loved — D
16. Lucille — D+
17. Crying, Waiting, Hoping — B-
18. To Know Her Is To Love Her — B-
19. Lend Me Your Comb — E
20. Oh Carol — E
21. I'm Gonna Sit Right Down And Cry — B-

Although entitled **Original Audition Tape - Circa 1962**, only one cut, *Love Of The Loved*, is actually from the January 1, 1962 audition for Decca Records. The remaining cuts are from various BBC and Radio Luxembourg broadcasts from 1962 and 1963.

Original Audition Tape - Circa 1962 (LP) (front)

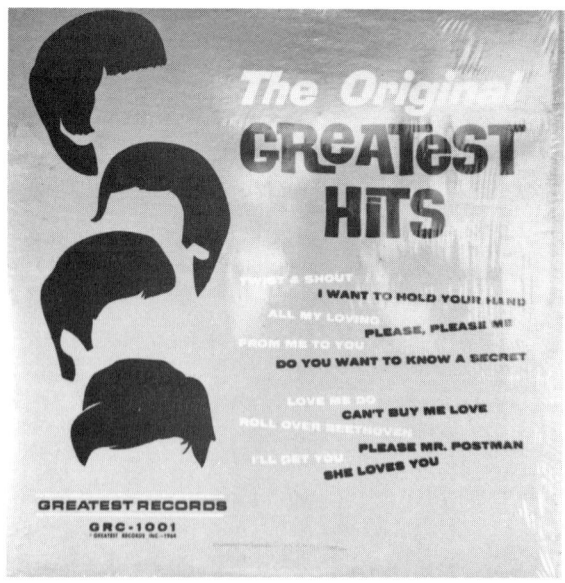

The Original Greatest Hits (LP) (front)

An Audiophile's Guide to the Sound of the Fab Four

Comments:
This record can only be described as fair at best. The eight cuts earning B grades are more than offset by the four cuts rated D or poorer. Two cuts, *Crying, Waiting, Hoping* and *To Know Here Is To Love Her*, are available in superior form on singles, as Deccagone PRO 1105 and Deccagone PRO 1106. *A Shot Of Rhythm And Blues (Live)* is a sonic disaster, but the performance and crowd sounds make it interesting and worthwhile. It sounds as if it were recorded from a room other than where the Beatles were playing, or through a closed wooden door into the concert hall.

I Just Don't Understand has a double rating due to the fact that midway through the song the quality gets much worse, perhaps due to problems with the tape machine. *Lucille*, as sonically poor as it is, is remarkable in the fact that Paul's lead vocal sounds very similar to his late-seventies version of the song performed with Rockestra at the "Concerts For The People of Kampuchea." His voice and vocal styling have stayed intact through more than two decades of performing.

This record is a perfect example of a fence sitter: some will like it and some will hate it, depending on the level of interest in the specific songs. The sonic merits on this LP are not very attractive, but the song selection might be.

The Original Greatest Hits Greatest Records GRC 1001

You Can't Do That #439

Ratings:
Side One
1. *Twist And Shout* — A-
2. *I Want To Hold Your Hand* — B+
3. *All My Loving* — B
4. *Please Please Me* — B-
5. *From Me To You* — B-
6. *Do You Want To Know A Secret* — B-

Side Two
7. *Love Me Do* — C+
8. *Can't Buy Me Love* — A-
9. *Roll Over Beethoven* — A-
10. *Please Mr. Postman* — A-
11. *I'll Get You* — A-
12. *She Loves You* — A-

The first of the Beatles bootlegs, this was issued during the height of Beatlemania in America in 1964. All cuts are dubs from legitimate releases. *Love Me Do* is the original English single version with Ringo playing drums, probably dubbed from the Canadian single.

Comments:
Being the first of the Beatles bootlegs, this record now changes hands for more than $50 among collectors. In general, it is a good-sounding album. Musically, however, the value of this album is almost nil.

All of the cuts are commercially available, and in better sonic form. The release of **The Beatles Rarities** (U.S. Capitol SHAL 12060) has made the version of *Love Me Do* with Ringo on drums commonplace, and this cut had previously been this LP's only claim to musical fame. Cuts 4 through 7 suffer from a lack of high frequencies and hiss. In fact, *Please Please Me*, *From Me To You*, and *Do You Want To Know A Secret* are so lacking in high frequency response that they sound as if they were recorded at too slow a speed. The remaining eight cuts all sound very fine, however, and are only a notch below the mono versions of their commercial counterparts.

Top Of The Pops Highway Records HHCER 111

You Can't Do That #562
Fixing A Hole, page 237

Ratings:
Side One
1.	*People Say*	N/R
2.	*I'm Walking*	N/R
3.	*Hey Jude*	C-
4.	*Revolution*	C
5.	*Long Tall Sally*	C

Side Two
6.	*A Hard Day's Night*	C
7.	*Things We Said Today*	C
8.	*Shout*	C
9.	*Twist And Shout*	B
10.	*You Can't Do That*	B
11.	*All My Loving*	B

Top Of The Pops (LP) (front)

The Beatles On Stage In Japan, The 1966 Tour
(LP) (front)

12.	*She Loves You*	B
13.	*Things We Said Today*	B
14.	*Roll Over Beethoven*	B

People Say and *I'm Walking* are not by the Beatles. *Shout* is from the Murray the K fan club record, *Hey Jude* is from "The David Frost TV Show" (BBC), and all other cuts are from various "Top of The Pops" BBC radio shows or the Hollywood Bowl concert of August 23, 1964.

Comments:

The selections on this LP that are by the Beatles (cuts 3-14) fall into two categories: songs recorded in the studio and songs recorded live at the Hollywood Bowl, 1964. The Hollywood Bowl songs (cuts 9-14) are actually quite good. The sound of screaming fans is a large part of the songs, and in spite of the fact that the vocals overpower the music, the performance and sound quality deserve the solid B rating. The studio songs, on the other hand, are only fair at best. In fact, four of them are available on 7-inch bootlegs (see reviews) in dramatically superior form. *Revolution* is available on a single from *Strawberry Fields Forever* (SFF/SOK 21) and the three "Top Of The Pops" songs (cuts 5-7) are available on an EP (Capitol P9431). The remaining cut, *Hey Jude* (from "The David Frost Show"), suffers from treble distortion and sounds if the record is playing slightly too slowly.

The Beatles On Stage In Japan, The 1966 Tour TAKRL 1900

You Can't Do That #080

Ratings:
Side One
1.	*Rock And Roll Music*	B
2.	*She's A Woman*	B
3.	*If I Needed Someone*	B
4.	*Day Tripper*	B
5.	*Baby's In Black*	B
6.	*I Feel Fine*	B

Side Two
7.	*Yesterday*	B
8.	*I Wanna Be Your Man*	B

9.	*Nowhere Man*	B
10.	*Paperback Writer*	B
11.	*I'm Down*	B

This LP was recorded during the Beatles' final tour at Budokan Martial Arts Hall in Tokyo, Japan on July 2, 1966.

Comments:
Sonically this album is rather good. Musically, however, it shows the Beatles at their worst! Compared to the Hollywood Bowl performances of 1964 and 1965, this is awful. Most of the vocals are off key, especially *If I Needed Someone* and the background in *Paperback Writer*. Instrumentals are sloppy at times, too. The only highlight of this album is the version of *Yesterday*, a rarity since drums and guitars replace the strings found on the original studio recording.

Other than a lack of bass (Paul's bass and Ringo's bass drum are at times hard to notice) and a bit too much screaming from the audience, this disc earns a solid B rating. Vocals are clean and instruments are generally well recorded. This LP paints a true but unfortunate picture of how poorly the Beatles played at this concert.

Judy Kustom Records ASC-003

You Can't Do That #307
Fixing A Hole, page 142

Ratings:
Side One

1.	*Judy! Judy!*	C+
2.	*Lady Mother*	B-
3.	*Ballad*	B-
4.	*Rain*	B-
5.	*Brown Shoes*	B
6.	*This Guy*	B+

Side Two

7.	*All You Need*	B+
8.	*Inert Lightnin'*	C
9.	*I'm An Opulent Man*	B-
10.	*I'm Laid*	B

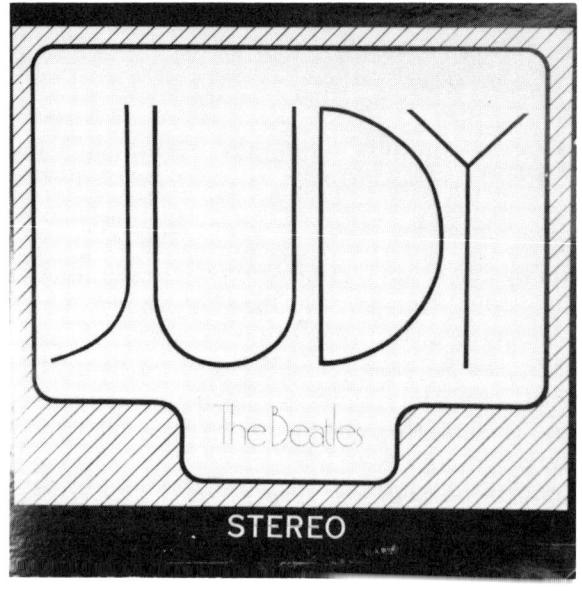

Judy (LP) (front)

Have You Heard The Word (LP) (front)

An Audiophile's Guide to the Sound of the Fab Four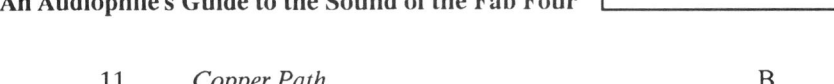

11. *Copper Path* B
12. *Raspberry Gardens* B+

Only cut 4 is the actual title of the song on the disc, although it doesn't take a genius to figure out the correct titles of the remaining cuts. All of the songs are dubs from legitimate releases. Why these puzzle-like titles are used is unknown, although two possibilities can be offered: 1) to fool prospective buyers into thinking that unreleased material is presented on the disc, or, 2) to avoid potential legal problems with this (obviously illegal) disc.

Comments:
In similar fashion to **The Original Greatest Hits** LP (see review), this album has become a valuable collectors item. In this case it is due to the fact that this was one of the earliest Beatles bootlegs with a laminated cover.

Sonically, most of the cuts on this record are of good quality. Only *Hey Jude* (referred to as *Judy! Judy!*) and *The Inner Light* (referred to as *Inert Lightnin'*) are not up to par. Both suffer from a lack of high frequencies, in many places sounding slightly closed-in. *The Inner Light* also is distorted at times, earning it a C, the lowest rating on the disc.

Contrary to the marking on the album's cover, this record is in mono, not stereo.

Have You Heard The Word Contra Band Music 3624

You Can't Do That #262
Do You Want To Know A Secret, page 142

Ratings:
Side One
1. *Have You Heard The Word* C
2. *You Really Got A Hold On Me* B
3. *The Long And Winding Road* B
4. *Cha Cha Cha* B
5. *Maxwell's Silver Hammer* B
6. *Piano Boogie* B-
7. *Besame Mucho* B
8. *Octopus's Garden* B
9. *I Me Mine* B
10. *Don't Let Me Down* B

Side Two
11.	*I Forgot To Remember To Forget Her*	B-
12.	*Twist And Shout*	B
13.	*Roll Over Beethoven*	B
14.	*Long Tall Sally*	B
15.	*Dizzy Miss Lizzy*	B
16.	*Lucille*	C

Most of this recording is either from the **Let It Be** sessions (cuts 2-10) or from BBC radio (cuts 11 and 16), although one dub from a legitimate release is included (*Dizzy Miss Lizzy*). Three live cuts and the much disputed *Have You Heard The Word* (see review of the single of the same name) complete this record.

Comments:
This is generally a good-sounding album, with only the title cut (*Have You Heard The Word*) and the closing cut (*Lucille*) getting as low as a C rating. The **Let It Be** cuts are of good quality, but are all available on other bootleg albums. The three live cuts sound good and are dynamic performances by the Beatles. Their origins, however, are clouded in mystery. Charles Reinhart in *You Can't Do That* credits *Twist And Shout* as being recorded at the Indra Club, 1962; *Roll Over Beethoven* as the Kaiserkeller, 1962; and *Long Tall Sally* as the Top Ten Club, 1963. The quality of these three songs is quite good, almost too good to believe that two of the recordings were made in Germany in 1962. It is generally thought that the Star Club LP marks the only aural souvenir of the Beatles' visits to Germany.

Outtakes Vol. 1 TMOQ 519

You Can't Do That #442

Ratings:
Side One
1.	*Do You Want To Know A Secret*	B-
2.	*You Really Got A Hold On Me*	B-
3.	*Hippy Hippy Shake*	B-
4.	*Misery*	B-
5.	*Money*	C
6.	*Till There Was You*	C

Outtakes Vol. 1 (LP) (front)

Outtakes Vol. 1 (LP) (back)

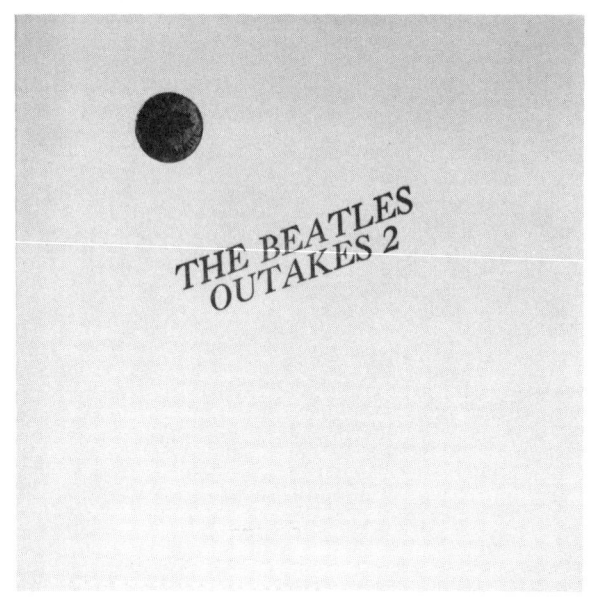

Outtakes Vol. 2 (LP) (front)

Outtakes Vol. 2 (LP) (back)

An Audiophile's Guide to the Sound of the Fab Four

    Side Two
7.   From Me To You   C
8.   Roll Over Beethoven   C
9.   Love Me Do   C+
10. Kansas City   C+
11. Long Tall Sally   C
12. Please Please Me   C+

All of these songs are studio outtakes of unknown origin, except cut 3, which was performed live on the BBC in 1962. The original pressing of this LP was on yellow vinyl; it is long out of print.

Comments:
This album of mostly studio outtakes suffers from small problems of distortion (especially on vocals), random crackling noises, lack of deep bass, and a problem in high-end reproduction. There is a general lack of high frequency content in this record, causing Ringo's cymbals to be barely noticeable on some cuts, and vocals to sound recessed and closed-in on others. In summation, the sound quality of this record is good in spots, but generally only fair overall.

Outtakes Vol. 2   TMOQ 520

You Can't Do That **#443** (listed as second edition TMOQ 71049)

    Ratings:
        Side One
1.   She Loves You   B
2.   Words Of Love   C
3.   She's Got The Devil In Her Heart   C-
4.   Anna   C
5.   Money   C
6.   There's A Place   C-

        Side Two
7.   Honey Don't   C-
8.   Chains   C-
9.   I Saw Her Standing There   C
10. I'm Sure To Fall   C
11. Lucille   C
12. Boys   C

The Decca Tapes (Picture disc) (front)

The Decca Tapes (Picture disc) (back)

All of these songs are studio outtakes of unknown origin, except cuts 10 and 11, which were performed live on the BBC. The original pressing of this LP was on blue vinyl; it is long out of print.

Comments:
This album is of similar quality to **Outtakes Vol. 1**, with distortion, random crackling noises, lack of deep bass, and lack of high frequency content. Cut 11, *Lucille*, is a better-sounding rendition than that on **The Original Audition Tape - Circa 1962** (see review). *Honey Don't*, cut 7, is a rare version with John singing the lead vocal. As with Volume 1, this is a fair-sounding album.

The Decca Tapes Circuit Records LK 4438

You Can't Do That #189
Do You Want To Know A Secret, page 111

Ratings:
Side One
1.	Hello Little Girl	A
2.	Three Cool Cats	A
3.	Crying, Waiting, Hoping	A
4.	Love Of The Loved	A
5.	September In The Rain	A
6.	Besame Mucho	A
7.	Searchin'	A

Side Two
8.	Like Dreamers Do	A-
9.	Money	A
10.	Till There Was You	A-
11.	Sheik Of Araby	A
12.	To Know Her Is To Love Her	A
13.	Take Good Care Of My Baby	A
14.	Memphis	A-
15.	Sure To Fall	A

This LP stems from the Decca audition, January 1, 1962. It contains the fourteen songs from the Deccagone singles series plus *Take Good Care Of My Baby*. This is one of the earliest bootleg picture discs, showing black and white photos of John, Paul, George, and Pete Best. The second picture disc pressing substituted a color photo of the Beatles (including Ringo) taken in Miami, 1964. A black vinyl edition with a laminated cover telling a fictitious story of the early days of the Beatles (how they came to be famous Decca recording artists) was issued at the time the second picture disc edition appeared.

Comments:
This is a great-sounding disc! It deviates from perfection in spots, but only for minor reasons. *Like Dreamers Do* shows a very slight depression of the high frequencies, *Till There Was You* has a lack of low bass in places, and *Memphis* has a low end that is fat and ill-defined at times. These problems, however would be almost unnoticeable except in direct comparison to the remaining songs on the LP. Sonically, this album probably comes as close to commercial standards as a bootleg can (albeit in mono, of course). Even the fact that this is a picture disc does not interfere with its sonic merits. The usual problems of ticks, pops, and hiss that tend to plague the picture disc genre are absent from this record (at least the copy reviewed here).

The combination of outstanding sonics and interesting material team up to make this quite an attractive album.

File Under: Beatles   Gnat Records GN-70075

Do You Want To Know A Secret, page 116

Ratings:
Side One

1.	Come And Get It	B-
2.	Shake, Rattle, & Roll	B
3.	Leave My Kitten Alone	B-
4.	I'm So Tired	B+
5.	Not Fade Away	B
6.	I Me Mine	B
7.	Third Man Theme	C+
8.	Bad To Me	C
9.	Christmastime (Is Here Again)	A-

Side Two
10.	*Goodbye*	B-
11.	*Blue Suede Shoes*	B
12.	*If You've Got Troubles*	B
13.	*Negro In Reserve*	C
14.	*That Means A Lot*	B-
15.	*Get Back*	A-
16.	*One After 909*	B+
17.	*I Dig A Pony*	B+
18.	Dialogue	B

Released in 1984, this is one of the "new generation" bootlegs. It consists entirely of studio material, most of which was newly unearthed and received its first release on this record. The package consists of a manilla file folder (hence the title) with a printed insert sheet. Also included, attached by a paper clip, is a 3" x 5" color snapshot and a strip of film from "A Hard Day's Night."

Come And Get It (cut 1) and *Goodbye* (cut 10) are demo performances by Paul recorded before he gave these songs to Badfinger and Mary Hopkin, respectively. *One After 909* (cut 16) is the original early 60s version, and *Leave My Kitten Alone* (cut 3) is the entire song (a piece of which was included on **The Beatles Live At Abbey Road Studios**). *Bad To Me* (cut 8) and *That Means A Lot* (cut 14) are Beatles versions of songs never officially released by the group. The remaining cuts are from various sources, such as a Christmas record performance (cut 9), the **Let It Be** sessions, and others.

Comments:

This is a first-rate bootleg. All but three songs (cuts 7, 8, and 13) rate B- or better, making this album a pleasure to experience. Its content comes from a variety of sources, which also proves interesting listening.

The sonic problems, which are minor, tend to revolve around the vocals in most instances. In general, vocals tend to be somewhat distant and very slightly muffled. This is especially true on *Come And Get It* (cut 1), *Bad To Me* (cut 8), and *That Means A Lot* (cut 14). Some cuts are also slightly thin in the bass, but again, these problems are minor.

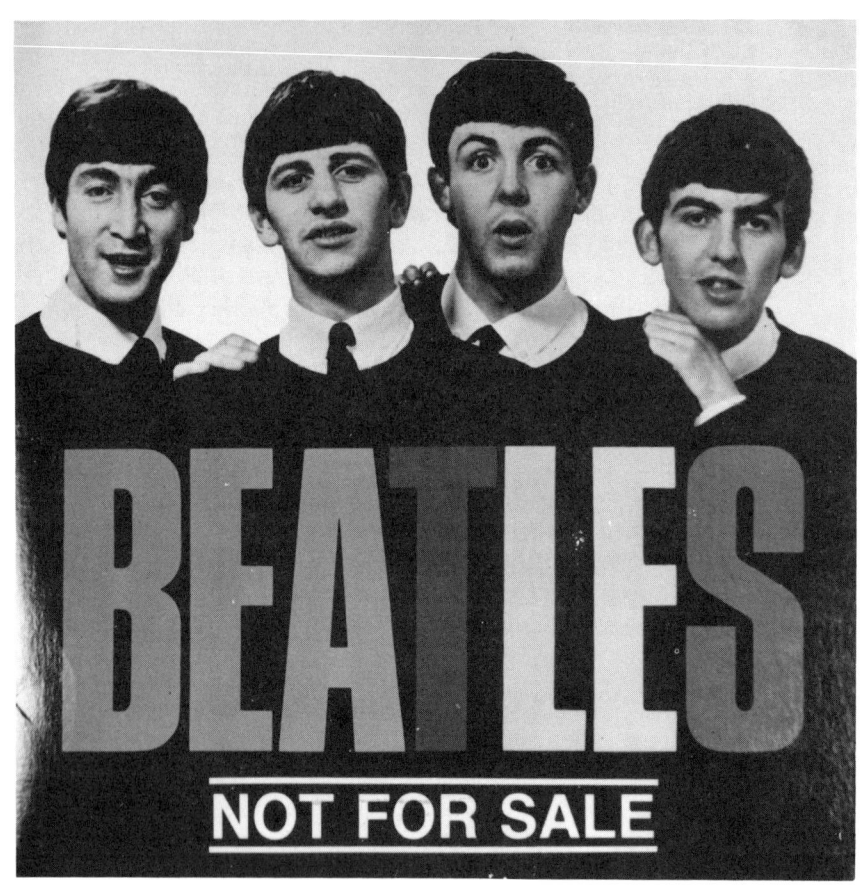
Not For Sale (LP) (front)

Not For Sale   Nems Records MOP 910

Do You Want To Know A Secret, page 173

Ratings:
Side One
1. *One After 909*   B
2. *Catswalk*   B+
3. *Bad To Me*   B-
4. *How Do You Do It*   A-
5. *Do You Want To Know A Secret*   A
6. *Leave My Kitten Alone*   B+
7. *If You've Got Trouble*   B
8. *Shout*   A-
9. *Medley (Love Me Do, Please Please Me, From Me To You, She Loves You, I Want To Hold Your Hand*   B

Side Two
10. *Yes It Is*   A
11. *Paperback Writer*   A-
12. *Your Mother Should Know*   A-
13. *Birthday*   B
14. *Goodbye*   B+
15. *I've Got A Feeling*   A
16. *I Me Mine*   A-
17. *A Day In The Life*   A

Another of the "new generation" bootlegs; here is a rundown of information on the songs included (as stated on the album's back cover):

Cut 1 - 1962 EMI studio rehearsal
Cut 2 - Instrumental; embryonic version of *Catcall* (later given by Paul to the Chris Barber Band)
Cut 3 - Original demo
Cut 4, 6, 7 - No origin stated
Cut 5 - Remixed version; no echo
Cut 8, 9 - Studio recordings for "Around The Beatles" TV special
Cut 10 - First time released in stereo

Not Guilty: The Beatles (LP) (front)

An Audiophile's Guide to the Sound of the Fab Four

Cut 11 - Remix; no echo (stereo)
Cut 12 - Original demo (mono)
Cut 13 - Vocal track reference demo (mono)
Cut 14 - Original demo (mono)
Cut 15 - Alternate take from **Get Back** sessions (mono)
Cut 16 - Basic tracks (stereo)
Cut 17 - Clan intro with countdown, remixed (stereo)

Comments:
Just as **File Under: Beatles**, this is another first-rate bootleg. Only one of the eighteen cuts earns as low as a B- grade. Six songs (cuts 1, 3, 6, 14, and 16) are common to this and **File Under: Beatles**, exemplifying the fact that new material is extremely difficult to find. Of these six, only *One After 909* (cut 1) fares worse on this LP.

How Do You Do It (cut 4) is the Decca audition performance of January 1, 1962, that is available both on a Deccagone single and the **Decca Tapes** picture disc LP, and is very well presented here (grade A-). Four cuts are remixes of familiar titles: *Do You Want To Know A Secret* (cut 5) earns an A, *Yes It Is* (cut 10) earns an A, *Paperback Writer* (cut 11) earns an A-, and *Your Mother Should Know* (cut 12) earns an A-. Each of these, as well as being fine-sounding, is sufficiently different from its normal version as to provide interesting listening.

Birthday (cut 10) has the vocals mixed significantly louder than the music. Unfortunately, this makes it sound absolutely ridiculous, as the vocals are actually a combination of screams and out-of-tune singing. The remaining songs, from various sources, are all exquisitely presented on this disc.

In summation, this is a can't-miss disc. Its contents are long (more than forty-five minutes), of varied origin, and sonically outstanding. Great listening!

NOTE: This album has been released on compact disc, with six additional cuts, as **Not For Sale** (Condor 1986).

Not Guilty: The Beatles   E.H.M.V. Records

Ratings:
Side One
1.	*Not Guilty*	C-
2.	*Rain*	C
3.	*You're Going To Lose That Girl*	C

4.	*Let It Be*	B
5.	*Paperback Writer*	B-
6.	*Rain*	B-
7.	*Rain*	B+
8.	*We Love You Beatles* - The Carefrees	N/R

Side Two

9.	*Twist And Shout*	B+
10.	*Roll Over Beethoven*	B+
11.	*I Wanna Be Your Man*	B
12.	*Long Tall Sally*	B+
13.	*Medley (Love Me Do, Please Please Me, From Me To You, She Loves You, I Want To Hold Your Hand*	B+
14.	*Can't Buy Me Love*	B
15.	*Shout*	B

This 1985 bootleg features material from the "Around The Beatles" Rediffusion TV Special filmed April 27 and 28, 1964, and various studio outtakes and remixes. It was issued in two versions: one with a laminated color jacket, and one with a white jacket and insert. It is the latter version that is reviewed here. As all of Side Two is from the TV special, here are the descriptions of the cuts on Side One as stated on the album's insert sheet:

1. George; lead guitar by George and John; unreleased
2. John (with Paul and George)
3. John (with George and Paul); mix without bongos
4. Paul (with John and George); no fadeout, no trumpets
5. Paul (with John and George); different take
6. Backing vocals only
7. John (with Paul and George); different take

Comments:
This 1985 bootleg is another example of an interesting collection of material from various sources. Virtually the whole gamut is covered, from television performances (all of Side Two), to movie material (*Let It Be*), to unreleased recordings (*Not Guilty*), to studio outtakes (most of Side One).

Side One opens with *Not Guilty*, the Beatles' version of George's song later released on the **George Harrison** LP. This was recorded during the **White Album** sessions and is different than the official (and familiar) version. As well as being performed at a faster tempo, this version contains a lengthy instrumental ending. Unfortunately, the sound quality doesn't do justice to the song. Vocals are somewhat muffled, and both frequency extremes are restricted in extension (rating C-).

Rain is presented three times here (cuts 2, 6, and 7). Cut 2 has the lead vocals echoed and mixed into the background rather than being up front, and is limited in high frequency content (rating C). Cut 6 is actually the different take that is listed as cut 7. This version has the background vocals presented forward in the mix and earns a B- rating, while cut 7 (listed as cut 6), although lacking the lead vocal part, is very clean and extended at both ends of the frequency spectrum. While earning a B+ rating, it is doubtful that this version, *sans* vocals, will be entertaining for more than a listen or two. In fact, this cut is an example of what a bootlegger will do to create enough material to fill out an album. Close scrutiny reveals that this version is actually the left channel only from the version of *Rain* on the U.S. **Hey Jude** album.

You're Going To Lose That Girl (cut 3) is an alternate mix without bongos. As with the previous cuts, it is lacking at both ends of the frequency range, earning a C rating. Although a cursory investigation revealed nothing, this cut may also be just a doctored copy of a legitimate release.

Cut 4, *Let It Be*, is a typical good-sounding song taken from the miles of available tape from the first two weeks in January 1969, at the Twickenham Film Studios.

Side Two is the highlight of this album. All of the Beatles cuts are very well presented, earning B of B+ ratings. The live for TV performances are also very good, creating an exciting listening experience. This definitely is sonically superior to the original TV broadcast, making the listener feel that he or she is sitting front row center in the studio at the performance.

The Beatles Conquer America NEMS Records SHU 6465

Do You Want To Know A Secret, page 81

Ratings:
    Side One
1.   Derrick Rudy Inteviews the Beatles:
    The Beatles Open-End Interview   A-

"The Ed Sullivan Show," February 9, 1964
2.   *All My Loving*   B
3.   *Till There Was You*   B

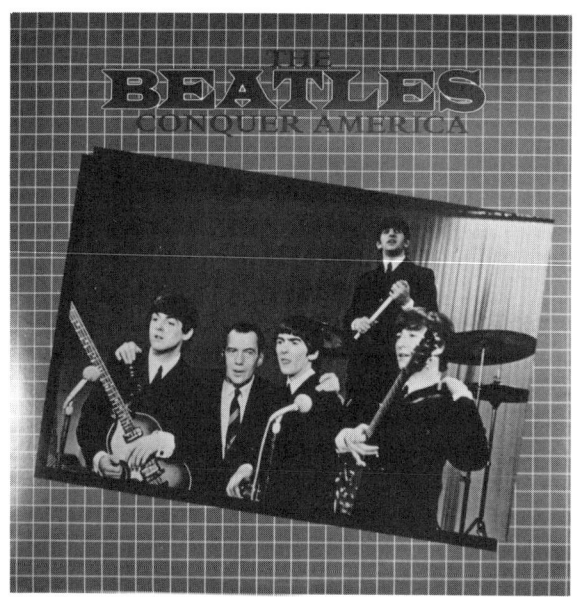

The Beatles Conquer America (LP) (front)

The Beatles Conquer America (LP) (back)

An Audiophile's Guide to the Sound of the Fab Four

4.	*She Loves You*	B
5.	*I Saw Her Standing There*	B
6.	*I Want To Hold Your Hand*	B
7.	The WWDC Interview	A

Side Two
"The Ed Sullivan Show," February 16, 1964

8.	*She Loves You*	B-
9.	*This Boy*	B-
10.	*All My Loving*	B-
11.	*I Saw Her Standing There*	B-
12.	*From Me To You*	B-
13.	*I Want To Hold Your Hand*	B
14.	Beatles Farewell To Miami (WQAM radio)	B+

Side Three
"The Ed Sullivan Show," February 23, 1964

15.	*Twist And Shout*	B+
16.	*Please Please Me*	B+
17.	*I Want To Hold Your Hand*	B+

"Shingdig," January 20, 1965

18.	*Kansas City/Hey Hey Hey Hey*	B
19.	*I'm A Loser*	B+
20.	*Boys*	B
21.	The Fab Four On Film	A

Side Four
"The Ed Sullivan Show," September 12, 1965

22.	*I Feel Fine*	A-
23.	*I'm Down*	A-
24.	*Act Naturally*	A-
25.	*Ticket To Ride*	A-
26.	*Yesterday*	A
27.	*Help!*	A-
28.	Minneapolis Press Conference	C

This 1985 double disc set compiles the Beatles' 1964 and 1965 "Ed Sullivan Show" performances, the 1965 "Shindig" show, and various interviews. These interviews range from promotions sources ("The Beatles Open-End Interview" and "Fab Four On Film") to press conferences (Minneapolis) to radio programs (WWDC and WQAM). This album is from the same people who produced the **Not For Sale** LP.

Comments:
This is generally a fine-sounding album, as well as being a great compilation of Beatles TV performances. Side One presents the Beatles' first "Ed Sullivan Show" appearance (February 9, 1964), sandwiched between two interviews. The disc opens with Derrick Rudy (who wrote the liner notes on the album jacket) reading the questions to "The Beatles Open-End Interview," a 7-inch promotional disc sent to disc jockeys in 1964. Other than some sibilant distortion in places, the sound is clear and the voices are easily understood. Interestingly, in response to a question about when the Beatles made their first record, Paul replies 1963. The five songs on this side all earn B grades, generally being well presented but lacking in extension at both frequency extremes. Remembering that this performance was meant to be heard on a TV set, and not on a high-quality audio system, makes this problem understandable. The WWDC interview that closes this side is a typical one with the Beatles in fine comic form (rating A).

The second "Ed Sullivan Show" (February 16, 1964) presented on Side Two does not fare quite as well sonically as Side One. As well as lacking at the frequency extremes, this side is plagued with random pops, ticks, clicks, and distortion. Also, Paul's microphone is dead through the first half of *I Saw Her Standing There* (cut 11). Only *I Want To Hold Your Hand* (cut 13) earns a B grade, with all others on this side earning B- due to the noise problem. Closing the side is the "Beatles Farewell To Miami," a telephone interview recorded for radio station WQAM (rating B+).

The third "Ed Sullivan Show" (February 23, 1964) on Side Three is slightly better sounding than the previous two shows. All three songs earn B+ ratings, mainly due to the fact that the high frequencies are more extended, adding some much needed "shimmer" to the sound. The three "Shindig songs are, unfortunately, very similar in sound to the first two Ed Sullivan Shows," and also have too much crowd noise. "The Fab Four On Film," which closes this side, is a dub from the Capitol 12-inch promotional single *The Beatles' Movie Medley* and earns an A rating.

Side Four, from the September 12, 1965, "Ed Sullivan Show," is the highlight of this double-disc set. Five of the six cuts earn A- ratings, while *Yesterday*, cut 26, earns an A. These songs are all very well presented, with excellent response at both ends of the frequency spectrum. Paul, accompanied by a string section, performs a breathtaking rendition of *Yesterday*, which earns an A grade to the "you are there" quality of the vocals. *Ticket To Ride* (cut 25) is different than the familiar studio version in that is has an

An Audiophile's Guide to the Sound of the Fab Four

extra long instrumental introduction. Closing out the album is a Minneapolis press conference, which unfortunately is not very well recorded. It is difficult at times to understand both the questions and the answers. Ironically, John responds to one question by saying: "We'll never start our own label." It was a short three years later that Apple was founded, which of course was the beginning of the end for the group.

All in all, this is a very good album, both for its sonic quality and TV performance material.

The Beatles Stockholm & Blackpool   Savage Records PLD 6365

Do You Want To Know A Secret, page 222

Ratings:
Side One
1.	*I Saw Her Standing There*	B-
2.	*From Me To You*	B
3.	*Money*	B-
4.	*Roll Over Beethoven*	B-
5.	*You Really Got A Hold On Me*	B
6.	*She Loves You*	B
7.	*Twist And Shout*	B+

Side Two
8.	*I Feel Fine*	C
9.	*I'm Down*	C-
10.	*Act Naturally*	C-
11.	*Ticket To Ride*	C
12.	*Yesterday*	C
13.	*Help!*	C+

This 1985 release contains excerpts from two live performances, Stockholm, Sweden on October 15, 1963 (cuts 1-7) and Blackpool, England on June 21, 1966 (cuts 8-13). The Blackpool (?) performance is listed as the first live public performance. Unfortunately, none of this can be believed, since the Beatles played in Sweden from October 24-29, 1963, and the only performance in England in 1966 was May 1 at the Empire Pool, Wembley, according to *The Beatles Again?!*, by Castleman & Podrazik (Popular Culture, Ink., originally published by Pierian Press, 1977).

85

The Beatles Stockholm & Blackpool (LP) (front)

The Beatles Budokan 1966 (LP) (front)

An Audiophile's Guide to the Sound of the Fab Four

Comments:
Side One of this album contains the same performance as that presented on the Johnny & The Moondogs: Silver Days Air Time album. Generally, this side sounds fairly good. The strongest point of this live recording is the vocals, which are up front and clear. Instrumentation is problematical at times, with the worst recordings, *I Saw Her Standing There* (cut 1), *Money* (cut 3), and *Roll Over Beethoven* (cut 4), exhibiting problems at both frequency extremes. Incidentally, this performance was recorded October 24, 1963, not the 15th as stated on the album insert.

Sonically, Side Two is not as good as Side One. A low frequency (60 Hz) buss is audible throughout this side, as is a siren-like whistle. This whistle is very pronounced on *I'm Down* (cut 9) and *Act Naturally* (cut 10), making these songs hard to tolerate at even a moderate listening level.

George introduces *Yesterday* (cut 12) as the first live public performance. This is an interesting recording, since it contains strings as does the commercial studio version. Unless the Beatles had a string quartet on hand, a tape must have been used. All other live versions of *Yesterday* feature John, George, and Ringo accompanying Paul instead of the more familiar string section.

Ringo nervously introduces himself as vocalist on *Act Naturally*, a chore usually left to Paul or John. This small bit of Ringo's personality coming through in his comments is a nice highlight on an otherwise fair-sounding album side.

In summation, this is not a bad album. The Stockholm concert is sonically good and is a much better than average performance by the Fab Four. The Blackpool concert is not as good sonically, but is listenable and interesting in places. In trying to track down the exact location of this concert, confusion arises from the fact that a stage comment made by Paul mentions Blackpool, although the entire sentence is not understandable. Hence the origin of this performance must be considered unknown.

The Beatles Budokan 1966 Savage Records L4342

Ratings:
  Side One
  1. Rock & Roll Music   C+
  2. She's A Woman   C+
  3. If I Needed Someone   B-
  4. Day Tripper   B-

5.	*Baby's In Black*	C+
6.	*I Feel Fine*	C+

Side Two
7.	*Yesterday*	B-
8.	*I Wanna Be Your Man*	B-
9.	*Nowhere Man*	B-
10.	*Paperback Writer*	C
11.	*I'm Down*	C+

This 1985 release is billed as the ". . . complete afternoon performance recorded by SONY/DENKI Audio-Video Mobile Unit at Nippon Budokan Arena Tokyo, Japan, 2:00 P.M. July 2nd 1966," even though the venue is actually called the Budokan Martial Arts Hall. This disc is pressed on green vinyl.

Comments:

This album contains a different performance from the Budokan 1966 shows than that presented on **The Beatles On Stage in Japan, The 1966 Tour** (TAKRL 1900). As with that performance, the Beatles did not do a good job.

Sonically, this album is only fair. The frequency range is generally restricted at both ends, with Paul's bass and Ringo's bass drum almost entirely nonexistent, and Ringo's cymbals missing from many of the cuts. Presentation of vocals is variable, depending upon who is singing the lead part. Paul's microphone is either non-functional or so poorly mixed as to be almost unnoticeable (his vocals sound at times as if they were being picked up by John's microphone instead of his own).

If I Needed Someone (cut 3) is so badly performed as to be laughable, and John and Paul make vocal blunders on *Day Tripper* (cut 4) and *Nowhere Man* (cut 9). The only interesting parts of this album are *She's A Woman* (cut 2) and *I'm Down* (cut 11), which feature guitar work that differs from the familiar commercial releases.

The real value of this album lies in its presentation of the Beatles at their worst in a live performance. It is easy to see why the touring stopped less than two months after this show, at the end of August 1966.

The Beatles Mach Shau! Savage Records SC 12620

Ratings:
Side One
1. A Taste Of Honey — C
2. Till There Was You — C
3. Where Have You Been All My Life — C-
4. Lend Me Your Comb — C-
5. Your Feets Too Big — C-
6. Talkin' Bout You — D
7. To Know Her Is To Love Her — C
8. Everybody's Trying To Be My Baby — C-
9. Matchbox — D
10. Little Queenie — D
11. Ain't Nothing Shakin — C-
12. Roll Over Beethoven — D

This 1985 album is billed as a previously unreleased complete and uncensored Beatles performance in Hamburg 1962. It was recorded by Adrian Barber, the so-called source of the legitimate **The Beatles Live at the Star Club in Hamburg, Germany, 1962**, between December 21 and 31, 1962, at the Star Club. The album's liner notes explain how Ted "Kingsize" Taylor came to possess the tapes that were eventually issued, and how this tape is one that was not given to Taylor. The accuracy of the liner notes is uncertain; it especially is questionable how a "complete" performance could have lasted only about forty minutes (as this album does), since the legitimate Hamburg albums contained a total of thirty-two songs (the combination of unique songs from the U.S. and German LP issues).

Comments:
Although not earning high grades, this is not a bad album. The best songs, *A Taste Of Honey* (cut 1), *Till There Was You* (cut 2), and *To Know Her Is To Love Her* (cut 3), sound very fine. They only earn C grades due to the lack of any low frequency energy, a problem that is prevalent throughout this album. Songs earning C- grades suffer from recessed vocals and slight amounts of distortion. The four cuts earning D grades are plagued by an abundance of ill-defined high-frequency "hash" and almost inaudible vocals.

This is not an album that bears frequent playing from start to finish, but for occasional listening it is a real eye-opener. The feeling of an uninter-

The Beatles Mach Shau! (LP) (front)

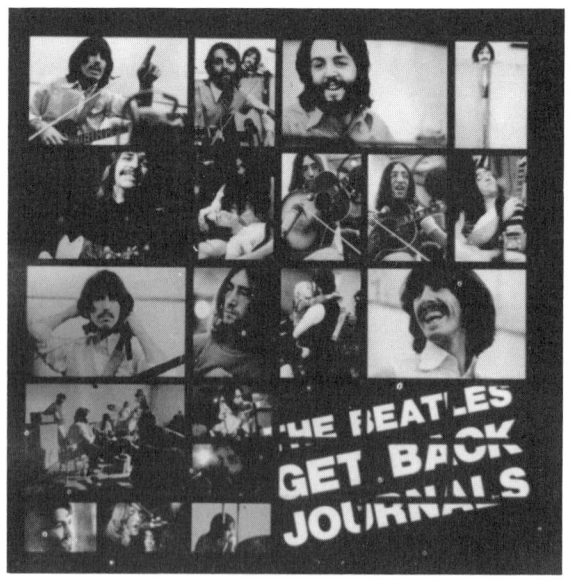

The Get Back Journals (12 LPs) (front)

rupted live performance is present throughout this album, due to the inclusion of between-song tuning, chatting with the audience, and general fooling around by the Beatles. The listener feels transported to Hamburg, as if he or she were sitting amongst the evening's crowd in the smoke-filled Star Club.

Listening to this album is a total contrast to either of the two albums recorded at Budokan Hall in Tokyo, 1966. Here, the Beatles sound like an up-and-coming band struggling to put on a good show for the audience. The playing is not very polished, but this is probably because the boys were not yet skilled as musicians. The Tokyo concerts from 1966 sound like a war-tired group playing poorly because they are just not enthusiastic about, or even interested, in performing.

This album bills the performance as "uncensored," and although foul language is not present in the included stage comments, a very surprising (even startling!) incident is. In late 1982, a German girl from Hamburg named Bettina Huebers filed a paternity suit against Paul McCartney. She was born December 18, 1962, two months prematurely, to Erika Wohlers. (Simple mathematics confirms that she was conceived during the time the Beatles were in Hamburg, since their first 1962 engagement at the Star Club was from April 23 to June 4.)

In 1967 Paul McCartney ". . . agreed to pay 30,000 Deutsche Marks, then about $7,500 - to support Bettina, reportedly without directly admitting paternity" (Clive Freeman, *People Magazine*, August 9, 1982, page 25). Although Paul eventually won the law suit, this album adds new light to the case.

Amongst the many stage comments present in this album, Paul mentions the name Bettina three times! Since the album's liner notes mention this recording as originating from the time period December 21-31, 1962 (after Bettina's birth), do Paul's stage comments confirm his knowledge of Bettina?

You decide.

The Get Back Journals Trade Mark Of Quality

Do You Want To Know A Secret, page 126

Ratings:
Side One
1.	*Tennessee*	A-
2.	*House Of The Rising Sun*	A-
3.	*Commonwealth*	A-
4.	*White Power*	A-

5.	Winston, Richard, and John	A-
6.	Hi Ho Silver	A-
7.	For You Blue	A-
8.	Let It Be	A-

Side Two

9.	Get Back	A-
10.	Don't Let Me Down	A-
11.	On Our Way Back Home	A-
12.	Don't Let Me Down	A-
13.	Suzy Parker	A-
14.	I've Got A Feeling	A-
15.	No Pakistanis	A-

Side Three

16.	Let It Be	A-
17.	Be Bop A Lula	A-
18.	She Came In Through The Bathroom Window	A-
19.	High Heeled Sneakers	A-
20.	I Me Mine	A-
21.	I've Got A Feeling	A-

Side Four

22.	She Came In Through The Bathroom Window	A-
23.	Penina	A-
24.	Shaking In The Sixties	A-
25.	Good Rocking Tonight	A-
26.	Across The Universe	A-
27.	Two Of Us	A-
28.	I Threw It All Away	A-
29.	Momma You've Been On My Mind	B-
30.	Domino	A-

Side Five

31.	Early In The Morning	A-
32.	Hi Ho Silver	A-
33.	Stand By Me	A-
34.	Hare Krishna	A-
35.	Two Of Us	A-
36.	Don't Let Me Down	A-
37.	I've Got A Feeling	A-
38.	One After 909	A-

Side Six

39.	Too Bad About Sorrows	A-
40.	She Said, She Said	A-
41.	Mean Mr. Mustard	A-

42.	All Things Must Pass	A-
43.	A Fool Like Me	A-
44.	You Win Again	A-
45.	She Came In Through The Bathroom Window	A-
46.	Watching Rainbows	A-
47.	Instrumental	A-

Side Seven

48.	Two Of Us	A-
49.	Jealous Guy	A-
50.	I Shall Be Released	A-
51.	Sun King	A-
52.	Don't Let Me Down	A-

Side Eight

53.	Don't Let Me Down	A-
54.	Tea For Two	A-
55.	Whole Lotta Shakin	A-
56.	All Shook Up	A-
57.	True Love	A-
58.	Blue Suede Shoes	A-
59.	Three Cool Cats	A-
60.	Blowin In The Wind	A-
61.	Lucille	A-

Side Nine

62.	I'm So Tired	A-
63.	Ob-La-Di, Ob-La-Da	A-
64.	Third Man Theme	A-
65.	Negro In Reserve	A-
66.	Don't Let Me Down	A-
67.	One After 909	A-
68.	The Right String, But Wrong Yo Yo	A-
69.	Singing The Blues	A-

Side Ten

70.	Bring It On Home	B
71.	Hitchhike	B
72.	You Can't Do That	B
73.	Hippy Hippy Shake	B
74.	Two Of Us	A-
75.	All Along The Watchtower	A-
76.	Short Fat Fanny	A-
77.	Midnight Special	A-
78.	Money	A-
79.	Gimme Some Truth	A-

Side Eleven
80.	Get Back	A-
81.	Bad Boy	A-
82.	Sweet Little Sixteen	A-
83.	Round & Round	A-
84.	Almost Grown	N/R
85.	No Particular Place To Go	N/R

Side Twelve
86.	Paul & Rich Duet	A-
87.	Woman	A-
88.	Back Seat Of My Car	A-
89.	It's Just For You	A-
90.	Dialogue (with Peter Sellers)	A-

Side Thirteen
91.	Take This Hammer	A-
92.	Johnny B. Goode	A-
93.	Dialogue/Paul	A-
94.	I Shall Be Released	A-
95.	I've Got A Feeling	A-
96.	I Had A Dream (Dialogue)	A-

Side Fourteen
97.	Every Night	A-
98.	Dig A Pony	A-
99.	Down In Mississippi	A-
100.	Mad Man A Comin'	A-
101.	I Dig A Pony	A-
102.	High-Heeled Sneakers	A-
103.	I've Got A Feeling	A-

Side Fifteen
104.	All I Want To Do	B-
105.	Roll Over Beethoven	B-
106.	Too Bad About Sorrows	B-
107.	I Dig A Pony	B-
108.	You Got Me Thinking	A-
109.	I've Got A Feeling	A-

Side Sixteen
110.	She Came In Through The Bathroom Window	A-
111.	Octopus' Garden	A-
112.	Get Back	A-

Side Seventeen
113.	Help/Please Please Me	A-
114.	Dialogue	A-

115.	*Ob-La-Di, Ob-La-Da*	A-
116.	*Get Back*	A-
117.	*Soldier of Love*	A-
118.	*Jealous Guy*	A-
119.	*Two Of Us*	A-

Side Eighteen

120.	*Let It Be*	A-
121.	*Maxwell's Silver Hammer*	A-
122.	*When I'm Sixty Four*	A-
123.	*I Me Mine*	A-

Side Nineteen

124.	Dialogue	A-
125.	*I Me Mine* (First Rehearsal)	A-
126.	Dialogue	A-
127.	*I Me Mine* (continued)	A-
128.	*Let It Be*	A-
129.	Live Show Discussion	A-
130.	Dialogue	A-

Side Twenty

131.	*Teddy Boy* (Original Take)	A-
132.	*Two Of Us*	A-
133.	Dialogue	A-
134.	*Polythene Pam*	A-
135.	*Two Of Us*	A-
136.	*Maggie Mae*	A-
137.	Playback	A-

Side Twenty-One

138.	*One After 909*	A
139.	Instrumental	A
140.	*Save The Last Dance For Me*	A
141.	*Don't Let Me Down*	A
142.	*I Dig A Pony*	A
143.	*I've Got A Feeling*	A
144.	*Get Back*	A

Side Twenty-Two

145.	*For You Blue*	A
146.	*Teddy Boy*	A
147.	*On Our Way Home*	A
148.	*Maggie Mae*	A
149.	*Can You Dig It!*	A
150.	*Let It Be*	A
151.	*The Long & Winding Road*	A

152.   *Get Back* (Reprise)   A

Of the many "Let It Be" bootlegs available, **The Get Back Journals** is the definitive statement on the subject. This eleven-record boxed set, while slightly overlapping with other previously released bootleg material, presents as much as (or more than) you'd ever want to hear from the Twickenham Studios sessions in January 1969.

The first three disks have been previously released as **The Black Album** (see review below), while disk eleven is available separately as the **Get Back** album. Disks four through ten present previously unreleased music and conversation recorded during the filming of the movie "Let It Be."

Comments:

Disk 1 is pressed on smokey brown/tan vinyl with black swirls. This is actually record #1 of **The Black Album**. The sound quality is uniformly excellent, with all songs earning A- grades due to small amounts of background hiss.

Disk 2 is pressed on pink translucent vinyl with black swirls. This is identical in content to record #2 of **The Black Album**. Small amounts of background hiss prevent A grades from being awarded to most songs. *Momma You've Been On My Mind* earns B- because George's vocals are almost inaudible in many places, although his guitar sounds quite good.

Disk 3 is pressed on clear vinyl. This is record #3 of **The Black Album,** and as with the first two disks, is excellent-sounding. Again, only slight amounts of background hiss mar absolute perfection.

Disk 4 is pressed on clear vinyl with purple streaks and blotches. Again, a very fine-sounding record with slight amounts of hiss. *Two Of Us* is a working session that lasts about twelve minutes, and shows the song taking shape and being polished. *Jealous Guy* is an early bersion of the song later released on John's **Imagine** LP. It has different lyrics, with "Child Of Nature" being the working title. *Sun King* is a faster instrumental version of the song eventually to appear on **Abbey Road**. *Don't Let Me Down* runs about ten minutes (continued from Side Seven to Side Eight), and is significantly faster with different guitar work than the official version.

Disk 5 is pressed on pink translucent vinyl with purple streaks and blotches. This is another fine-sounding record, with most cuts earning A-grades. The first four songs on Side Ten are hampered by extraneous swishing noises, and therefore only rate B. *Gimmie Some Truth* is a very early version of John's song later released on the **Imagine** LP. Here Paul and John share the vocals, with Paul making suggestions to John during the actual songwriting process. (Paul never received official writing credit.)

Disk 6 is pressed on clear vinyl. Side Eleven is actually mislabelled, because *Almost Grown* and *No Particular Place To Go* are missing, and a version of Get Back is heard instead. *Woman* is the song written by Paul (as Bernard Webb), and released by Peter and Gordon). *Back Seat Of My Car* is an early version with only Paul (playing piano). A fine-sounding record.

Disk 7 is pressed on clear vinyl. All songs earn A- grades, as usual, due to background hiss present at most times. *Every Night* is an early version of Paul's song later issued on the **McCartney** album.

Disk 8 is pressed on clear vinyl. The first four songs on Side Fifteen earn only B- grades because of swishing noises that are either in the original tape (most probably) or are due to pressing problems in the making of the record. *Get Back* is a working/practice session that lasts about fifteen minutes.

Disk 9 is pressed on tan translucent vinyl. All songs earn A- grades. As on Disk 4, *Jealous Guy* is "Child Of Nature."

Disk 10 is pressed on tan translucent vinyl with black blotches. As with the other disks, tape hiss is the only sonic problem evident on the record. *Teddy Boy* lasts about ten-and-a-half minutes of practicing/rehearsing before disintegrating into total fooling around.

Disk 11 is the **Get Back** album, and is pressed on tan translucent vinyl with black blotches. It Is the **Let It Be** album as originally intended - song line-up intact and untouched by Phil Spector. It is stated that this record was mastered from the second generation master tape, and its sound quality proves it. All cuts earn solid A grades; this is definitely a commercial quality recording.

The songs presented vary slightly from the officially released versions. *On Our Way Home* was released as *Two Of Us*, and is slower in temp here than on the commercial LP. *Can You Dig It* is actually a long version (about four minutes) of the song *Dig It*. *Let It Be* contains a different guitar solo than on the legitimate single version. The other cuts are generally unpolished performances, *sans* overdubs, of the remaining LP songs, with the exception of *Save The Last Dance For Me* and "Instrumental," which each run about one minute and were removed from the album before it was commercially released.

In summation, **The Get Back Journals** presents more than eight hours of the Beatles during their tumultuous two weeks at the Twickenham Film Studios in January 1969. It is a most interesting sonic picture of the breakup of the group, presented over eleven fine-sounding records.

Nothing Is Real (LP) (front)

Nothing Is Real (LP) (back)

An Audiophile's Guide to the Sound of the Fab Four

Nothing Is Real Nems BUD 280

Do You Want To Know A Secret, page 177

Ratings:
Side One
1. Introduction — B+
2. *Strawberry Fields Forever* (Take One) — B+
3. *Strawberry Fields Forever* (Unreleased Version #2) — B+
4. *Strawberry Fields Forever* (Backing Tracks) — A-
5. *Strawberry Fields Forever* (Unreleased Version #3) — A-
6. *Strawberry Fields Forever* (Unreleased Version #4) — B+
7. *Strawberry Fields Forever* (Completed Master) — A

Side Two
8. *Not Guilty* — B-
9. *I'm Only Sleeping* — B
10. *Hey Jude* — B+
11. *Revolution* — A-
12. *While My Guitar Gently Weeps* — B
13. *Christmastime Is Here Again* — A

This 1985 release is highlighted by six versions of *Strawberry Fields Forever* that trace the son's development in the studio from beginning to end. The second side presents various material, to quote the album's cover, "Although several of the songs...have previously appeared on unauthorized albums, they are featured here in the best-ever sound quality to dates."

Comments:
This is a fine-sounding album, with only one cut earning as low as B-. Side One opens with "Introduction," which features George Martin explaining the creation of *Starwberry Fields Forever* from two different recordings. "Take One" is mostly John on acoustic guitar, although some drums and electric guitar are present. A slight amount of hiss is audible throughout the song; hence, the grade is only B+. The stereo has been faked by boosting the highs on the right channel and cutting them on the left. "Unreleased Version #2" is a more finished performance of the song, with all of

Sessions (LP) (front)

An Audiophile's Guide to the Sound of the Fab Four

the Beatles playing. Hiss is evident as in "Take One." This cut is in true stereo, however. "Backing Tracks" is comprised of the orchestration and Ringo's drums in stereo, minus the Beatles' guitars and vocals. A very slight depression of the high frequencies causes this to earn A-. "Unreleased Version #3 is in true stereo, and is faster than the official release. It contains all of he instruments, and earns A-. "Unreleased Version #4" is another different performance of the song. It sounds as if it is a recording of a record - possibly an acetate - as ticks and pops are heard in the beginning of recording (not the LP pressing). While sonically good, the extraneous noises cause a B+ grade. "Completed Master" is a commercial-quality recording only very slightly different, in fact, than the officially-released version.

Not Guilty is another fake stereo recording that has slightly muffled vocals and a depressed high end. It is the least desirable cut on this album, but still earns B-. *I'm Only Sleeping* is an alternate mono mix that is totally missing the low frequencies. It is also slightly depressed in the high end, and earns only a B grade. *Hey Jude* is a rehearsal that consists almost entirely of the "na na" ending of the song. It shares the lack of low end with *I'm Only Sleeping*, but its good high end helps it to earn B+. *Revolution* is a good-quality mono presentation lacking just a little weight at the low end. It is almost a commercial quality recording; grade A-. *While My Guitar Gently Weeps* is only George on the acoustic guitar. This is Take 1, when George first played it to the group in the studio. It features a verse that was left off the official edition. Vocals are distant, slightly echoed, and a little muffled. Unfortunately, this only earns a B grade, as it is a unique performance befitting a first-rate sonic presentation. *Christmastime Is Here Again* is the full-length version (six-and-a-half minutes) that was heavily edited for inclusion in the 1967 fan club Christmas flexi-disk. Sonically it is first-rate (grade A), but musically it is repetitive at best.

In summation, **Nothing Is Real** is a real gem!

Sessions Parlophone 0C 064 2402701

Do You Want To Know A Secret, page 205

Ratings:
Side One
1.	Come And Get It	B-
2.	Leave My Kitten Alone	B+
3.	Not Guilty	B
4.	I'm Looking Through You	A-
5.	What's The New Mary Jane	A-

Side Two

6.	*How Do You Do It*	A-
7.	*Besame Mucho*	A-
8.	*One After 909*	A
9.	*If You've Got Troubles*	A-
10.	*That Means A Lot*	B-
11.	*While My Guitar Gently Weeps*	B
12.	*Mailman Bring Me No More Blues*	B
13.	*Christmas Time (Is Here Again)*	A

This 1985 album is the bootleg version of the ill-fated Parlophone "Sessions" project that never saw the light of day. Material covers the period from 1962 through 1969. It includes alternate takes (*I'm Looking Through You* and *While My Guitar Gently Weeps*), previously unreleased recordings (*Besame Mucho, If You've Got Troubles*, and *Leave My Kitten Alone*), and recordings officially released by artists other than the Beatles (*Come And Get It, That Means A Lot,* and *How Do You Do It*).

According to the album's liner notes, recording dates for the various songs are as follows:

Besame Mucho - June 6, 1962
How Do You Do It - November 26, 1962
One After 909 - March 5, 1963
Leave My Kitten Alone - August 5, 1964
That Means A Lot - Spring 1965
I'm Looking Through You - Recorded during the "Rubber Soul" sessions
Christmastime Is Here Again - November 28, 1967
While My Guitar Gently Weeps - July 25, 1968
Not Guilty - August 7, 1968
What's The New Mary Jane - August 14, 1968
Mailman Bring Me No More Blues - January 1969 during the "Let It Be" sessions
Come And Get It - Sometime in 1969

Comments:

This album, containing material that spans the length of the Beatles' recording career, is both interesting and fine-sounding. *Come And Get It,* Paul's song for Badfinger, is tied for honors as the worst-sounding song on the album, yet it still earns a B- rating and is quite listenable. In stereo, its problems are slightly recessed vocals, fat ill-defined bass, and a slightly closed top end. *That Means A Lot,* the other song earning B-, has different prob-

An Audiophile's Guide to the Sound of the Fab Four

lems, including unclear vocals and harsh-sounding sibilants when the music gets loud. It is in reprocessed stereo with boosted highs in the right channel. *Not Guilty*, in stereo, earns a B due to recessed and cloudy vocals. *While My Guitar Gently Weeps*, in mono, also earns a B due to recessed vocals. It is also sounds somewhat "soft," exemplified by the lack of transient bite in George's guitar work. It is a great song, however, being Take 1 as first performed by George for the other Beatles in the studio. It is a solo acoustic performance, and includes one more verse than the officially-released version (which was Take 44). The remaining B-graded song, *Mailman Bring Me No More Blues*, suffers from ill-defined bass and slightly overbearing lower midrange.

The remaining songs earn B+ or better grades. All are quite enjoyable, and the best of them could pass for legitimate commercial releases. Highlights include: *Besame Mucho* - a different version than the January 1, 1962, Decca Audition performance; *One After 909* - the original 1963 recording; and, *I'm Looking Through You* - an early studio version before the "middle 8" was written.

In summation, this is an excellent album. It is the kind that you could tape and play in your car for non-Beatles-fanatic friends. They'd probably like the music and never know from the sound quality that it is a bootleg.

NOTE: This album has been released on compact disc three times: (1) **Sessions** (EMI CDP 7 48001 2), with eighteen cuts including eight from the LP; (2) **Sessions** (Disques du Monde SS 87 1967), featuring the entire album plus one additional cut; (3) **Sessions** (Condor 1991), also the entire album plus thirteen additional cuts.

The Beatles At Shea Trade Mark Of Quality Records

Ratings:

Side One
1. *I'm Down* — C-
2. *Spoken* — B
3. *Twist And Shout* — C-
4. *I Feel Fine* — C-
5. *Dizzy Miss Lizzy* — C-
6. *Ticket To Ride* — C

Side Two
7. *Act Naturally* — C-
8. *Can't Buy Me Love* — C+
9. *Baby's In Black* — C+
10. *A Hard Day's Night* — C+

The Beatles At Shea (LP) (front)

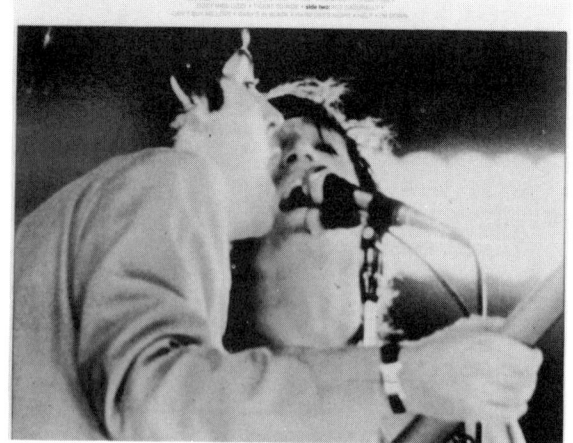

The Beatles At Shea (LP) (back)

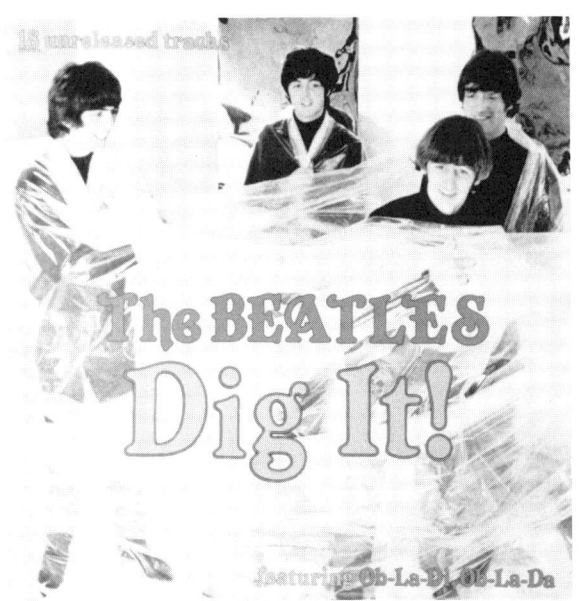

Dig It! (LP) (front)

Dig It! (LP) (back)

11. *Help* C+
12. *I'm Down* C

This album is the soundtrack from the 1965 TV documentary "The Beatles At Shea." It is in mono.

Comments:
This album can be described as fair-sounding at best. The songs earning a C- grade suffer from lack of low bass, missing highs, no evidence of Ringo's drumming, and an overabundance of audience participation (screaming). *Ticket To Ride* earns C because Ringo's drumming is inaudible. The four cuts earning C+ do so because the audience screaming is very much reduced in volume. The format of the TV special started with the concert's final song (*I'm Down*), and ended at the same place. Before the concert's first song (*Twist And Shout*) are bits of spoken wisdom from each member of the Beatles, stage announcements from Murray The K, and Ed Sullivan's introduction of the group. The second appearance of *I'm Down* includes a voice-over by George, before the song fades out well before its conclusion.

This is not a very good-sounding record. If you've seen the TV special, the album may serve as a pleasant reminder, but otherwise it can be avoided.

Dig It Nems Records FAB-1234

Do You Want To Know The Secret, page 113

Ratings:
Side One
1. *That's All Right* B-
2. *I'll Be On My Way* B
3. *Twist And Shout* A-
4. *Roll Over Beethoven* A-
5. *I Wanna Be Your Man* A-
6. *Can't Buy Me Love* A-
7. *She's A Woman* B-
8. *Ticket To Ride* B-
9. *Long Tall Sally* B-
10. *Yes It Is* A
Side Two
11. *Magical Mystery Tour* B
12. *Ob-La-Di, Ob-La-Da* A

An Audiophile's Guide to the Sound of the Fab Four

13.	*Christmas Time Is Here Again*	A
14.	*Oh Darling*	B-
15.	*Across The Universe*	A-
16.	*Lady Madonna*	B
17.	*I Want You (She's So Heavy)*	D
18.	*Dig It*	A

This 1987 release presents material from various sources, as follows:
That's All Right - BBC Radio performance
I'll Be On My Way - BBC Radio performance
Twist And Shout - Studio recording (without audience) made for the "Around The Beatles" TV special
Roll Over Beethoven - Studio recording (without audience) made for the "Around The Beatles" TV special
I Wanna Be Your Man - Studio recording (without audience) made for the "Around The Beatles" TV special
Can't Buy Me Love - Studio recording (without audience) made for the "Around The Beatles" TV special
She's A Woman - Live performance for 1965 *New Musical Express* Awards Show
Ticket To Ride - Live performance for 1965 *New Musical Express* Awards Show
Long Tall Sally - Live performance for 1965 *New Musical Express* Awards Show
Yes It Is - True stereo version
Magical Mystery Tour - Film soundtrack version
Ob-La-Di, Ob-La-Da - Early outtake
Christmas Time Is Here Again - Short version intended for **Sessions** LP
Oh Darling - Outtake vocal track by Paul (without any instrumentation)
Across The Universe - Early version without overdubs
Lady Madonna - Unfinished version without saxophone
I Want You (She's So Heavy) - John during an interview with an Israeli journalist
Dig It - Full version from the "Let It Be" sessions

Comments:
This fine-sounding album is another qiality release from NEMS Records. All cuts earn A through B- grades, except *I Want You (She's So Heavy)*, which earns D because it is very distorted and unclear. It is a very

107

short (less than one minute) impromptu performance by John during an interview with an Israeli journalist. The two BBC performances are interesting and sound good, but seem out-of-place on this album. The fit much better in **The Beatles At The BEEB** series (see reviews below).

This album has many highlights. *Dig It* is a super-long version (8:23) recorded during the "Let It Be" sessions. The officially-released edition can be heard as a small section of this one. The studio recordings made for the "Around The Beatles" TV special in 1964, *Twist And Shout, Roll Over Beethoven, I Wanna Be Your Man*, and *Can't Buy Me Love* give the listener a chance to hear the Beatles in a live performance without the usual audience participation. The performances of the songs are absolutely first-rate.

She's A Woman, from the 1965 *New Musical Express* Awards Show, while earning only a B- due to veiled vocals, indistinct bass, and audience screaming, is very interesting because the ending is very different than the commercially-released version. *Oh Darling!* is an outtake of Paul's vocal track without any instrumentation at all. It is easy to hear from this version the strain in Paul's vocal cords had to endure to get this song to sound right.

In total, this is a very good record. Can you *Dig It*?

NOTE: This album has been released on compact disc as **Dig It** (Condor 1987), including fourteen cuts from the album plus twelve others.

The Black Album   TWK 0169 AIYHO-10

Ratings:
Side One
1.	*Tennessee*	A-
2.	*House Of The Rising Sun*	A-
3.	*Commonwealth*	A-
4.	*White Power*	A-
5.	*Winston, Richard, and John*	A-
6.	*Ho Ho Silver*	A-
7.	*For You Blue*	A-
8.	*Let It Be*	A-

Side Two
9.	*Get Back*	A-
10.	*Dont Let Me Down*	A-
11.	*On Our Way Home*	A-
12.	*Don't Let Me Down*	A-
13.	*Suzy Parker*	A-
14.	*I've Got A Feeling*	A-
15.	*No Pakistanis*	A-

Side Three
16. *Let It Be* — A-
17. *Be Bop A Lula* — A-
18. *She Came In Through The Bathroom Window* — A-
19. *High Heeled Sneakers* — A-
20. *I Me Mine* — A-
21. *I've Got A Feeling*

Side Four
22. *She Came In Through The Bathroom Window* — A-
23. *Penina* — A-
24. *Shaking In The Sixties* — A-
25. *Good Rocking Tonight* — A-
26. *Across The Universe* — A-
27. *Two Of Us* — A-
28. *I Threw It All Away* — A-
29. *Momma You've Been On My Mind* — B-
30. *Domino* — A-

Side Five
31. *Early In The Morning* — A-
32. *Hi Ho Silver* — A-
33. *Stand By Me* — A-
34. *Hare Krishna* — A-
35. *Two Of Us* — A-
36. *Don't Let Me Down* — A-
37. *I've Got A Feeling* — A-
38. *One After 909* — A-

Side Six
39. *Too Bad About Sorrows* — A-
40. *She Said, She Said* — A-
41. *Mean Mr. Mustard* — A-
42. *All Things Must Pass* — A-
43. *A Fool Like Me* — A-
44. *You Win Again* — A-
45. *She Came In Through The Bathroom Window* — A-
46. *Watching Rainbows* — A-
47. *Instrumental* — A-

This three-record set of "Let It Be" film session material is packaged in similar fashion to **The Beatles** (the "White Album"), with a solid black cover with the words THE BEATLES in raised letters. It Includes a large collage-type poster with the "Let It Be" movie script on the back. Originally pressed on black vinyl and

Return To Abbey Road (LP) (front)

Return To Abbey Road (LP) (back)

then reissued in translucent multi-color, it is the reissue that is reviewed here. This material is also available as the first three records of **The Get Back Journals** (see review above).

Return To Abbey Road NW-8

Do You Want To Know A Secret, page 198

Ratings:
   Side One
   1.   *Something*   B+
   2.   *Maxwell's Silver Hammer*   A-
   3.   *Oh Darling*   A-
   4.   *Octopus's Garden*   B
   Side Two
   5.   *Because*   C+
   6.   *You Never Give Me Your Money*   B
   7.   *Sun King*   B
   8.   *Mean Mr. Mustard*   B+
   9.   *Polythene Pam*   B-
   10. *She Came In Through The Bathroom Window*   B
   11. *Golden Slumbers*   B-
   12. *Carry That Weight*   B-
   13. *Her Majesty*   A

This collection of studio material recorded during the making of the **Abbey Road** LP and the "Let It Be" sessions features a cover photograph of the Beatles crossing Abbey Road. Three things make the photo interesting: the Beatles are walking across the LP cover from right to left (the opposite direction of the **Abbey Road** LP cover), Paul is wearing sandals (instead of being barefoot), and the photograph was later used on the cover of the HMV **Abbey Road** Compact Disc Box in England.

Comments:
   Although this album is good-sounding, all of its material is available elsewhere. Cuts 1 through 4, 6, and 11 through 13 are also contained in the **No. 3 Abbey Road** LP (see review above). The remaining songs can be found in **The Get Back Journals** eleven-record box set (see review above).
   The most interesting cut on this album is *Something*. This is a tape

reduction of Take 36 onto Take 37, performed on July 11, 1969. Most of the instrumentation is the same as the commercially-released version, although the mix is different. During the mixdown, the length of this song was reduced from 7:48 to 5:32. It contains an instrumental coda that was later removed from the song before its official release. A B+ grade is earned due to small amounts of distortion in spots, along with a slight lack of high-frequency response.

Maxwell's Silver Hammer is lacking in final overdubs. A very small amount of hiss causes an A- grade. *Oh Darling* features a different vocal track by Paul. It is slightly deficient in the bass end; grade A-. *Octopus's Garden* is missing the "water" sounds, and has different guitars and a different vocal by Ringo. The sound gets garbled in a few places, but the B rating is mainly due to the veiled sound of Ringo's vocals. *Because* earns the lowest rating of any song on this album (C+). It is a very short (less than one minute) vocal-only performance that sounds as if you're hearing it through a wooden door.

You Never Give Me Your Money is different in instrumentation and vocals than the official edition. It is hissy and lacking in deep bass, and therefore earns only a B grade. *Sun King* is a guitar only instrumental track with talking in the background. It is also hissy and earns a B grade. *Mean Mr. Mustard* is an early version without much of its final instrumentation. It is very slightly deficient at both ends of the frequency spectrum; grade B+. The vocals are not yet finalized, because Polythene Pam, as mentioned in the line "...his sister Pam works..." is not called Pam, but Shirley!

Polythene Pam is a very primitive version that is mostly John with sparse instrumentation. It sounds slightly muffled and distant, and earns a B- grade. *She Came In Through The Bathroom Window* is a slower version that sounds distant, and is lacking in both the high and low frequencies; grade B. *Golden Slumbers* and *Carry That Weight* both feature different vocals and instrumentation, but suffer from tape dropouts and distortion, earning only B- grades. *Her Majesty* is the "true" version as originally recorded - without the opening guitar chord and with the closing acoustic guitar chord. It is the best-sounding song on the album; grade A.

In summation, this is a good-sounding album of material available elsewhere. For owners of **No. 3 Abbey Road** and **The Get Back Journals**, its only virtue is its front cover. For others, this collection of studio outtakes of material from the **Abbey Road** album - although some were recorded during the "Let It Be" sessions - is quite interesting.

An Audiophile's Guide to the Sound of the Fab Four

1967 Parlophone PCS 1967

Fixing A Hole, page 189

Ratings:
Side One
1. *A Day In The Life* — C+
2. *Strawberry Fields Forever* — B+
3. *Only A Northern Song* — A
4. *Penny Lane* — B+
5. *All You Need Is Love* — A
6. *It's All Too Much* — B
7. *A Day In The Life* — A

Side Two
8. *Magical Mystery Tour* — B
9. *The Fool On The Hill* — B
10. Instrumental — C+
11. *Blue Jay Way* — A
12. *Your Mother Should Know* — B-
13. *I Am The Walrus* — A-
14. *Christmas Time Is Here Again* — A-

The jacket of this 1988 album is very similar to the legitimate **Sgt. Pepper** album, except that both the front and back photographs are alternate shots. The material is from many sources, as follows:

A Day In The Life - Demo acetate
Strawberry Fields Forever - Demo acetate
Only A Northern Song - Original mono version, never available in the U.S.
Penny Lane - Original mono promotional version
All You Need Is Love - Live performance from the "Our World" telecast
It's All Too Much - Unreleased version
A Day In The Life - Remixed version with clean intro
Magical Mystery Tour - Film soundtrack
The Fool On The Hill - Demo acetatee
Instrumental - "Magical Mystery Tour" film soundtrack
Blue Jay Way - Rare mono version with different sound effects
Your Mother Should Know - Demo acetate
I Am The Walrus - Demo acetate
Christmas Time Is Here Again - Complete version

Comments:
This good-sounding album presents material from the year 1967, comprising the "Sgt. Pepper" and "Magical Mystery Tour" recording sessions, plus the "Our World" live TV performance. *A Day In The Life* (#1) only earns a C+ grade due to popping and crackling sounds, veiled vocals, slightly fat bass, and lack of high frequencies. The noises arise from the fact that this track originates from a demo acetate. This song is very interesting, however, because it includes a vocal track that is different than the commercially-released version of this song. These vocals contain significantly different echo effects, as well as different lyrics in a few places.

Strawberry Fields Forever is another demo acetate, although it does not suffer from extraneous surface noise. Although fine-sounding (B+), this track is better heard on the **Nothing Is Real** LP (see review above), where the creation and development of this song is presented across the entire side of an album.

Only A Northern Song, in mono, is slightly different than the stereo version. It is of true commercial quality; grade A. This version had previously been available only on the English monaural pressing of the **Yellow Submarine** album. *Penny Lane* is the mono promotional version with the trumpet ending. It earns B+, but since the Beatles **Rarities** LP makes this available in stereo, the value of this cut is rather small. *All You Need Is Love* is the live performance from the "Our World" telecast, in mono. It sounds very similar to the commercial release of this song, although some of the final overdubs are not yet included. Grade A.

"Instrumental," a short snippet (less than one minute) of incidental music from the "Magical Mystery Tour" film, earns only a C+ because it is very hissy and lacking at both ends of the frequency spectrum. The remaining cuts all earn in the B- to A range. They are various demo acetates, mono versions, and remixes. Some of them are available on other bootlegs, as follows:

A Day In The Life (#2) is on **Not For Sale**
Magical Mystery Tour is on **Dig It**
The Fool On The Hill is on **Ultra Rare Trax Vol. 1 & Vol. 2**
Christmastime Is Here Again is on **File Under: Beatles**

While this album is generally a good-sounding one, its value is not quite top shelf. Since a good bit of its material is available elsewhere, a Beatles fan with a large bootleg collection will already own much of this material. The demo acetate of *A Day In The Life* is quite interesting, as are the outtake photos on the front and back covers.

This record would make a fine addition to a beginning bootleg col-

1967 (LP) (front)

Meet The BEEB (LP) (front)

lection, but has very little place in a large one.

Meet The BEEB BEEB Transcription Records BB2190

Fixing A Hole, page 181

Ratings:
Side One
1.	*Dream Baby*	D+
2.	*Memphis Tennessee*	C-
3.	*Please Mr. Postman*	D+
4.	*Ask Me Why*	D+
5.	*Besame Mucho*	D+
6.	*A Picture Of You*	D+
7.	*Some Other Guy*	C-
8.	*Keep Your Hands Off My Baby*	C-
9.	*Beautiful Dreamer*	C
10.	*From Me To You*	D+

Side Two
11.	*I Saw Her Standing There*	C
12.	*Misery*	C
13.	*Too Much Monkey Business*	C
14.	*I'm Talking About You*	C
15.	*Please Please Me*	C
16.	*Hippy Hippy Shake*	C
17.	*I Saw Her Standing There*	D+
18.	*A Shot Of Rhythm And Blues*	D
19.	*There's A Place*	E
20.	*My Evelyne*	E

This album contains material predating Volume 1 of **The Beatles At The BEEB** series, as well as other BEEB performances not included in the series. Cuts 1 through 6 have Pete Best on drums, and are also included on **The Lost BEEBs** album (see review below). The origin of the material is as follows:

Cuts 1 - 3: "Teenagers Turn," recorded March 7 and broadcast March 8, 1962

Cuts 4 - 6: "Here We Go Again," broadcast June 15, 1962

Cuts 7 - 9: "Saturday Club," recorded January 22 and broadcast January 26, 1963

An Audiophile's Guide to the Sound of the Fab Four

Cut 10: "Easy Beat," broadcast April 7, 1963
Cuts 11 - 16: "Saturday Club," broadcast live March 16, 1963
Cuts 17 - 19: "Easy Beat," broadcast July 21, 1963
Cut 20: Unknown BBC program, broadcast sometime in 1963 (probably not the Beatles)

Comments:
This is not a good-sounding record. The best of its twenty songs only earn C grades. Sonic problems include lack of bass, lack of treble extension, instrumentation not audible or ill-defined, recessed vocals, volume fading up and down, and an overabundance of midrange energy. The greater the number of these problems, or the greater the magnitude of these problems, the lower the song's grade.

Does this record offer the Beatles fan anything of value? Yes. The first six songs on Side One represent the group's two 1962 BBC radio appearances with Pete Best on drums. The album's final cut, *My Evelyne*, is actually *Abilene* (the city in Texas). It is not the Beatles. Its sound is so bad as to be almost unlistenable, but it is interesting to hear a time or two.

By the way, although this album contains material predating **The Beatles At The BEEB** series, it is not a harbinger of things to come. Starting with the first record, **The Beatles At The BEEB** disks are ear-opening albums!

The Lost BEEBs Tiger Beat Records TBR/LP2

Fixing A Hole, page 165

Ratings:
Side One
1. *Dream Baby* — D+
2. *Memphis Tennessee* — C-
3. *Please Mr. Postman* — C-
4. *Ask Me Why* — E
5. *Besame Mucho* — D+
6. *A Picture Of You* — D+

Side Two
7. *Misery* — B-
8. *The Hippy Hippy Shake* — B-
9. *Money (That's What I Want)* — B
10. *Till There Was You* — C-
11. *A Shot Of Rhythm And Blues* — B-

117

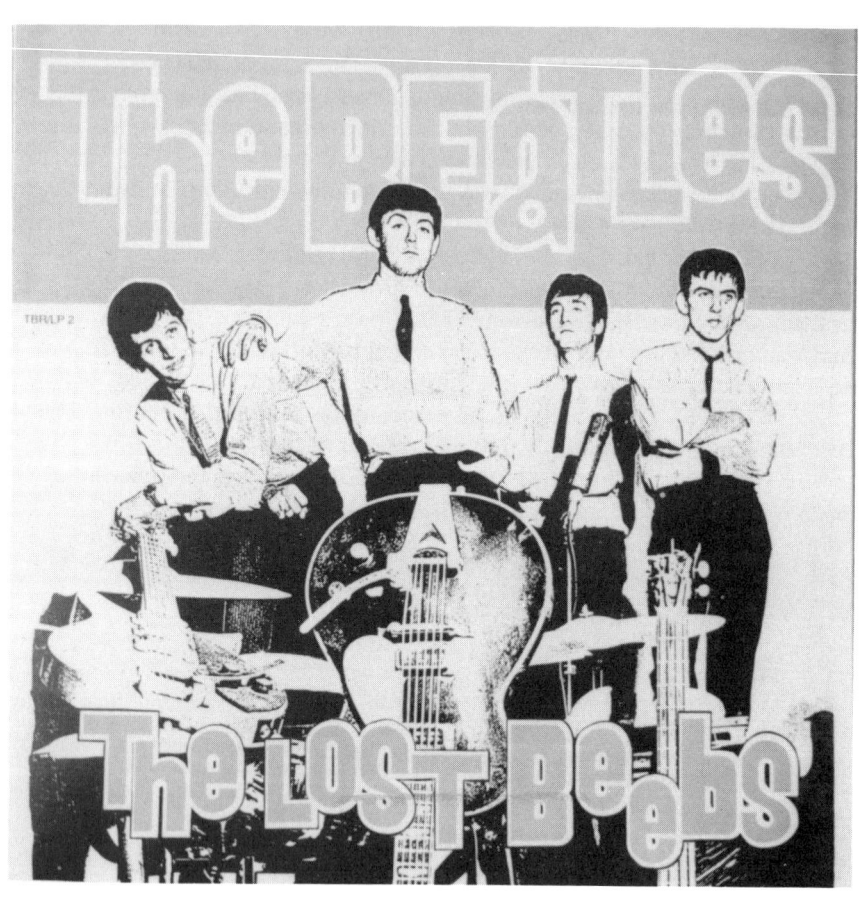

The Lost BEEBs (LP) (front)

12. *Money (That's What I Want)*   C

This album is presented as a "...companion volume to the fine Beatles At The BEEB series." It contains material from 1962 and 1963. Cuts 1 through 6 have Pete Best on drums, and are also included on the **Meet The BEEB** album (see review above). The origin of the material is as follows:

Cuts 1 - 3: "Teenagers Turn," recorded March 7 and broadcast March 8, 1962

Cuts 4 - 6: "Here We Go Again," broadcast June 15, 1962

Cuts 7 - 8: "Pop Go The Beatles," recorded May 24 and broadcast June 4, 1963

Cuts 9 - 10: "Saturday Club," recorded June 24 and broadcast June 29, 1963

Cut 11: "Pop Go The Beatles," recorded July 10 and broadcast July 23, 1963

Cuts 12 - 13: "Pop Go The Beatles," recorded August 1 and broadcast August 27, 1963

Cut 14: "Pop Go The Beatles," recorded August 1 and broadcast September 3, 1963

Comments:

As with the **Meet The BEEB** LP, this album presents the Beatles' two 1962 BBC appearances with Pete Best on drums. Unfortunately, the sound quality is as bad on this album as it is on that one. A lack of audible instrumentation, distorted vocals, no treble, harsh sound when instruments are audible, and a lack of deep base plague each of the songs on Side One of this record. The problems are bad in all cases, as only *Memphis Tennessee* and *Please Mr. Postman* earn C- ratings.

Side One closes out with four-and-a-half minutes of phone chat between the Beatles and Brian Matthew aired on the BBC on Saturday, February 8, 1964. This was recorded on Friday, February 7, after the Beatles landed in New York City to start their first American visit.

Side Two sounds considerably better than Side One. *Misery* and *Hippy Hippy Shake*, recorded in May of 1963, have "up front" vocals and acceptable levels of bass and treble information. Distortion in small amounts cause the B- ratings for these songs. The next cut, *Money*, is the best-sounding song on this album. It is free of any distortion, and earns a B grade.

The final five songs on this album all earn in the range of B- to C-. All exhibit some distortion on vocals or instrumentation. The presentation of the frequency extremes separates these songs, with *A Shot Of Rhythm And Blues* having the best bass and getting a B- grade.

While only Side Two of this album is sonically worth repeated listening, this record is definitely preferred over **Meet The BEEB** if you'd like to have the Beatles' 1962 BBC appearances on vinyl.

The Beatles At The BEEB Volume 1 Beeb Transcription Records 2172

Do You Want To Know A Secret, page 72

Ratings:
Side One
1.	*I Saw Her Standing There*	B+
2.	*Do You Want To Know A Secret*	B+
3.	*Boys*	A-
4.	*Long Tall Sally*	A-
5.	*From Me To You*	A-
6.	*Money (That's What I Want)*	B+
7.	*Side By Side*	N/R
8.	*Too Much Monkey Business*	A-
9.	*Boys*	A
10.	*I'll Be On My Way*	A
11.	*From Me To You*	A

Side Two
12.	*Some Other Guy*	A-
13.	*A Taste Of Honey*	B+
14.	*Thank You Girl*	A-
15.	*From Me To You*	A-
16.	*Twist And Shout*	C+
17.	*From Me To You*	C+
18.	*Please Please Me*	C-
19.	*I Saw Her Standing There*	C-

This album is the first of the BEEB series, and contains performances from 1963 as follows:
- Cuts 1 - 6: "Saturday Club," recorded May 21 and broadcast May 25, 1963
- Cuts 7 - 11: "Side By Side," recorded April 4 and broadcast June 24, 1963
- Cuts 12 - 15: "Easy Beat," recorded June 19 and broadcast June 23, 1963
- Cuts 16 - 17: "Swinging Sound '63," broadcast live April 18, 1963

An Audiophile's Guide to the Sound of the Fab Four

Cuts 18-19: "Steppin' Out," recorded May 21 and broadcast June 3, 1963

Comments:
This mono album is a fine start to **The Beatles At The BEEB** LP series. Things begin with six songs recorded for "Saturday Club" on May 21, 1963. *I Saw Her Standing There* features excellent frequency balance and clear, forward vocals. It contains a guitar solo by George that is different than that of the commercial version of this song. Only a couple of tape drop outs cause the grade to be B+. *Do You Want To Know A Secret* earns B+ due to hiss at its start, although it is generally fine sounding. *Boys, Long Tall Sally*, and *From Me To You* are excellent sounding songs (A-), with performances differing from their more familiar commercial versions. *Boys* features a different guitar solo by George, and *Long Tall Sally* and *From Me To You* are performed faster than usual. *Misery* is plagued by a brief fade out in the tape at the beginning, but still earns a B+

Side By Side is a very short theme song with some lyrics sung by the Fab Four. It is too short to be given a sonic rating. The four songs from this radio show are both great performances and sonically excellent. *Too Much Monkey Business*, a Chuck Berry song never officially released by the group, features a fine lead vocal performance by John. Its grade is A- because the bass is slightly ill-defined at times. *I'll Be On My Way* is a startlingly good rendition of the song given to Billy J. Kramer. It is slower than his familiar version, and has more sparse instrumentation;grade A. *Boys* and *From Me To You* are both just about perfect, and also earn A grades.

The four songs recorded live before a studio audience for the "Easy Beat" program open Side Two of this album in grand fashion. *Some Other Guy* is a Beatles concert mainstay from their Cavern Club shows. A small amount of hiss causes this good performance to earn oly A-. *A Taste Of Honey* gets B+ due to some audible distortion in places. *From Me To You* and *Thank You Girl* are both A- songs, with *Thank You Girl* differing from its commercial edition because John doesn't play the harmonica this time.

Twist And Shout and *From Me To You*, broadcast live on April 18, 1963, on the "Swinging Sound '63" show, are not very good sounding. Vocals are slightly muffled, bass is ill-defined, treble is not very extended, and during vocal passages most of the instrumentation drops out (becomes inaudible). These C+ songs sound as if they were recorded with a low quality microphone in the audience.

The album finishes with *Please Please Me* and *I Saw Her Standing There*, recorded live before an audience for the "Steppin' Out" show. These are the worst-sounding songs on the record, each earning a C- rating. Both are very distorted at times, and lack extension at both frequency extremes. While not

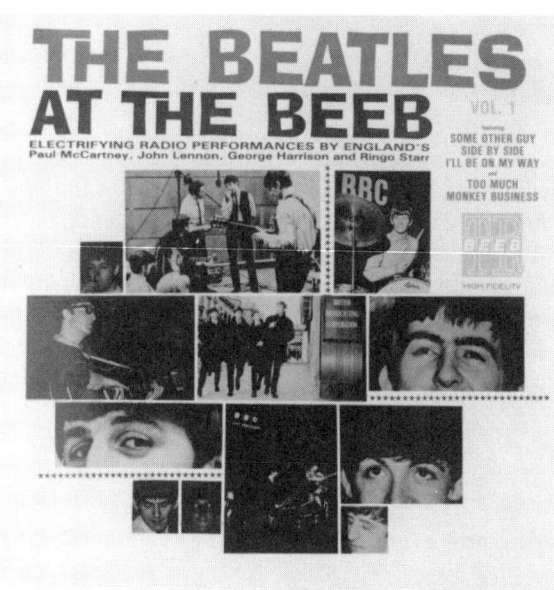

The Beatles At The BEEB Volume 1 (LP) (front)

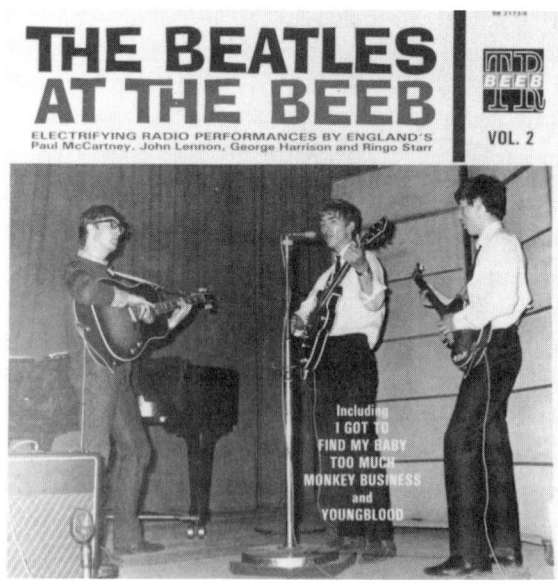

The Beatles At The BEEB Volume 2 (LP) (front)

being very good sounding, *I Saw Her Standing There* does have some interesting guitar work by George.

In summation, this album makes a fine start to **The Beatles At The BEEB** series. Fourteen of the eighteen songs earn B+ or better grades as the Beatles generally give rousing performances for their radio audiences. Highlights of this record are the three songs never officially released, *Too Much Monkey Business*, *I'll Be On My Way*, and *Some Other Guy*.

NOTE: This album has been released on compact disc as **The Beatles At The BEEB Volume 1** (Pyramid RFT CD005).

The Beatles At The BEEB Volume 2 Beeb Transcription Records 2173

Do You Want To Know A Secret, page 73

Ratings:
   Side One
   1. *I've Got To Find My Baby*   A-
   2. *Memphis, Tennessee*   A
   3. *From Me To You*   A-
   4. *Roll Over Beethoven*   B+
   5. *Long Tall Sally*   A-
   6. *A Taste Of Honey*   A-
   7. *Chains*   B+
   8. *Thank You Girl*   A-
   9. *Boys*   A-
   Side Two
   10. *Too Much Monkey Business*   A-
   11. *I Got To Find My Baby*   A-
   12. *Youngblood*   A
   13. *'Till There Was You*   A-
   14. *Baby It's You*   A-
   15. *Love Me Do*   B-
   16. *Everybody's Trying To Be My Baby*   C
   17. *Do You Want To Know A Secret*   C
   18. *You Really Got A Hold On Me*   C-

This album is the second of the BEEB series, and contains performances from 1963 as follows:
   Cuts 1 - 4: "Saturday Club," recorded June 24 and broadcast June 29, 1963
   Cuts 5 - 9: "Side By Side," recorded April 1 and broadcast May 13,

1963
Cuts 10 - 15: "Pop Go The Beatles" (#2), recorded June 1 and broadcast June 11, 1963
Cuts 16 - 18: "Pop Go The Beatles" (#1), recorded May 24 and broadcast June 4, 1963

Comments:
This second album in **The Beatles At The BEEB** series presents performances recorded for the BBC in the spring and summer of 1963. It is an excellent album, with fourteen songs earning B+ or better grades, and fifteen of the eighteen songs rated above C.

The record opens with four songs from "Saturday Club." *I Got To Find My Baby* is the Beatles' version of a 1960 Chuck Berry song with John on lead vocal. It is an outstanding performance kept from perfection by a very slightly depressed high end; grade A-. *Memphis, Tennessee* is next, another previously unreleased song written by Chuck Berry. This version is very similar to that from the Decca Audition of January 1, 1962, and earns a perfect A rating. *From Me To You* earns an A- because it is slightly lightweight in character and ill-defined at the top end. The "Saturday Club" show ends with *Roll Over Beethoven*, which only gets a B+ because George's voice fades down in volume and the instrumentation gets sparse during the first half-minute of the song. The remainder of the song is sonically excellent, and contains different guitar work than the official version.

The next five songs are from the "Side By Side" show recorded on April 1, 1963. All earn A- grades except *Chains*, which gets B+due to hiss and recessed vocals during the chorus. *Long Tall Sally* has great vocals by Paul, and different guitars than the official version, but is kept from perfection by a depressed low end in places. *Thank You Girl* is slightly lacking in bass and, as in Volume 1, John does not play the harmonica. *Boys* begins with a wonderful introduction by Ringo, who says that if the album (**Please Please Me**) is selling, then *Boys* is "...the track that's selling it!" It is slightly bass shy and fades out early, but has different guitar work by George than the commercial version.

The six songs from "Pop Go The Beatles" (#2) all earn B- to A grades, with *Love Me Do* getting B- because of a depressed high end, recessed vocals, and some distortion. *Youngblood*, a song performed only once on the BBC, earns a perfect A grade. *Too Much Monkey Business* gets A- due to a deficient high end. *I Got To Find My Baby* and *'Till There Was You* both get A- because of bass problems, and *Baby It's You* gets A- since the tape drops in level briefly in the first half-minute of the song.

The album's final three songs, from "Pop Go The Beatles" (#1), all suffer from a whining/buzzing in the background. *Everybody's Trying To Be My Baby* and *Do You Want To Know A Secret* both have problems in the treble region, and get C grades. *You Really Got A Hold On Me* is the least sonically desirable song on the album. Its C- grade is caused by a lack of bass, muffled background vocals, and unclear instrumentation.

Despite the fact that the final three songs are only fair sounding, this is an excellent album. With this, **The Beatles At The BEEB** series is "2 for 2"!

NOTE: This album has been released on compact disc as **The Beatles At The BEEB Volume 2** (Pyramid RFT CD006).

The Beatles At The BEEB Volume 3 Beeb Transcription Records 2174

Do You Want To Know A Secret, page 74

Ratings:
   Side One
1. *Pop Go The Beatles* — A
2. *A Shot Of Rhythm And Blues* — A-
3. *Memphis, Tennessee* — A-
4. *Happy Birthday Paul* — N/R
5. *A Taste Of Honey* — A-
6. *Sure To Fall* — A
7. *Money (That's What I Want)* — A-
8. *I Saw Her Standing There* — B+
9. *Anna (Go To Him)* — B+
10. *Boys* — A-
11. *Chains* — A-
   Side Two
12. *P.S. I Love You* — A-
13. *Twist And Shout* — A-
14. *That's Alright Mama* — B-
15. *There's A Place* — B-
16. *Carol* — A-
17. *Soldier Of Love* — A
18. *Lend Me Your Comb* — A-
19. *Clarabella* — A-
20. *Pop Go The Beatles* — A-

This album is the third of the BEEB series, and contains performances from 1963 as follows:
   Cuts 1 - 7: "Pop Go The Beatles" (#3), recorded June 1 and broadcast June 18, 1963

Cuts 8 - 13: "Pop Go The Beatles" (#4), recorded June 17 and broadcast June 25, 1963
Cuts 14 - 19: "Pop Go The Beatles" (#5), recorded July 2 and broadcast July 16, 1963

Comments:
This third album in **The Beatles At The BEEB** series consists of three "Pop Go The Beatles" shows recorded in June and July of 1963. Cuts 1 through 7 were recorded June 1, and broadcast June 18. The record starts with the show's theme, *Pop Go The Beatles*. It is a short piece (about a half-minute) that is perfect; grade A. The remaining rated songs from the show all earn A- or A grades. *A Shot Of Rhythm And Blues* is a never officially recorded song that earns A- due to a small deficiency at the low end. *Memphis, Tennessee* is a short version (joined in progress) that gets A- because of hiss. *Happy Birthday Paul* is not rated because it is just a short *a capella* birthday wish. *A Taste Of Honey* earns A- due to small amounts of hiss, and too full bass at times. *Sure To Fall* is perfect, and gets an A grade. *Money (That's What I Want)* earns an A- because it is slightly depressed at the high end. It features a guitar introduction instead of the familiar piano intro.

Songs 8 throuh 13 were recorded on June 17, and broadcast on June 25, 1963. *I Saw Her Standing There* and *Anna (Go To Him)* both earn B+ because they are lacking at the high end and are too full and fat-sounding in the mid bass. The remaining four songs from this show all earn A- ratings, with *Boys*, *Chains*, and *Twist And Shout* being deficient at the high end, and *P.S. I Love You* exhibiting small amounts of hiss throughout its length.

The final seven songs were performed on July 2, and broadcast on July 16. *That's Alright Mama* is the Beatles' performance of the Big Boy Crudup song made famous by Elvis Presley. It gets B- because it is somewhat distorted at times, and has a fat-sounding bass guitar. *There's A Place* sounds very similar to *That's Alright Mama*, and gets the same grade. *Carol*, another of the Beatles' many Chuck Berry covers, gets an A- because of deficient bass. *Soldier Of Love*, with John on lead vocal, gets a perfect A rating. *Lend Me Your Comb* and *Clarabella* are premier radio performances of these songs by the group. Both get A- due to deficiencies at the bass end. *Pop Go The Beatles* is the longest recorded version of this song (1:05), and gets an A- because it is fat in the bass.

What can be said in summing up this record? It is the best of the series so far, with all cuts earning B- or better. Containing many unique songs in great sound quality, this is a can't miss album!

NOTE: This album has been released on compact disc as **The Beatles At The BEEB Volume 3** (Pyramid RFT CD007).

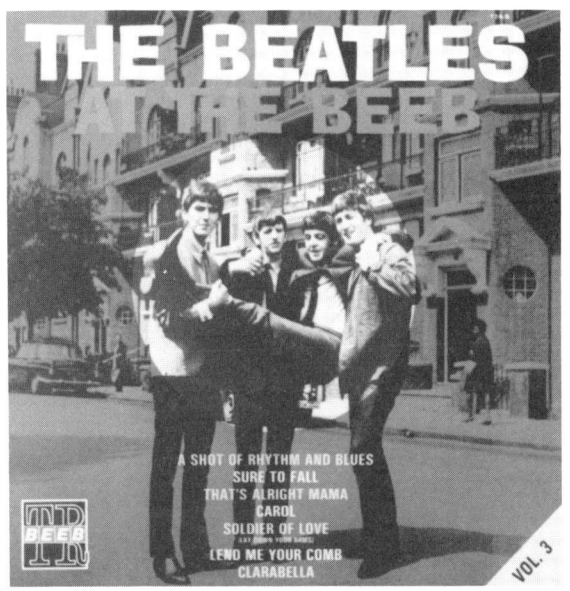

The Beatles At The BEEB Volume 3 (LP) (front)

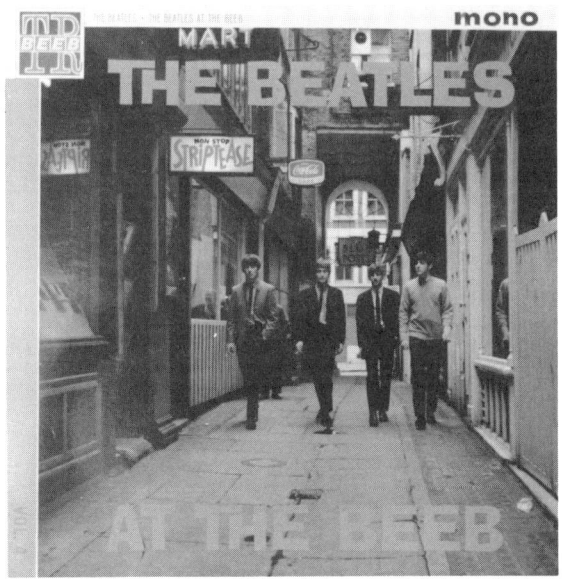

The Beatles At The BEEB Volume 4 (LP) (front)

The Beatles At The BEEB Volume 4   Beeb Transcription Records 2175

Do You Want To Know A Secret, page 76

Ratings:
Side One
1.	*Sweet Little Sixteen*	B
2.	*Nothin' Shakin' (But The Leaves On The Tree)*	C-
3.	*Lonesome Tears In My Eyes*	A-
4.	*So How Come (No One Loves Me)*	A-
5.	*Memphis, Tennessee*	A-
6.	*Do You Want To Know A Secret*	B
7.	*Till There Was You*	B+
8.	*Matchbox*	B+
9.	*Please Mr. Postman*	B+
10.	*The Hippy Hippy Shake*	B+

Side Two
11.	*Pop Go The Beatles*	A
12.	*I'm Gonna Sit Right Down And Cry Over You*	A-
13.	*Crying, Waiting, Hoping*	A-
14.	*Kansas City/Hey-Hey-Hey-Hey*	A-
15.	*To Know Her Is To Love Her*	A
16.	*The Honeymoon Song*	A
17.	*Twist And Shout*	A
18.	*Pop Go The Beatles*	A-

This album is the fourth of the BEEB series, and contains performances from 1963 as follows:
    Cuts 1 - 4: "Pop Go The Beatles" (#6), recorded July 10 and broadcast July 27, 1963
    Cuts 5 - 10: "Pop Go The Beatles" (#7), recorded July 10 and broadcast July 30, 1963
    Cuts 11 - 18: "Pop Go The Beatles" (#8), recorded July 16 and broadcast August 6, 1963

Comments:
    This fourth album in **The Beatles At The BEEB** series upholds the high sonic and performance standards set by the first three records. Of the eighteen songs presented here, seventeen earn B- or better grades. As well as being sonically excellent, this album contains eight songs performed only once for the BBC. It is this unique material that makes this such a wonderful record.

An Audiophile's Guide to the Sound of the Fab Four

Sweet Little Sixteen leads off the first of the three "Pop Go The Beatles" shows presented here. John sings lead on this performance, which earns a B due to hiss and small amounts of distortion. This, like the following three songs, was performed only once for the BBC and is available nowhere else. *Nothin' Shakin' (But The Leaves On The Tree)* has George on lead vocal on the worst-sounding song on this record. Its C grade is caused by large amounts of hiss, recessed and distorted vocals, and deficiencies at both ends of the frequency spectrum. *Lonesome Tears In My Eyes* features a fine vocal by John, and good sonics. Only a slight depression in the bass keeps this song from perfection; grade A-. *So How Come (No One Loves Me)* closes this "Pop Go The Beatles" episode in great style. Only a slightly ill-defined bass end makes the grade A-.

The next six songs come from the second of the "Pop Go The Beatles" shows on this record. Being the second show for the group recorded that day (July 10), the boys did not perform any unique material. *Memphis, Tennessee* is slightly deficient at the top end, and earns an A-. *Do You Want To Know A Secret* gets a B because the recording is slightly hissy, deficient at the top end, and has a couple of tape drop outs. *Till There Was You* has slightly fat bass, and is deficient in the treble; grade B+. *Matchbox* is the first BBC performance of the song by the group, and gets a B+ grade due to deficient treble and overemphasized bass. *Please Mr. Postman* and *Hippy Hippy Shake* sound very similar to *Matchbox*, and also earn B+.

Side Two of this album consists entirely of the "Pop Go The Beatles" program recorded on July 16. It starts and finishes with the show's theme song, although the closing edition is the long (1:05) version. Its A- is caused by a decrease in level in the left channel. The six songs between the themes all earn A- or A grades. *To Know Her Is To Love Her*, *The Honeymoon Song*, and *Twist And Shout* are absolutely perfect, and get an A. Both *To Know Her Is To Love Her* and *The Honeymoon Song* are one-time BBC performances. *I'm Gonna Sit Right Down And Cry Over You* is a unique appearance earning A- because of a slightly deficient high end. Another unique BBC song, *Crying, Waiting, Hoping*, earns A- because the bass is a little too full at times. The album is rounded out by *Kansas City/Hey-Hey-Hey-Hey*, an A- song also due to a high end frequency.

In conclusion, **The Beatles At The BEEB Volume 4** is an outstanding album. It has a great cover photograph, presents eight songs never performed elsewhere, and is sonically excellent. A must have!

NOTE: This album has been released on compact disc as **The Beatles At The BEEB Volume 4** (Pyramid PYCD018).

The Beatles At The BEEB Volume 5 Beeb Transcription Records 2176

Do You Want To Know A Secret, page 77

Ratings:
    Side One
1. *Pop Go The Beatles* — B
2. *Long Tall Sally* — A-
3. *Please Please Me* — A-
4. *She Loves You* — A-
5. *You Really Gotta Hold On Me* — A-
6. *I'll Get You* — A-
7. *I Got A Woman* — A-
8. *Pop Go The Beatles* — B
9. *She Loves You* — B
10. *Words Of Love* — B
    Side Two
11. *Glad All Over* — C+
12. *I Just Don't Understand* — C+
13. *Devil In Her Heart* — C+
14. *Slow Down* — C
15. *Ooh! My Soul* — B
16. *Don't Ever Change* — C
17. *Twist And Shout* — C
18. *There's A Place* — B
19. *Honey Don't* — B+
20. *Roll Over Beethoven* — B+

This album is the fifth of the BEEB series, and contains performances from 1963 as follows:
    Cuts 1 - 8: "Pop Go The Beatles" (#9), recorded July 16 and broadcast August 13, 1963
    Cuts 9 - 14: "Pop Go The Beatles (#10), recorded July 16 and broadcast August 20, 1963
    Cuts 15 - 17: "Pop Go The Beatles" (#11), recorded August 1 and broadcast August 27, 1963
    Cuts 18 - 20: "Pop Go The Beatles" (#12), recorded August 1 and broadcast September 3, 1963

Comments:
    This fifth album in **The Beatles At The BEEB** series features shows #9 through #12 of "Pop Go The Beatles," recorded in July and August, and

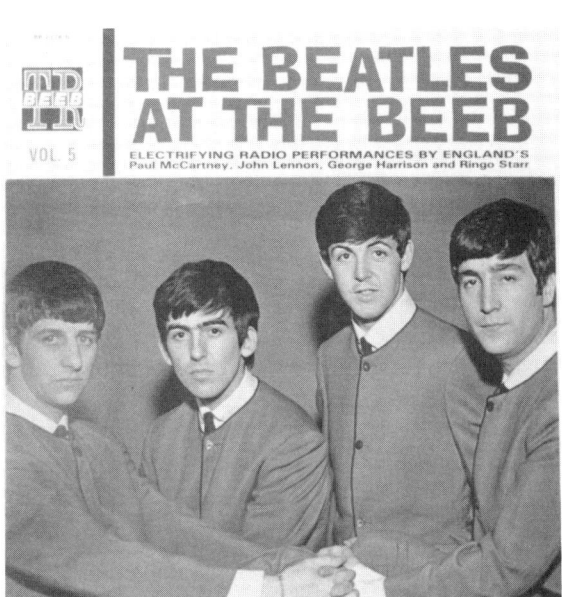

The Beatles At The BEEB Volume 5 (LP) (front)

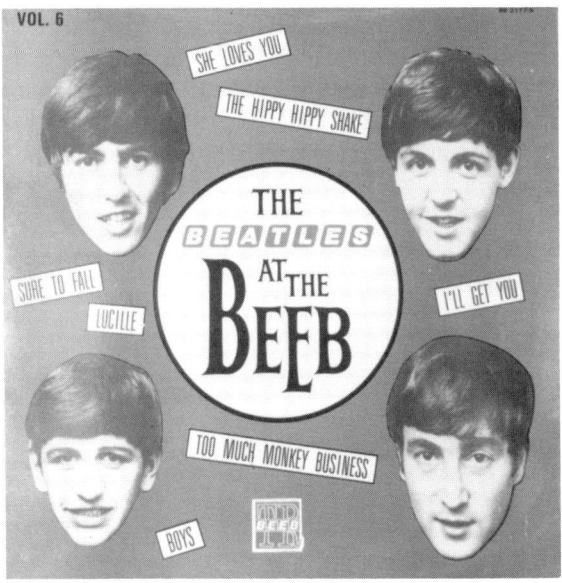

The Beatles At The BEEB Volume 6 (LP) (front)

broadcast in August and September of 1963.

Show #9, recorded July 16, is the high point of this record. Its six songs (not counting the opening and closing themes) all earn A- grades. Only a small amount of background hiss ruins perfection for these tunes. *Long Tall Sally* features guitar playing by George that is different than the commercial version, and *I Got A Woman* is an unreleased song performed for the first time on the BBC.

Show #10 is not as good sonically at #9. *She Loves You* and *Words Of Love* earn B grades because of background hiss, slightly harsh vocals, and a deficiency in the bass. These songs have a "lightweight" sound because of the lack of deep bass. *Glad All Over*, *I Just Don't Understand*, and *Devil In Her Heart* get C+ grades because of major problems with hiss. Although the full frequency range is well presented, the level of hiss is so great as to be intrusive on the music. These songs are listenable, however, which is good because *Glad All Over* and *I Just Don't Understand* are first-time BBC performances of these unreleased Beatles songs.

Show #11 opens in the middle of *Ooh! My Soul*, a Little Richard song. Only a minute-and-a-half of it is presented here. Slightly distorted vocals cause it to receive a B grade. *Don't Ever Change* and *Twist And Shout* earn C ratings due to obtrusive amounts of hiss and "lightweight" sound.

Show #12 closes the album with three songs broadcast September 3, 1963. *There's A Place* is slightly lacking in the bass, and is a little hissy; grade B. *Honey Don't* and *Roll Over Beethoven* are hiss free, but lacking in the low frequencies, causing B+ ratings. *Honey Don't* is unique because John handles the lead vocal rather than Ringo, a departure from the commercial release.

All in all, this is a fine record. Fourteen of its twenty songs earn B- or better grades, five songs were never officially released by the group, and one features a unique performance with a different lead singer. This album would make a fine addition to any collection.

NOTE: This album has been released on compact disc as **The Beatles At The BEEB Volume 5** (Pyramid RFT CD014).

The Beatles At The BEEB Volume 6 Beeb Transcription Records 2177

Do You Want To Know A Secret, page 78

Ratings:
Side One
1.	Too Much Monkey Business	A-
2.	Love Me Do	B+
3.	She Loves You	B+

An Audiophile's Guide to the Sound of the Fab Four

4.	*I'll Get You*	A-
5.	*A Taste Of Honey*	A-
6.	*The Hippy Hippy Shake*	A-
7.	*Chains*	B+
8.	*You Really Got A Hold On Me*	A-
Side Two		
9.	*Misery*	A-
10.	*Lucille*	A-
11.	*From Me To You*	A-
12.	*Boys*	B+
13.	*She Loves You*	B+
14.	*Ask Me Why*	A-
15.	*Devil In Her Heart*	A-
16.	*I Saw Her Standing There*	A-
17.	*Sure To Fall*	A-
18.	*Twist And Shout*	A-

This album is the sixth of the BEEB series, and conatins performances from 1963 as follows:
Cuts 1 - 6: "Pop Go The Beatles" (#13), recorded September 3 and broadcast September 13, 1963
Cuts 7 - 12: "Pop Go The Beatles" (#14), recorded September 3 and broadcast September 17, 1963
Cuts 13 - 18: "Pop Go The Beatles" (#15), recorded September 3 and broadcast September 24, 1963

Comments:
This sixth album in **The Beatles At The BEEB** series presents shows #13 through #15 of "Pop Go The Beatles." These final three shows of the series were recorded in one marathon day between 2:00 PM and 10:30 PM in a London BBC studio.
Thirteen of the eighteen songs on this album earn A- grades, with the remaining five rated B+. This excellent-sounding record is the first in the series with all songs earning at least B+. Almost all songs offer identical sonic presentation, with both ends of the frequency spectrum being very slightly deficient in level.
Love Me Do and *She Loves You*, from show #13, earn B+ due to minor problems with the presentation of vocals. When John, Paul, and George sing three-part harmony or chorus, the vocal level increases and gets slightly distorted. *Chains*, from show #14, is slightly hissy at the beginning and mildly deficient in level of the lead vocal. *Boys*, from show #14, and *She Loves You*, from show #15, are lacking at the high end so that Ringo's cymbals are hard to detect.

Because this album sounds so good, its highlights must be found in the performances. Four songs featured here were never officially released by the group. They are *Too Much Monkey Business*, *The Hippy Hippy Shake*, *Lucille*, and *Sure To Fall*. Of the "normal" Beatles songs, the most interesting is *I Saw Her Standing There*, which features a fine guitar solo by George that is totally different than that on the commercial release.

In summation, this is a great record! It contains eighteen well-performed, sonically outstanding songs, including four never officially released by the Beatles.

NOTE: This album has been released on compact disc as **The Beatles At The BEEB Volume 6** (Pyramid RFT CD015).

The Beatles At The BEEB Volume 7   Beeb Transcription Records 2178

Fixing A Hole, page 79

Ratings:
    Side One
1.	*I Saw Her Standing There*	B+
2.	*Memphis, Tennessee*	A-
3.	*Happy Birthday*	N/R
4.	Rick Nelson: *Fools Rush In*	N/R
5.	Joe Brown and his Bruvers: *Sally Ann*	N/R
6.	Joe Brown and his Bruvers: *Autumn Leaves*	N/R
7.	Bobby Vee: *Take Good Care Of My Baby*	N/R
8.	Everly Brothers: *All I Have To Do Is Dream*	N/R
9.	*Lucille*	B+

    Side Two
10.	*I Saw Her Standing There*	B
11.	*Love Me Do*	B
12.	*Please Please Me*	B
13.	*From Me To You*	B+
14.	*She Loves You*	B
15.	*From Me To You*	C
16.	*She Loves You*	C
17.	*Till There Was You*	C
18.	*Twist And Shout*	C
19.	*Twist And Shout*	D+

This album is the seventh of the BEEB series, and contains perform-

ances from 1963 as follows:
Cuts 1 - 3: "Saturday Club," recorded September 7 and broadcast October 5, 1963
Cuts 4 - 8: As noted above, not by the Beatles.
Cut 9: "Saturday Club," recorded September 7 and broadcast October 5, 1963
Cuts 10 - 14: "Easy Beat," recorded October 16 and broadcast October 20, 1963
Cuts 15- 18: "The Royal Variety Performance," recorded November 4, 1963
Cut 19: An unidentified "Easy Beat" performance.

Comments:
This seventh album of **The Beatles At The BEEB** series presents material from three different sources, "Saturday Club," "Easy Beat," and the "Royal Variety Performance 1963." It also presents seven songs not by the Beatles, making this album the leanest (in terms of material) of any of the BEEB records. To make matters worse, this album is the least sonically desirable record in the series up to this point.

The three songs from "Saturday Club" earn B+ or A- grades. All are slightly deficient in the lower frequencies, with *Memphis, Tennessee* getting the A- because of its fine treble presentation. *I Saw Her Standing There* and *Lucille* are also mildly lacking at the top end.

The five songs from "Easy Beat" all share problems at the high frequencies. These songs sound slightly dark and "closed in," with cymbals being all but inaudible at times, and harmonica not having its characteristic transient bite. *From Me To You* earns B+ to the other songs' B because it is better in the bass end. The four songs from the "Royal Variety Performance" can be described as fair at best. All are quite weak in the bass, and have instrumentation too low in volume in relation to their vocals. *She Loves You* and *Twist And Shout* are slightly distorted on vocals. This performance is interesting, however, as it contains John's famous "rattle your jewelery" remark.

Unfortunately, seven is not a lucky number for **The Beatles At The BEEB** series. This album offers no songs available elsewhere, and in general is not good sounding. This can only be recommended for those who feel they must have the entire BEEB series.

NOTE: This album has been released on compact disc as **The Beatles At The BEEB Volume 7** (Pyramid RFT CD019).

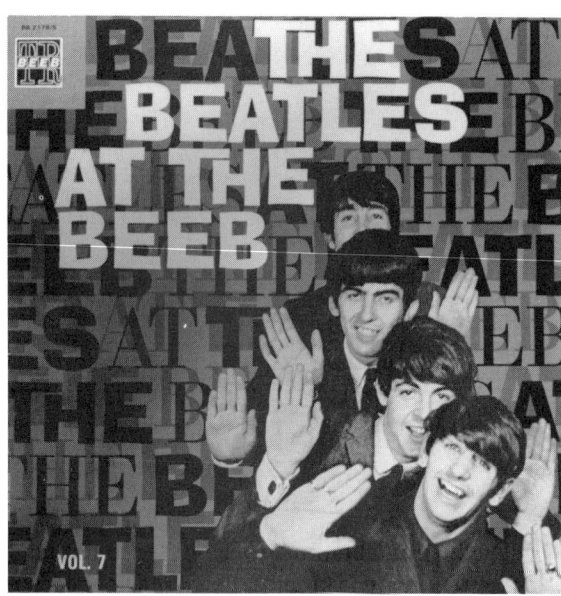

The Beatles At The BEEB Volume 7 (LP) (front)

The Beatles At The BEEB Volume 8 (LP) (front)

An Audiophile's Guide to the Sound of the Fab Four

The Beatles At The BEEB Volume 8 Beeb Transcription Records 2179

Fixing A Hole, page 81

Ratings:
Side One
#	Title	Rating
1.	This Boy	B+
2.	All I Want For Christmas Is A Bottle	N/R
3.	I Wanna Hold Your Hand	B+
4.	Till There Was You	B
5.	Roll Over Beethoven	B+
6.	She Loves You	B+
7.	Beatles Crimble Medley: Love Me Do - Please Please Me - From Me To You - She Loves You - I Wanna Hold Your Hand - Rudolf The Red-Nosed Reindeer	N/R
8.	From Us To You	C-
9.	She Loves You	C
10.	All My Loving	C
11.	Roll Over Beethoven	B
12.	Till There Was You	B
13.	Boys	B

Side Two
#	Title	Rating
14.	Money	B
15.	I Saw Her Standing There	B+
16.	Tie Me Kangaroo Down, Sport	B
17.	I Wanna Hold Your Hand	B+
18.	Murray The K: Interview	N/R
19.	WINS Radio, New York: Beatles Sweatshirt Plug	N/R
20.	Kennedy Airport: Interview with Teenagers	N/R
21.	Kennedy Airport: Arrival of Beatles Plane	N/R
22.	Fans in front of Plaza Hotel, Manhattan	N/R
23.	Beatle Chat	N/R

This album is the eighth of the BEEB series, and contains material from 1963 and 1964 as follows:
   Cuts 1-8: "Saturday Club," recorded December 17 and broadcast December 21, 1963
   Cuts 9-18: "From Us To You" (#1), recorded December 18 and broadcast December 26, 1963
   Cuts 19-23: "Saturday Club," broadcast February 8, 1964 - Report from Malcolm Davis in New York

Comments:

This eighth album in **The Beatles At The BEEB** series presents two musical performances for the 1963 Christmas season, as well as a broadcast of interviews and news reports about the Beatles' arrival in America in February of 1964.

The five rated songs from "Saturday Club" all earn B or better, although they exhibit dissimiliar sonic characteristics. *This Boy* is slightly hissy, and has indistinct bass; grade B+. *I Want To Hold Your Hand* is also somewhat hissy and slightly deficient in the high frequencies; grade B+. *Till There Was You* shares the hiss and high frequency problems, but also briefly fades in volume in the song's middle; grade B. *Roll Over Beethoven* and *She Loves You* are both hiss-free, but sound lightweight due to a lack of bass; grade B+.

The songs from "From Us To You" get sonically better as the show progresses. *From Us To You* (C-) and *She Loves You* (C) have recessed vocals, and are not quite in balance between vocals and instruments. *All My Loving* (C) is also out of balance, but does not have recessed vocals. *Roll Over Beethoven* (B), *Till There Was You* (B), and *Boys* (B) present wide frequency range, but sound as if the entire performances are recessed and distant from the listener.

Money (B) has slightly recessed vocals, but its bass presentation is good. *Tie Me Kangaroo Down, Sport* is a two-and-a-half minute ditty with Rolf Harris singing lead and the Beatles joining in for the chorus. It is mostly voice with little music, and earns a B grade. Rolf sings a special lyric about the Beatles. *I Saw Her Standing There* (B+) has a tad too much treble, and *I Wanna Hold Your Hand* (B+) has vocals louder than its music.

This album ends with six segments totaling eight-and-a-half minutes covering the Beatles' arrival in the U.S.A., February 7, 1964. It starts with an interview with Murray The K, continues with coverage of the plane landing in Kennedy Airport, fan interviews, and concludes with a Beatle chat.

The Beatles At The BEEB Volume 8 is definitely a fun album. It sounds good, has holiday frivolity in the between-song chatter, Rolf Harris' *Tie Me Kangaroo Down, Sport*, and presents a wonderful snippet of Beatles history from February 1964.

NOTE: This album has been released on compact disc as **The Beatles At The BEEB Volume 8** (Pyramid RFT CD016).

An Audiophile's Guide to the Sound of the Fab Four

The Beatles At The BEEB Volume 9   Beeb Transcription Records 2180

Fixing A Hole, page 82

Ratings:
   Side One
   1. *All My Loving*   C+
   2. *Money*   C+
   3. *The Hippy Hippy Shake*   C+
   4. *I Wanna Hold Your Hand*   C+
   5. *Roll Over Beethoven*   C+
   6. *Johnny B. Goode*   C+
   7. *I Wanna Be Your Man*   C+
   Side Two
   8. *From Us To You*   B-
   9. *You Can't Do That*   B-
   10. *Roll Over Beethoven*   B
   11. *Till There Was You*   B
   12. *I Wanna Be Your Man*   B-
   13. *Please Mr. Postman*   B-
   14. *All My Loving*   B
   15. *This Boy*   B
   16. *Can't Buy Me Love*   B
   17. *From Us To You*   B-

This album is the ninth of the BEEB series, and contains material from 1964 as follows:
   Cuts 1 - 7: "Saturday Club," recorded January 7 and broadcast February 15, 1964
   Cuts 8 - 17: "From Us To You" (#2), recorded February 28 and broadcast March 30, 1964

Comments:
   This ninth album in **The Beatles At The BEEB** series presents two performances from early 1964. The "Saturday Club" songs all earn C+, although they all sound somewhat different from each other. *All My Loving*, *Money*, and *Roll Over Beethoven* have harsh vocals, indistinct bass, and are slightly hissy. *The Hippy Hippy Shake* is mildly hissy, and has weak and indistinct bass. *I Wanna Hold Your Hand* is similar to *The Hippy Hippy Shake*, but is also indistinct in treble. *I Wanna Be Your Man* is weak in the bass, and gets harsh in the vocals when John and Paul sing along with Ringo. *Johnny B. Goode* is indistinct at both ends of the frequency spectrum, and has vocals that get harsh at times. It is a unique performance, however, feauring spirited guitar playing

139

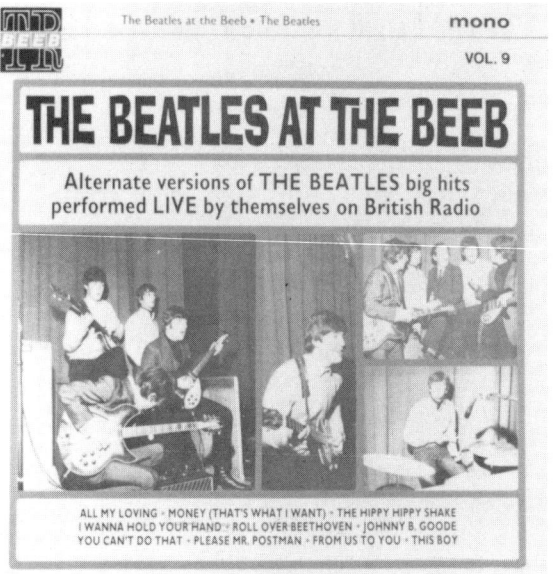

The Beatles At The BEEB Volume 9 (LP) (front)

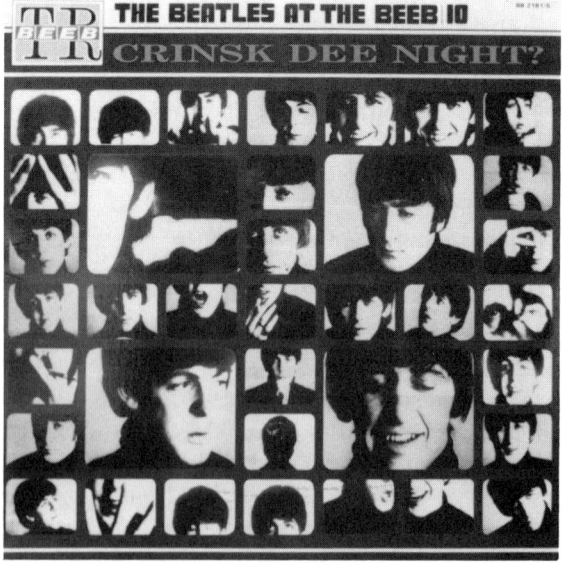

The Beatles At The BEEB Volume 10 (LP) (front)

by George and a fine vocal by John. Side One ends with a four-minute telephone conversation with Brian Matthew from Heathrow Airport in London. This was recorded just after the Beatles returned to England from their triumphant first trip to America

The songs from "From Us To You" earn B- or B grades. *From Us To You* (both versions), *I Wanna Be Your Man*, and *Till There Was You* are the only songs plagued by hiss on this side of the record. *You Can't Do That* is slightly harsh in the vocals, as are *Can't Buy Me Love* and *This Boy*. *Roll Over Beethoven* and *Please Mr. Postman* suffer from indistinct treble, and *All My Loving* has indistinct bass. All of these are quite listenable, as none of the problems mentioned here are very severe.

The Beatles At The BEEB Volume 9 can be called a fair album. Its seventeen songs are neither boring nor extraordinary, except for *Johnny B. Goode*, which was performed only this once on the BBC. Sonically, the album is just slightly below Volume 7, making this the least attractive record in the series so far. Do you want this record in your collection? If you'd like to hear the Beatles' remarks on their return to England in February 1964, together with a good version of *Johnny B. Goode*, yes! Otherwise, move on to other volumes in the series.

NOTE: This album has been released on compact disc as **The Beatles At The BEEB Volume 9** (Pyramid RFT CD017).

The Beatles At The BEEB Volume 10   Beeb Transcription Records 2181

Fixing A Hole, page 83

Ratings:
Side One

1.	*Everybody's Trying To Be My Baby*	B
2.	*I Call Your Name*	C-
3.	*I Got A Woman*	C-
4.	*You Can't Do That*	C-
5.	*Can't Buy Me Love*	C-
6.	*Sure To Fall (In Love With You)*	C-
7.	*Long Tall Sally*	B

Side Two

8.	*From Us To You*	B+
9.	*Whit Monday To You*	N/R
10.	*I Saw Her Standing There*	B
11.	*Kansas City/Hey-Hey-Hey-Hey*	B-

12.	*I Forgot To Remember To Forget*	B
13.	*You Can't Do That*	B
14.	*Sure To Fall (In Love With You)*	B-
15.	*Can't Buy Me Love*	B-
16.	*Matchbox*	B-
17.	*Honey Don't*	B
18.	*From Us To You*	N/R

This album is the tenth of the BEEB series, and contains material from 1964 as follows:

Cuts 1 - 7: "Saturday Club," recorded March 31 and broadcast April 4, 1964

Cuts 8 - 18: "From Us To You" (#2), recorded May 1 and broadcast May 18, 1964

Comments:

This tenth record in **The Beatles At The BEEB** series presents two performances from the spring of 1964. Side One contains a "Saturday Club" show broadcast April 4, and Side Two contains the third "From Us To You" show broadcast May 18.

Everybody's Trying To Be My Baby opens in fine style, as reflected in its B grade. It features guitar work by George that is quite different than that on the officially released version. The next four cuts all earn C- grades and are plagued by numerous problems. Bass is too full, treble is indistinct, and vocals are slightly distorted at times. *Sure To Fall* earns C because - although it shares some of the other songs's problems - its bass presentation is perfectly acceptable. *Long Tall Sally* closes Side One as it was opened, with a grade B song.

The songs on Side Two from "From Us To You" all earn B- or B grades. *I Saw Her Standing There* (B) is slightly hissy and not totally extended in the treble. *Kansas City/Hey-Hey-Hey-Hey* (B-) shares the hiss and treble problems, but also has harsh-sounding vocals at times. *I Forgot To Remember To Forget* and *You Can't Do That* both earn B grades. They have good bass presentation but are slightly hissy and not extended into the uppermost treble regions. *Sure To Fall, Can't Buy Me Love,* and *Matchbox* earn B- because they also have problems with the presentation of vocals. *Honey Don't*, the final song on the album, closes the record with a good-sounding performance. Although this album can only be described as fair-sounding, it is by no means unlistenable. Most of its sonic problems are mild in nature; the low grades are due to multiple problems being simultaneously present. The album does have value in the fact that it contains Beatles performances of songs never officially released: *I Got A Woman, Sure To Fall* (twice), and *I Forgot To Remember To Forget* (its only BBC performance). Also, contrary to the record jacket's liner

An Audiophile's Guide to the Sound of the Fab Four

notes, the version of *Honey Don't* from "From Us To You" has John singing the lead vocal, not Ringo (as he does in the officially-released version).
All in all, this is not a bad album!
NOTE: This album has been released on compact disc as **The Beatles Live At The BEEB Volume 10** (Pyramid PY CD024).

The Beatles At The BEEB Volume 11   Beeb Transcription Records 2182

Fixing A Hole, page 84

Ratings:
   Side One
   1. *Long Tall Sally* — B-
   2. *Things We Said Today* — C+
   3. *A Hard Day's Night* — B
   4. *And I Love Her* — B-
   5. *I Should Have Known Better* — B
   6. *If I Fell* — C
   7. *You Can't Do That* — C-
   Side Two
   8. *From Us To You* — B
   9. *Long Tall Sally* — B
   10. *If I Fell* — B+
   11. *I'm Happy Just To Dance With You* — A-
   12. *Things We Said Today* — B+
   13. *I Should Have Known Better* — B+
   14. *Boys* — B+
   15. *Kansas City/Hey-Hey-HeyHey-Hey* — B+
   16. *A Hard Day's Night* — B+
   17. *From Us To You* — B+

This album is the eleventh of the BEEB series, and contains material from 1964 as follows:
   Cuts 1 - 7: "Top Gear," recorded July 14 and broadcast July 16, 1964
   Cuts 8 - 16: "From Us To You" (#4), recorded July 17 and broadcast August 3, 1964

Comments:
   Record 11 in **The Beatles At The BEEB** series presents two performances recorded in July of 1964. Side One presents "Top Gear," broadcast July

The Beatles At The BEEB Volume 11 (LP) (front)

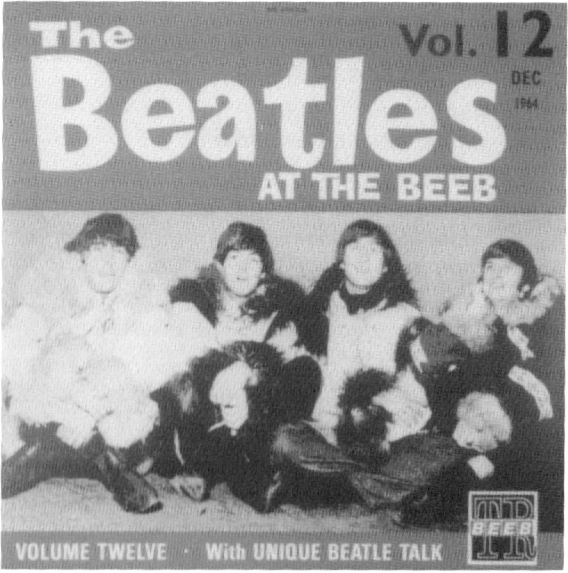

The Beatles At The BEEB Volume 12 (LP) (front)

An Audiophile's Guide to the Sound of the Fab Four

16, 1964. *A Hard Day's Night* earns a B grade due to slightly harsh vocals, mildly weak bass, and indistinct treble. *Long Tall Sally* (B-) also has weak bass, as well as being veiled. This song sounds as if a heavy curtain is hanging between the listener and the speakers. *Things We Said Today* (C+) again has weak bass and is veiled. It is also distorted during many vocal passages. These three songs are all available on the **Top Of The Pops** EP, where they all earn A- grades (see review above).

And I Love Her (B-) is weak at the low frequencies, has recessed vocals, and some distortion in places. *I Should Have Known Better* (B) is musically fine throughout the frequency spectrum, but has harsh vocals. *If I Fell* (C) and *You Can't Do That* (C-) are both too full in the bass, and have distorted vocals. *You Can't Do That* is also plagued by vocal drop-out on occasion.

Side Two, the "From Us To You" show broadcast on August 3, 1964, is quite good from start to finish. *I'm Happy Just To Dance With You* (A-) is the best of the lot, just missing a perfect grade because it is slightly "soft" sounding. The transient "snap" and aliveness of the commercial recording of this song are missing in this version. The B+ songs exhibit a variety of minor problems, from slightly recessed vocals to mildly overemphasized bass to indistinct and/or overly-bright treble. These problems do not greatly detract from the listener's oleasure, however. *Long Tall Sally*, grade B, is indistinct in the treble, and the vocals are too low in level.

In all, this is a fine album. Although presenting no unusual material, fouteen of its seventeen songs earn B- or better grades.

NOTE: This album has been released on compact disc as **The Beatles At The BEEB Volume 11** (Pyramid PY CD025).

The Beatles At The BEEB Volume 12   Beeb Transcription Records 2183

Ratings:
    Side One
1. *I'm A Loser* — C-
2. *Honey Don't* — C+
3. *She's A Woman* — C+
4. *Everybody's Trying To Be My Baby* — B
5. *I'll Follow The Sun* — C
6. *I Feel Fine* — B-

    Side Two
7. *Rock And Roll Music* — B+
8. *I'm A Loser* — B+
9. *Everybody's Trying To Be My Baby* — A-

10.	*I Feel Fine*	B+
11.	*Kansas City/Hey-Hey-Hey-Hey*	A-
12.	*She's A Woman*	B

This album is the twelfth of the BEEB series, and contains material from 1964 as follows:
Cuts 1 - 6: "Top Gear," recorded November 17 and broadcast November 26, 1964
Cuts 7 - 12: "Saturday Club," recorded November 25 and broadcast December 26, 1964
Also interspersed between the songs are introductions of the group and short segments of "Beatle Talk." Side One has a total of approximately six minutes of talk, and Side Two has about three minutes.

Comments:
Album 12 in **The Beatles At The BEEB** series presents two shows from the winter of 1964. Side One contains "Top Gear," broadcast November 26, and Side Two presents "Saturday Club," broadcast December 26, 1964.

"Top Gear" opens this record, unfortunately, in problematic fashion. Only two of the six songs earn B or B- grades. *Everybody's Trying To Be My Baby*, grade B, is generally good-sounding, but is very slightly distorted in the bass. *I Feel Fine*, grade B-, is somewhat harsh in the vocals, and has extraneous crackling sounds. *I'll Follow The Sun*, grade C, also has crackling sounds, as well as veiled vocals and bass which is too full at times. *I'm A Loser*, grade C-, has distorted vocals, weak and indistinct treble, and bass which is too full and distorted. *Honey Don't* earns a C+ grade due to very distorted bass, and *She's A Woman* earns C+ because its vocals are harsh and distorted.

In contrast to "Top Gear," the "Saturday Club" show is outstanding. All six of its songs earn B or better, with two earning A-. *She's A Woman* earns a B due to hiss at its beginning, occasional dropouts, and bass that is slightly full. *I Feel Fine* and *I'm A Loser* both earn B+, and share a problem with overly-full bass. *Rock And Roll Music*, the other song rated B+, has bass that is somewhat indistinct, along with vocals that are too low in level at times. *Everybody's Trying To Be My Baby* earns A- due to a small amount of overemphasis in the bass, and *Kansas City/Hey-Hey-Hey-Hey* earns A- because of a couple of tape dropouts.

This album can only be described as middle-of-the-road in nature. It has a good- and a bad-sounding side, and contains no unusual material. It is for those collectors who insist on owning the entire series of **The Beatles At The BEEB**; otherwise, it can be avoided.

NOTE: This album has been released on compact disc as **The Beatles At The BEEB Volume 12** (Pyramid PY CD032).

An Audiophile's Guide to the Sound of the Fab Four

The Beatles At The BEEB Volume 13 Beeb Transcription Records 2184

Ratings:
Side One
1. *Ticket To Ride* — C
2. *Everybody's Trying To Be My Baby* — B
3. *I'm A Loser* — B
4. *The Night Before* — B
5. *Honey Don't* — B
6. *Dizzy Miss Lizzie* — B
7. *She's A Woman* — B+
8. *Ticket To Ride* — B

Side Two
9. *She's A Woman* — C-
10. *Ticket To Ride* — C-
11. *Long Tall Sally* — D
12. *She Loves You* — C-
13. *You Can't Do That* — C-
14. *Twist And Shout* — C-
15. *Long Tall Sally* — C-

This album is the thirteenth of the BEEB series, and contains material from 1964 and 1965 as follows:
Cuts 1 - 8: "The Beatles (Invite You To Take A Ticket To Ride)," recorded May 26 and broadcast June 7, 1965.
Cuts 9 - 11: "New Musical Express 1964-65 Annual Poll-Winners All-Star Concert," performed live April 11, 1965
Cuts 12 - 15: New Musical Express 1963-64 Annual Poll-Winners All-Star Concert," performed live April 25, 1964
Also interspersed between the songs are introductions of the group, and a couple of minutes of "Beatle Talk."

Comments:
This thirteenth record in **The Beatles At The BEEB** series is, as of the time of this writing, the final release of the BBC radio performances. Thirteen proves to be a very unlucky number for the series, as this is the least sonically desirable record of all.
Side One presents "The Beatles (Invite You To Take A Ticket To Ride)," broadcast June 7, 1965. This is a good-sounding show, with all songs other than the brief introductory version of *Ticket To Ride* earning B or B+ grades. The B grade songs share common characteristics, including small deficiencies at both ends of the frequency spectrum, and slight problems with

The Beatles At The BEEB Volume 13 (LP) (front)

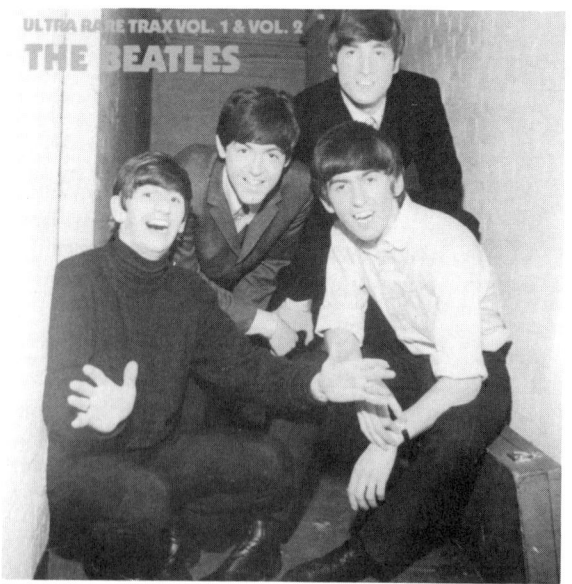

Ultra Rare Trax Vol. 1 & Vol. 2 (2 LPs) (front)

the presentation of vocals. *She's A Woman* earns the only B+ due to its fine bass, although its vocals are both slightly harsh-sounding and recessed. *I'm A Loser* is quite an ear-opener, as John, instead of singing "...beneath this mask I am wearing a frown," sings "...*beneath this wig I am wearing a tie.*"

Side Two consists of the Beatles' live performances at two *New Musical Express* Annual Poll-Winners All-Star Concerts. Cuts 9 to 11 are from the 1964-65 winners' show recorded April 11, 1965, and cuts 12 to 15 are from the 1963-64 winners' show recorded April 26, 1964. Songs from the 1965 performance earn C- grades due to veiled and recessed vocals, along with severe deficiencies at both ends of the frequency spectrum, except for *Long Tall Sally*, which earns D because it also has an oppressive amount of audience screaming. Songs from the 1964 performance all earn C- grades because they consist almost entirely of vocals. Instrumentation is generally too low in volume, at times bordering on inaudibility.

If you are not a completist and are willing to forego at least one album in the series, **The Beatles At The BEEB Volume 13** is the one to avoid.

NOTE: This album has been released on compact disc as **The Beatles At The BEEB Volume 13** (Pyramid PY CD033).

Ultra Rare Trax Vol. 1 & Vol. 2 STASH Records STASH 637

Ratings:
Side One
1.	*I Saw Her Standing There*	A
2.	*One After 909* [Take 2]	A
3.	*She's A Woman* [Take 2]	A
4.	*I'm Looking Through You* [Take 1]	A
5.	*If You've Got Troubles*	A
6.	*How Do You Do It*	A

Side Two
7.	*Penny Lane*	A
8.	*Strawberry Fields Forever* [Fast version]	A
9.	*From Me To You*	A
10.	*Besame Mucho*	A
11.	*The Fool On The Hill*	B
12.	*Paperback Writer*	A

Side Three
13.	*Can't Buy Me Love*	A
14.	*There's A Place* [Take 3]	A
15.	*There's A Place* [Take 4]	A

16.	*That Means A Lot*	B
17.	*Day Tripper* [I]	A
18.	*Day Tripper* [II]	A
19.	*I Am The Walrus*	A

Side Four

20.	*Misery* [Take 1]	A
21.	*Leave My Kitten Alone*	A
22.	*We Can Work It Out*	A
23.	*A Hard Day's Night*	A
24.	*Norwegian Wood (This Bird Has Flown)* [Take 4]	A

This 1988 release contains some newly-unearthed material previously unavailable outside the Abbey Road Studios' vaults. The best description of the material can be found on the album's back cover, quoted as follows [sic]:

I Saw Her Standing There [Take 2]: Recorded on Feb. 11th 1963 from "Please Please Me" sessions. Continued from warming up, they start a great live performance in the studio. John makes a mistake and with lyrics, and Paul makes a mistake with some bass lines. No echo effects.

One After 909 [Take 2]: Recorded on March 5th 1963 from "From Me To You" session. Composed by John Lennon in late 50's-early 60's in the period of The Quarrymen (pre-Beatles). Released on the **Let It Be** album in 1970, but this take is absolutely different.

She's A Woman [Take 2]: Recorded in Sept.-Oct 1964. No lead guitar, piano, or additional vocals. No fade-out at the end. Very primitive version.

I'm Looking Through You [Take 1]: Recorded in Oct. 1965 from "Rubber Soul" session. No chorus yet. Beginning with percussion, vocals on single track. No fade out at the end.

If You've Got Troubles: Previously unreleased song by The Beatles. Recorded in Oct. 1965 from "Rubber Soul" session. Ringo Starr on lead vocal.

How Do You Do It: Previously unreleased song by The Beatles. Recorded on Sept. 4th 1962, from "Please Please Me" session. Prepared as a second single, but never released.

Penny Lane: Recorded Dec. 29th 1966. Basically same version as on the **Rarities** album, but including dialogue and Paul's count in the beginning. An absolutely different mono mix!

Strawberry Fields Forever: There're two takes for *Strawberry Fields*

Forever. The previously released version consists of Take I and II with controlled speed, and it is also remixed. This version on this disk is take II, with a different mix. Recorded in December 1966.

From Me To You: Recorded on March 4th-5th 1963. Beginning with Paul's count "1, 2 ,3, 4!", no harmonica. Absolutely different.

Besame Mucho: Basically unreleased song. Recorded on June 6th 1962, with Pete Best on drums. A different take from "Decca Tapes."

The Fool On The Hill: Recorded in Sept. 1967. Demo version. Paul performs solo with the piano.

Paperback Writer: Recorded in April 1966. Beginning with Paul's count "1, 2, 3, 4!" on the right channel. Same as the single, but different mix, no echo effects on vocals and no fade-outs at the end.

Can't Buy Me Love: Recorded on Jan. 29th 1964. Absolutely different with no echo effects. Wonderful choral vocals by John & George. Paul makes a mistake with some lyrics. Supposed to be THE BEST TAKE!

There's A Place [Take 3]: Recorded on February 11th 1963, from "Please Please Me" session. Intro vocals only.

There's A Place [Take 4]: Continued from Take 3. Absolutely different with no harmonica or piano. Great live performance in the studio!

That Means A Lot: Previously unreleased song. Recorded in Feb. 1965, from "2nd Help" session. Paul McCartney on lead vocals.

Day Tripper [I]: Recorded on Oct. 16th 1965. Instrumental without tambourine or lead guitar. Absolutely different, supposed to be the first basic. Not complete.

Day Tripper [II]: Continued from [I]. Starting with Paul's count "1, 2, 3, 4!". Basically same version as the previously released one, but no additional vocals dubbed by Paul. No fade-out at the end.

I Am The Walrus: Recorded in Sept. 1967, from "Magical Mystery Tour" sessions. Un-edited & long version without strings, bass guitar, choral, or side vocals.

Misery [Take 1]: Recorded on Feb. 11th 1963, from "Please Please Me" session. Absolutely different without piano or echo effects.

Leave My Kitten Alone: Previously unreleased song. Recorded

Aug. 5th 1964, from "For Sale" session. John Lennon on lead vocals.

We Can Work It Out: Recorded on Oct. 20th 1965. Beginning with Paul's count "1, 2, 3, 4!," and it has louder keyboards sound. Vocals on both channels. Fade-out at the end.

A Hard Day's Night: Recorded on April 16th 1964, from "A Hard Day's Night" sessions. Live performance in the studio. Absolutely different without acoustic or gat [sic] guitars, or piano.

Norwegian Wood (This Bird Has Flown) [Take 4]: Recorded in Oct. 1965, from "Rubber Soul" sessions. Basically same as the released take, though John makes a mistake with his acoustic guitar twice in the intro, and says "I Showed Ya!" in the end part. George Martin replies "GREAT, FINE!". Un-edited version.

Comments:

Very little needs to be said about this two-record set, other than that at the time of its release (fall 1988) it earned the crown as king of all Beatles bootlegs. Not only does it present previously unreleased material, it does so in almost perfect fashion. Only two of the twenty-four cuts earn B grades, the others are all absolutely perfect!

The Fool On The Hill is Paul's demo version on acoustic piano. Taken from an acetate, it has a small amount of hiss audible throughout the song. Both ends of the frequency spectrum are also slightly depressed in level. These problems are small, however, allowing the song to earn a B grade.

That Means A Lot is the Beatles' version of John and Paul's song for P.J. Proby. It only earns a B grade due to small amounts of distortion on lead vocals, slightly oberbearing midrange, and a lack of deep bass. Again, these problems are not severe and do not detract from the listener's potential enjoyment of the music.

The rest of this album is absolutely unbelievable. Alternate mixes, live performances in the studio, and works in progress presented in perfect sound. A Beatle fan's dream!

NOTE: This album has been released on compact disc as follows: (1) **Ultra Rare Trax Vol. 1** (Swingin' Pig TSP-CD-001); (2) **Ultra Rare Trax Vol. 2** (Swingin' Pig TSP-CD-002); (3) **Back Track** ([No label] BT62672 (includes both LPs plus three extra cuts).

An Audiophile's Guide to the Sound of the Fab Four

Ultra Rare Trax Vol. 3 & Vol. 4   The Swingin' Pig Records   BEEB Transcription Records TR 2190

Fixing A Hole, page 247

Ratings:
   Side One
1. *12 Bar Original*   A-
2. *Help* (Takes 1 Through 5)   A
3. *I Feel Fine* (Takes 6 and 7)   A
   Side Two
4. *Day Tripper* (Takes 1 Through 3)   A
5. *We Can Work It Out* (Takes 1 and 2)   A
6. *Yes It Is* (Takes 1 and 2)   A
   Side Three
7. *One And One Is Two*   D+
8. *Do You Want To Know A Secret* (Track 2,
    Take 8)   A
9. *She's A Woman* (Take 7)   A
10. *Hold Me Tight*   A-
11. *Ticket To Ride*   A
    Side Four
12. *Yes It Is*   A
13. *There's A Place*   A
14. *A Taste Of Honey*   A
15. *There's A Place* (Track 2, Take 11)   A
16. *I Saw Her Standing There* (Track 2, Take 10) A
17. *Misery* (Takes 2 Through 6)   A

Although the album jacket contains no liner notes, here is a brief rundown of those songs with their take numbers identified or whose origins can be identified.
   12 Bar Original - Two takes of this were recorded on November 4, 1965. Take 1 was a breakdown and Take 2 ran 6:36. The mono version presented here fades out at about 3:50, and therefore must be the mono remix of Take 2, created November 30, 1965.
   Help (Takes 1 Through 5) - Recorded April 13, 1965. Vocals were not added until Take 9.
   I Feel Fine (Takes 6 and 7) - Recorded October 18, 1964. Vocals were not added until Take 9.

153

Day Tripper (Takes 1 Through 3) - Recorded October 16, 1965. This song was finished with overdubs onto Take 3.

We Can Work It Out (Takes 1 and 2) - Recorded October 20, 1965. Overdubs were later added on October 29.

Yes It Is (Takes 1 and 2) - Recorded February 16, 1965. The official version consists of Take 14 plus overdubs.

Do You Want To Know A Secret (Track 2, Take 8) - Recorded February 11, 1963. Take 8 was an overdub of harmoney vocals and two drumsticks being tapped together onto Take 6.*

She's A Woman (Take 7) - Recorded October 8, 1964. Take 6 had overdubs added and later became the official release, but Take 7 was recorded before Take 6 was determined to be "best."

Hold Me Tight - Recorded September 12, 1963. At this session, Takes 20 - 29 were recorded. The official version was an edit of Takes 26 and 29. The Take number of the version presented here is not identified.

Ticket To Ride - Recorded February 15, 1965.

A Taste Of Honey (Track 2, Take 2) - Recorded February 11, 1963. This is an overdub onto Take 5.*

There's A Place (Track 2, Take 11) - Recorded February 11, 1963. This is an overdub of harmonica onto Take 10.*

I Saw Her Standing There (Track 2, Take 10) - Recorded February 11, 1963. This is an overdub of handclapping onto Take 1.*

Misery (Takes 2 Through 6) - Recorded February 11, 1963. These Takes were recorded at double speed (30 ips) to facilitate the later overdubbing of piano.

* - Although these takes are overdubs, the record presents the entire contents (all of the tracks) of the tape. During the overdubbing process, the Beatles heard the tape through headphones so that the new track being recorded would not be contaminated by the already existing material.

Comments:
This second two-record set in the **Ultra Rare Trax** series continues in the excellent fashion of Volumes 1 and 2. It presents previously unreleased material and studio working-sessions in almost perfect sound quality. Only three of the seventeen cuts earn less than a perfect A rating!

12 Bar Original is an instrumental recorded in November 1965. Prior to this album, this song was never available outside of the Abbey Road Studios' tape vaults. It earns an A- due to some extraneous crackling noises at its start.

Ultra Rare Trax Vol. 3 & Vol. 4 (2 LPs) (front)

Ultra Rare Trax Vol. 5 & Vol. 6 (2 LPs) (front)

One And One Is Two is a demo featuring Paul on acoustic guitar and vocals of a Lennon-McCartney song recorded by The Strangers with Mike Shannon. It is very hissy and heavily distorted on the vocals. It lasts approximately 1:45 and earns a D+ rating. *Hold Me Tight* is the only other cut missing a perfect rating. Its A- is due to a lack of deep bass, along with vocals being too low in level to be in balance with the instruments.

Help (Takes 1 Through 5) is about 6:10 of work on the backing instrumental track, with only Take 5 being a complete run through. *I Feel Fine* (Takes 6 and 7) is approximately 5:30 long, and contains an instrumental which breaks down (Take 6), and a version with vocals (Take 7). Something is wrong here, because according to *The Beatles: Recording Sessions* by Mark Lewisohn, the vocals were not added until Take 9. *Day Tripper* (Takes 1 Through 3) lasts about 6:20, and is actually two breakdowns and a completed version. The completed version is Take 3 *with overdubs*, because the vocals were not recorded simultaneously with the instruments.

The remainder of this album presents the recording process for various other songs. Instrumentals, breakdowns, and multiple run attempts at getting things right. Some of the songs are the same as on **Ultra Rare Trax Volume 1 and Volume 2**, although different Takes are presented here. The most unique and interesting of the bunch is *She's A Woman*, which includes an almost six-minute version highlighted by a three-minute ending of instrumental jamming and Paul's howling vocals.

As with the first album in the **Ultra Rare Trax** series, this set is absolutely unbelievable!

NOTE: This album has been released on compact disc as **Hold Me Tight** (Condor 1990), without *One And One Is Two*.

Ultra Rare Trax Vol. 5 & Vol. 6   The Swingin' Pig records   BEEB Transciption Records TR 2191

Fixing A Hole, page 249

Ratings:
Side One
1.	*All You Need Is Love*	A
2.	*Norwegian Wood*	A
3.	*Not Guilty*	A
4.	*Because* (Vocals only)	A

Side Two
5.	*Lady Madonna*	A

6.	*Rain*	A
7.	*A Day In The Life*	A
8.	*What's The New Mary Jane*	A

Side Three

9.	*Hello Goodbye*	A-
10.	*Paperback Writer* (Instrumental)	A-
11.	*Paperback Writer*	A
12.	*Hey Jude*	A-
13.	*I Hate To See*	A-

Side Four

14.	*Strawberry Fields Forever* (Take 1)	A-
15.	*Strawberry Fields Forever* (Take 2)	A-
16.	*Strawberry Fields Forever* (Take 3)	A-
17.	*Strawberry Fields Forever* (Take 4)	A
18.	*Strawberry Fields Forever* (Take 5)	A-
19.	*Strawberry Fields Forever* (Take 6)	A-
20.	*Strawberry Fields Forever* (Take 7)	A-
21.	*Strawberry Fields Forever* (Take 8)	A-
22.	*Strawberry Fields Forever* (Take 9)	A

This late-1988 release continues the **Ultra Rare Trax** series of rare studio outtakes. As with Volumes 3 and 4, the album's jacket has no liner notes. Here is a brief rundown of those songs whose origins can be identified.

All You Need Is Love - This is the live "Our World" TV broadcast from June 25, 1967. The recording is Take 58 of the song.

Norwegian Wood - Although this song doesn't include a "Take" number announcement, based on the description in *The Beatles: Recording Sessions*, by Mark Lewisohn, this is probably Take 1 recorded on October 12, 1965.

Not Guilty - This is an overdub onto Take 102, recorded on August 12, 1968.*

Because - Recorded August 1, 1969, this is most likely an overdub onto Take 16.* On August 4, 1969, two more layers of three-part harmony were recorded, giving the final version nine-part harmony!

Lady Madonna - Recorded February 3, 1968, this is probably an overdub onto Take 3.*

Rain - This unidentified performance originates from either April 14, 1966, when Takes 1 - 5 were recorded, or April 16, 1966, when overdubs were added to Take 5, and Takes 6 and 7 were recorded.

A Day In The Life - This was probably recorded on January 20, 1967, as this was when Paul's "...woke up, got out of bed..." vocals were first added as an overdub onto Take 6.*

What's The New Mary Jane - This is Take 4, recorded August 14, 1968.

Hello Goodbye - This is Take 1, recorded October 2, 1967.

Paperback Writer (Instrumental) - This is Take 1, recorded April 13, 1964.

Paperback Writer - This is probably one of the stereo remixes from Take 2 created on October 31, 1966.

Hey Jude - This is Take 6, recorded July 29, 1968. This is a live in-the-studio recording.

Strawberry Fields Forever (Take 1) - Recorded November 24, 1966.

Strawberry Fields Forever (Takes 2 - 4) - Recorded November 28, 1966.

Strawberry Fields Forever (Takes 5 - 7) - Recorded November 29, 1966.

Strawberry Fields Forever (Take 25) - Recorded December 9, 1966, this is actually an overdub onto Take 25.*

Strawberry Fields Forever (Take 26) - Recorded December 15, 1966, this is actually an overdub onto Take 26.*

* - Although these takes are overdubs, the record presents the entire contents (all of the tracks) of the tape. During overdubbing process, the Beatles heard the tape through headphones so that the new track being recorded would not be contaminated by the already existing material.

Comments:

This third two-record set in the **Ultra Rare Trax** series completes (as of the time of this writing) the collection of rare and previously unreleased studio ottakes and working sessions. Of the twenty-two cuts on the album, ten earn A grades and twelve earn A-. In all cases but one the A- rating is due to the presence of audible hiss in the recording. Because the overall sonic quality of this set is excellent, descriptions of only the most interesting songs are presented here.

All You Need Is Love is the entire Beatles segment from the "Our World" television special. Including announcing and George Martin's technical direction, it lasts six-and-a-half minutes and earns an A- grade due to a slight weakness in the bass frequencies. It is in mono.

Norwegian Wood contains different instrumentation and lyrics than the official version.

Not Guilty is the complete version with instrumental ending, and lasts about 4:20.

Because presents only the vocals sung in beautiful three-part harmony by John, Paul, and George.

Hello Goodbye is "introduced" by the engineer as "Hello Hello Take 1." This is an instruments-only run-through with a long ending, and lasts about five minutes.

Paperback Writer (Instrumental) breaks down after about forty seconds, and *Paperback Writer* with vocals is missing the echo effects and is identical to the version included on **Ultra Rare Trax Volume 1 & Volume 2.**

Hey Jude is a slightly shorter version than the commercial release (5:40), and is different in both lyrics and instrumentation.

Strawberry Fields Forever is presented in nine takes covering the entire fourth side of the album. Take 1 lasts about 3:10, and has beautiful background harmony vocals. This is significantly simpler than the official version, but absolutely wonderful! Takes 2 and 3 are abbreviated instrumentals. Take 7 is announced as "Remix from four-track Take 6." Take 25 presents the strings and percussion without vocals, and starts with a count-off. Take 26 is actually Take 25 with both vocals and guitars added. Even though this progression through the development of *Strawberry Fields Forever* lasts more than twenty minutes, it ends before the song is finished. George Martin later would work his famous magic of editing together Takes 7 and 26 (even though they were recorded at different speeds)!

Summing up this record is easy - GREAT! As with the other **Ultra Rare Trax** sets, this contains priceless material beautifully presented.

Off White Maclen Records WHT 868

Fixing A Hole, page 190

Ratings:
Side One
1.	*The Continuing Story Of Bungalow Bill*	C+
2.	*Cry Baby Cry*	C+
3.	*Sexie Sadie*	C
4.	*Yer Blues*	C
5.	*Dear Prudence*	C+
6.	*Julia*	B-
7.	*I'm So Tired*	B-

Side Two
8.	*Child Of Nature*	B

9.	*While My Guitar Gently Weeps*	B
10.	*Lady Madonna*	C+
11.	*Everybody's Got Something To Hide Except Me And My Monkey*	B-
12.	*Goodbye*	B
13.	*Honey Pie*	C+
14.	*What's The new Maryjane?*	B
15.	*Revolution*	B

This 1988 release was issued on white vinyl in its original pressings. It contains material from the "White Album" recording sessions and associated time period (hence the title). While some of the material is familiar *(While My Guitar Gently Weeps* and *What's The new Maryjane?),* much of it is available for the first time on this album.

Comments:

This fair-sounding mono album features mostly John Lennon performing demo versions of songs from the "White Album." In order to make things interesting, our friendly bootleggers have spliced extraneous sounds onto the beginning of most of the songs, such as jet plane noises on *Bungalow Bill,* bells on *Julia,* and birds on *Child Of Nature.*

The Continuing Story Of Bungalow Bill features John on guitar and vocals, and a background chorus of voices. It earns a C+ grade because it has no deep bass, no upper treble, and is distorted in places. The volume also fades in and out as if the music first gets closer, then farther away from the microphone. *Cry Baby Cry, Dear Prudence, Lady Madonna,* and *Honey Pie* share the problems mentioned above, and therefore also earn C+ grades. *Sexie Sadie* and *Yer Blues* are also lacking in deep bass and upper treble, but are free from distortion and get C grades.

The remaining songs all earn B- or better grades. *Julia, I'm So Tired,* and *Everybody's Got Something To Hide Except Me And My Monkey* earn B- due to generally better vocal presentation than the previously discussed songs. The songs earning B grades are the best of those on this album, and possess better extension at the frequency extremes than all the others.

In summation, this record is gimmicky (spliced in tape sounds) and only fair-sounding, but it contains much new material and therefore may prove to be an interesting addition to a Beatles collection.

NOTE: This album has been released on compact disc as **Off White** ([No label] WHT 868) with seven extra cuts.

Quarrymen Rehearse With Stu Sutcliffe Spring 1960 Pre Beatle
Records VD 15/16

Fixing A Hole, page 200

Ratings:
Side One
1.	*Hallelujah, I Love Her So*	C-
2.	*The One After 909 Ver. 1*	C-
3.	*I'll Always Be In Love With You*	C+
4.	*You'll Be Mine*	C-
5.	*Matchbox*	C+
6.	*You Just Don't Understand*	C
7.	*Some Days*	C-
8.	*Thinking Of Linking*	C+

Side Two
9.	*I'll Follow The Sun*	C
10.	*The One After 909 Ver. 2*	C-
11.	*Hey Darling*	C-
12.	*You Must Lie Everyday*	D+
13.	*The Guitar Bop*	C-
14.	*When Your Heartaches Begin*	C-
15.	*Hello, Little Girl*	C+
16.	*That'll Be The Day*	C

This album is one of two releases from tapes of the Quarrymen recorded in the spring of 1960. This single LP is a condensed version of a two-record set that also includes several additional instrumentals. Vocals are performed as follows:
Paul - Cuts 1, 6, 7, and 9
John - Cuts 3, 14 and 16
George - Cut 5
John (+Paul) - Cuts 2 and 15
Paul (+John) - Cut 10
Paul (+George) - Cut 11

Comments:
This album is a double-edged sword if there ever was one. While sonically it is only fair at best, historically it is very important. This is a very crude home recording made, as the title says, in the the spring of 1960. It predates the Beatles' first EMI recording sessions by two years.
All cuts on this album are lacking significantly at both ends of the

QUARRYMEN REHEARSE WITH STU SUTCLIFF SPRING 1960

Quarrymen Rehearse With Stu Sutcliffe Spring 1960
(LP) (front)

frequency spectrum. All vocals sound very recessed, obviously because the vocalists were not located close enough to the microphone to be recorded clearly. The difference between those songs earning C+ and C- grades is the fact that when levels get high on vocals the sound gets harsh and distorted. It is the level of harshness and distortion that determines the final grade for each song. *You Must Lie Everyday* is the worst-sounding cut of all. Because of a severe drop in volume during the song it only earns a D+ grade.

That'll Be The Day is a brief thirty-second snippet of the song, followed by Paul McCartney saying "That was the first record we ever did - The Beatles...." This must have been done after Paul recovered the only existing copy of this record after successful legal action.

While the playing is very raw and simple, the Beatles' songwriting talents are always in evidence with the inclusion of three Lennon-McCartney originals. *Hello Little Girl* is slower than the Decca Tapes version, while *The One After 909* is similar to the first recording of the song made by the Beatles in 1963. *I'll Follow The Sun* is musically similar but lyrically different than the 1964 officially-released version.

This record would make a valuable addition to any Beatles collection, as it presents the first recordings made by John, Paul, and George. While not sonically good, it is certainly listenable. By the way, the cover sports the first-ever color photograph of the Beatles, taken by Mike McCartney.

Ratings Summaries

Presented here in tabular form are summary ratings for all the bootleg records reviewed in this section. In formulating the summary ratings two changes have been made in comparison to the reviews presented in section: 1) letter grades have been changed to number scores, and 2) individual cuts on a disc are not included, only an average score for all cuts on a disc.

The numerical scoring system is as follows:

Letter Grade	Numerical Score
A	4.00
A-	3.67
B+	3.33
B	3.00
B-	2.67
C+	2.33
C	2.00
C-	1.67
D+	1.33
D	1.00
D-	0.67
E+	0.33
E	0.00

Table 1 below presents the ratings for 7-inch discs in the same order in which the reviews were presented, while Table 2 presents the ratings in numerical order from highest to lowest.

Table 3 below presents the ratings for 12-inch discs in the same order in which the reviews were presented, while Table 4 presents the ratings in numerical order from highest to lowest.

TABLE 1
7-inch Ratings in Review Order

TITLES	# cuts on disc	page # of review	RATING
How Do You Do It/Revolution (Live)	2	7	3.84
Three Cool Cats/Hello Little Girl	2	10	4.00
Sheik Of Araby/September In The Rain	2	10	3.84
Memphis/Love Of The Loved	2	13	3.84
Searchin'/Like Dreamers Do	2	13	3.67
Sure To Fall/Money	2	15	3.84
Crying, Waiting, Hoping/Till There Was You	2	18	3.67
To Know Him Is To Love Him/Besame Mucho	2	18	4.00
The Beatles By Royal Command (EP)	4	21	2.25
Top Of The Pops (EP)	4	24	3.67
Exclusive! Beatles Interviews 1966	2	24	3.67
Television Outtakes (EP)	5	26	2.61
Souvenir Of Their Visit To America (EP)	4	28	2.67
Strawberry Fields Forever/Penny Lane	2	28	3.67
Have You Heard The Word/Futting Around	2	30	2.67
Twickenham Jams (EP)	6	30	2.58
Love Of The Loved/Love Of The Loved	2	32	1.67
The Really Big Shew (EP)	5	34	1.40
From Us To You, A Parlophone Rehearsal Session (10-inch)	13	34	1.97

TABLE 2
7-inch Ratings in Numerical Order

TITLE	# cuts on disc	page # of review	RATING
Three Cool Cats/Hello Little Girl	2	10	4.00
To Know Him Is To Love Him/Besame Mucho	2	18	4.00
How Do You Do It/Revolution (Live)	2	7	3.84
Sheik Of Araby/September In The Rain	2	10	3.84
Memphis/Love Of The Loved	2	13	3.84
Sure To Fall/Money	2	15	3.84
Searchin'/Like Dreamers Do	2	13	3.67
Crying, Waiting, Hoping/Till There Was You	2	18	3.67
Top Of The Pops (EP)	4	24	3.67
Exclusive! Beatles Interviews 1966	2	24	3.67
Strawberry Fields Forever/Penny Lane	2	28	3.67
Souvenir Of Their Visit To America (EP)	4	28	2.67
Have You Heard The Word/Futting Around	2	30	2.67
Television Outtakes (EP)	6	26	2.61
Twickenham Jams (EP)	6	30	2.58
The Beatles By Royal Command (EP)	4	21	2.25
From Us To You, A Parlophone Rehearsal Session (10-inch)	13	34	1.97
Love Of The Loved/Love Of The Loved	2	32	1.67
The Really Big Shew (EP)	5	34	1.40

TABLE 3
12-inch Ratings in Review Order

TITLE	# cuts on disc	page # of review	RATING
Hahst Az Sun (Two Weeks In January, 1969)	29	37	3.53
The Beatles Live At Abbey Road Studios	25	39	3.02
Johnny & The Moondogs: Silver Days Air Time	17	41	3.37
Casualties	15	45	3.89
EMI Outtakes	11	47	2.30
Beautiful Dreamer	18	49	2.17
No. 3 Abbey Road	8	51	3.71
The Beatles Broadcasts	18	54	3.87
The Beatles Collector's Items	16	55	3.65
Don't Pass Me By	23	57	2.25
The Original Audition Tape - Circa 1962	21	59	1.92
The Original Greatest Hits	12	61	3.22
Top Of The Pops	12	62	2.47
The Beatles On Stage In Japan - The 1966 Tour	11	64	3.00
Judy	12	65	2.83
Have You Heard The Word	16	67	2.83
Outtakes Vol. 1	12	68	2.14
Outtakes Vol. 2	12	71	1.97
The Decca Tapes	15	73	3.93
File Under: Beatles	18	74	2.91
Not For Sale	17	77	3.47
Beatles: Not Guilty	14	79	2.83
The Beatles Conquer America	28	81	3.22
The Beatles Stockholm & Blackpool	13	85	2.46
The Beatles Budokan 1966	11	87	2.45
The Beatles Mach Shau!	12	89	1.53
The Get Back Journals	153	91	3.58
Nothing Is Real	13	99	3.41
Sessions	13	101	3.39
The Beatles At Shea	12	103	2.06
Dig It	18	106	3.21

An Audiophile's Guide to the Sound of the Fab Four

The Black Album	47	108	3.65
Return To Abbey Road	13	111	3.10
1967	14	113	3.31
Meet The BEEB	20	116	1.47
The Lost BEEBs	12	117	1.75
The Beatles At The BEEB Volume 1	19	120	3.11
The Beatles At The BEEB Volume 2	18	123	3.32
The Beatles At The BEEB Volume 3	19	125	3.58
The Beatles At The BEEB Volume 4	18	128	3.48
The Beatles At The BEEB Volume 5	20	130	2.98
The Beatles At The BEEB Volume 6	18	132	3.58
The Beatles At The BEEB Volume 7	13	134	2.69
The Beatles At The BEEB Volume 8	15	137	2.91
The Beatles At The BEEB Volume 9	17	139	2.63
The Beatles At The BEEB Volume 10	16	141	2.54
The Beatles At The BEEB Volume 11	17	143	2.96
The Beatles At The BEEB Volume 12	12	145	2.86
The Beatles At The BEEB Volume 13	15	147	2.31
Ultra Rare Trax Volume 1 & Volume 2	24	149	3.92
Ultra Rare Trax Volume 3 & Volume 4	17	153	3.80
Ultra Rare Trax Volume 5 & Volume 6	22	156	3.82
Off White	15	159	2.58
The Quarrymen Rehearse With Stu Sutcliffe Spring 1960	16	161	1.88

TABLE 4
12-inch Ratings in Numerical Order

TITLE	# cuts on disc	page # of review	RATING
The Decca Tapes	15	73	3.93
Ultra Rare Trax Volume 1 & Volume 2	24	149	3.92
Casualties	15	45	3.89
The Beatles Broadcasts	18	54	3.87
Ultra Rare Trax Volume 5 & Volume 6	22	156	3.82
Ultra Rare Trax Volume 3 & Volume 4	17	153	3.80
No. 3 Abbey Road	8	51	3.71
The Black Album	47	108	3.65
The Beatles Collector's Items	16	55	3.65
The Get Back Journals	153	91	3.58
The Beatles At The BEEB Volume 3	19	125	3.58
The Beatles At The BEEB Volume 6	18	132	3.58
Hahst Az Sun (Two Weeks In January, 1969)	29	37	3.53
The Beatles At The BEEB Volume 4	18	128	3.48
Not For Sale	17	77	3.47
Nothing Is Real	13	99	3.41
Sessions	13	101	3.39
Johnny & The Moondogs: Silver Days Air Time	17	41	3.37
The Beatles At The BEEB Volume 2	18	123	3.32
1967	14	113	3.31
The Beatles Conquer America	28	81	3.22
The Original Greatest Hits	12	61	3.22
Dig It	18	106	3.21
The Beatles At The BEEB Volume 1	19	120	3.11
Return To Abbey Road	13	111	3.10
The Beatles Live At Abbey Road Studios	25	39	3.02
The Beatles On Stage In Japan - The 1966 Tour	11	64	3.00
The Beatles At The BEEB Volume 5	20	130	2.98
The Beatles At The BEEB Volume 11	17	143	2.96
File Under: Beatles	18	74	2.91
The Beatles At The BEEB Volume 8	15	137	2.91
The Beatles At The BEEB Volume 12	12	145	2.86

Beatles: Not Guilty	14	79	2.83
Judy	12	65	2.83
Have You Heard The Word	16	67	2.83
The Beatles At The BEEB Volume 7	13	134	2.69
The Beatles At The BEEB Volume 9	17	139	2.63
Off White	15	159	2.58
The Beatles At The BEEB Volume 10	16	141	2.54
Top Of The Pops	12	62	2.47
The Beatles Stockholm & Blackpool	13	85	2.46
The Beatles Budokan 1966	12	87	2.45
The Beatles At The BEEB Volume 13	15	147	2.31
EMI Outtakes	11	47	2.30
Don't Pass Me By	23	57	2.25
Beautiful Dreamer	18	49	2.17
Outtakes Vol. 1	12	68	2.14
The Beatles At Shea	12	103	2.06
Outtakes Vol. 2	12	71	1.97
The Original Audition Tape - Circa 1962	21	59	1.92
The Quarrymen Rehearse With Stu Sutcliffe Spring 1960	16	161	1.88
The Lost BEEBs	12	117	1.75
The Beatles Mach Shau!	12	89	1.53
Meet The BEEB	20	116	1.47

SECTION TWO

Commercial Singles

> SECTION TWO

The Mass Market

GETTING TO KNOW YOUR DISCS

A record by the Beatles is much more than just a piece of plastic in a cardboard (or paper) cover. There is a wealth of information to be found if you know what to look for and where to find it. Since most of the reviews in this book are of imported (non-U.S.) records, the most important questions are "Where was this record made?" and "Where does it come from?" Surprising as it may seem, these two questions do not always have the same answer.

The simplest way to find the country of origin of a Beatles record is to read the album jacket and record label. Unfortunately, not every jacket or label explicitly states this information. It is always there, however, if you know how to find it. EMI, being a multinational company, has devised a numerical coding system to identify its branches throughout the world. Every country participating in the Common Market has a "C" code number uniquely its own. Here are just a few of the codes that you may come across while building your collection of Beatles records:

0C	= England
1C	= Germany
2C	= France
3C	= Italy
5C	= Holland
7C	= Sweden
10C	= Spain
14C	= Greece
31C	= Brazil

Many Beatles albums have common serial numbers around the (EMI) world, with only the code numbers differing. This code and serial number combination always appears somewhere on the album jacket, with one minor and one major exception.

The minor exception involves English pressings, which do not always use the "0C" code number. Each U.K. Beatles album has its own serial number, usually beginning with the letter "P." Actually, if an English album was issued in mono and stereo, each edition has a unique serial number; for example, **Sgt. Pepper's Lonely Hearts Club Band** is PCS 7027 (stereo) and PMC 7027 (mono).

Toshiba-EMI in Japan is the major exception to the "C" code number rule. Beatles records from Japan never have a "C" code number, only a special "Japan only" serial number. Records released on the Apple label have serial numbers beginning with "A" or "E," while records on the Odeon label have serial numbers beginning with "O" or "E." The "O" series, "OP" for albums and EPs and "OR" for singles, is out of print.

Although all Japanese Beatles records say "made in Japan" on the sleeve or jacket, many countries do not clearly state the place of origin. Going to the record store armed with your list of EMI codes will solve most, if not all, of the possible mysteries.

An important point must be made here. Deciphering the EMI code on the sleeve actually reveals only the origin of the sleeve itself. It is an approved practice for EMI countries to cross-package Beatles albums. This usually occurs when one country is starting a new printing run and either the production of records or album jackets falls behind schedule, or when two countries go into a joint production venture. This results in one country supplying the actual record and the other supplying the jacket and packaging. In this manner it has become possible to get a French pressing in an English or German jacket, or a New Zealand pressing in an Australian jacket. Therefore, you never really know what you're getting until you get the record home and open up the package.

READING THE RECORD

Reading a record, as strange as it sounds, can be a very informative endeavor for the Beatles collector. The label, as well as listing the album and/or song titles, has a great deal of information to reveal when closely scrutinized. The country of origin is usually available in one of two places. Around the edge of the label is generally a copyright statement of the following type: "All Rights of the Manufacturer and of the Owner of the Recorded Work Reserved. Unauthorized Public Performance, Broadcasting and Copying of this Record Prohibited." After this statement can usually be found "Made in [country name]." This "around the edge" writing may not appear on both sides of the disc, so look carefully. If the country of origin is not found here, then look for the "C" code number. This will definitely reveal the disc's origin, keeping in mind the exceptions of England and Japan.

As well as having the serial number and the "C" code from appropriate countries, the label usually lists the master number of the recording. This master number refers to the code number assigned by EMI to the master tape, or a copy of the master tape, that was used to cut the disc. (Actually, in almost all cases a copy of the master tape was used. This will be explained in SECTION THREE - FOR AUDIOPHILES ONLY.) Every pressing from a specific master tape will have the same master number, even if manufactured in different years. Here is an example: EMI England, in the 1960s, mixed both mono and stereo master tapes for the first ten Beatles albums, with only **Abbey Road** and **Let It Be** being "stereo only" releases. All mono masters had the prefix "XEX" and all stereo masters had the prefix "YEX." In 1981, when EMI reissued the Beatles' mono albums, the "XEX" prefix was brought back into use. Following this stereo/mono prefix is the tape number, for **Sgt. Pepper's Lonely Hearts Club Band** it is 637 for Side One and 638 for Side Two. Therefore, a mono **Sgt. Pepper** will have XEX637 and XEX638 on its labels and a stereo pressing will have YEX637 and YEX638.

After examining the label, the record itself remains. There are two distinct places to look at on a Beatles record: the grooves, and (what else is left?) the non-grooves! The non-groove refers to the space between the end of the last cut and the label. This is sometimes referred to as the "run out groove," but is not actually the groove in which we are interested. The flat space (land) between the end of the last cut and the label always has information printed there. The master number can always be found scratched or stamped in this area; Capitol in the U.S. usually has it scratched in while EMI in European countries usually has it stamped in. After the master number, sometimes separated by a dash, is usually found the cutting number. This is only found on the record, not on the label. This cutting number uniquely identifies the master lacquer that eventually led to the pressed record. Two pressings from the same tape may be different - due to different cutting techniques, equalization, or other reasons - so it is important to check the cutting number. For example, Side One of an English copy of **Sgt. Pepper's Lonely Hearts Club Band** (PCS 7027) from **The Beatles Collection** box set (Parlophone BC 13, cutting number YEX637-3) is a different cutting than Side One of the English **Sgt. Pepper Picture Disc** (Parlophone PHO 7027, cutting number YEX637-5). These two records may sound indistinguishable, and then again they may sound as different as night and day.

The master and cutting numbers provide useful information about a Beatles record. Many EMI countries use the English "XEX" and "YEX" mono/stereo prefixes, thus making it very easy to identify a stereo pressing if the label is lacking that message. The most famous and important of all examples showing the value of reading the master and cutting numbers involves the **Magical Mystery Tour** LP. Originally a double-EP set in England

(Parlophone (S)MMT 1/2), this was issued by Capitol Records in the United States as an LP (Capitol SMAL 2835). This American release was, and still is "synthetic" or "reprocessed" stereo. True stereo pressings are available, however, from Germany and Israel.

The problem for collectors in finding these true stereo pressings revolves around the fact that these discs have appeared on various labels at different times. In Germany, **Magical Mystery Tour** has appeared on both Odeon and Apple; in Israel it has appeared on both Parlophone and Portrait. The German disc has had two different serial numbers; the Israeli disc has the same serial number as the American "reprocessed" stereo release. How do you know if you have a true stereo pressing? Check the master number! The German and Israeli true stereo pressings of **Magical Mystery Tour** have the master number SHZE 327 stamped into the record. If this number is not found, then the record is not true stereo.

Other things may appear, at times, in this blank area of a record. "Mastered by Capitol" is usually stamped here on American releases. Many times the name or initials of the engineer who cut the master lacquer are scratched here - "Wally" or "J. Lemay" are frequently found on Capitol's American discs, and "SR/2" can be found on Mobile Fidelity Sound Lab discs. By the way, "SR/2" is translated into "cut by Stand Ricker at half-speed." This can be considered analogous to an artist's signature on a painting, because Ricker's discs are consistently outstanding in sonic quality: he is currently one of, if not the most highly regarded disc cutter in the business.

This blank area is sometimes even used to convey a message to the record-buying public. This was done twice on Beatles or solo Beatles records - "Phil + Ronnie" can be found on the American *The Long and Winding Road* single (Apple 2832), and "One World One People" can be found on the American *Starting Over* single (Geffen 49604). Of course, the most famous of all messages was actually the inner groove itself on the English (and other countries outside the U.S.) **Sgt. Pepper's Lonely Hearts Club Band** LP. Does anyone know what that message really says?

Looking at the grooves of a record can sometimes be a revealing experience. As an oversimplification, wide grooves can be quieter (less background noise), more dynamic (higher signal levels), contain lower frequency information, and be easier for a phono cartridge to track than narrow grooves. If you compare the English **Sgt. Pepper** LP (Parlophone YEX637 and YEX638) with the American pressing (Capitol SMAS 1-2653-A1#2 and SMAS 1-2653-B1#2) a major difference is evident. Although both pressings use about the same amount of available record space (the flat land around the label is about equal), the English pressing has no blank space between songs. This space, otherwise wasted, has been used to allow generally wider grooves to be cut. The American record has narrower grooves

because a good amount of space is wasted on the inter-song blank spaces.
These cutting differences are usually evident on 45 rpm singles issued by Capitol. Many collectors have tried to get versions of an American single with all possible label variations - yellow/orange swirl, orange Capitol, Apple, purple Capitol, etc. Many times a new pressing of a single will be a new master cutting; many U.S. singles have various editions still in print. A good example of this is the single *We Can Work It Out*. The orange Capitol label version, master number 45377-F10, has grooves that span only 5/8 inch on the record, while the purple Capitol label version, master number 45377-J10, has grooves that span 1 1/8 inches on the record. Looking at the two records side by side it is difficult to believe they both contain the same song.

It is quite easy to see that with the Beatles, there's more than just what's in the grooves!

SINGLES

What can be said about the Beatles as singles artists? Nothing special, only that they were the most successful group on the singles chart in the history of *Billboard* magazine and almost every other music trade publication around the world. Imagine what rock and roll radio was like the week of April 4, 1964, when the Beatles had the entire Top Five and twelve of the Top Hundred in *Billboard* magazine. The following week, April 11, 1964, even though two of their songs had dropped out of the Top Five, they established an all-time mark with fourteen songs in the Top Hundred. Not even the Bee Gees in their "Saturday Night Fever" heyday did that well!

More than albums or extended plays, the Beatles' singles have been issued, reissued, reissued again, recoupled, put in new picture sleeves, boxed, and so on *ad infinitum*. This certainly is a tribute to the staying power of the music - the 45 rpm single is generally not a lifetime catalogue item as is an album. The life of a successful single is usually three to five months on the chart, a year or so in the record bins, and then life as a "golden oldie" reissue if considered one of the artist's "greatest hits."

The fact that every Beatles single issued by EMI in England is still in print is a feather in the Beatles' cap and an excellent opportunity for the import collector. The original twenty-two English singles are as follows:

Title	Label	Serial	Released
Love Me Do/P.S. I Love You	Parlophone	R 4949	10/05/62
Please Please Me/Ask Me Why	Parlophone	R 4983	1/11/63
From Me To You/Thank You Girl	Parlophone	R 5015	4/12/63

She Loves You/I'll Get You	Parlophone	R 5055	8/23/63
I Want To Hold Your Hand/ This Boy	Parlophone	R 5084	11/29/63
Can't Buy Me Love/You Can't Do That	Parlophone	R 5114	4/20/64
A Hard Day's Night/Things We Said Today	Parlophone	R 5160	7/10/64
I Feel Fine/She's A Woman	Parlophone	R 5200	11/27/64
Ticket To Ride/Yes It Is	Parlophone	R 5265	4/09/65
Help!/I'm Down	Parlophone	R 5305	7/23/65
We Can Work It Out/Day Tripper	Parlophone	R 5389	12/03/65
Paperback Writer/Rain	Parlophone	R 5452	6/10/66
Yellow Submarine/Eleanor Rigby	Parlophone	R 5493	8/05/66
Penny Lane/Strawberry Fields Forever	Parlophone	R 5570	2/17/67
All You Need Is Love/ Baby, You're A Rich Man	Parlophone	R 5620	7/07/67
Hello, Goodbye/I Am The Walrus	Parlophone	R 5655	11/24/67
Lady Madonna/The Inner Light	Parlophone	R 5675	3/15/68
Hey Jude/Revolution	Apple	R 5722	8/30/68
Get Back/Don't Let Me Down	Apple	R 5777	4/11/69
The Ballad Of John And Yoko/ Old Brown Shoe	Apple	R 5786	5/30/69
Something/Come Together	Apple	R 5814	10/31/69
Let It Be/You Know My Name (Look Up The Number)	Apple	R 5833	3/06/70

Reviews of these records, as part of **The Beatles Singles Collection** from England and Japan, are the heart of this section, although singles from America (the Blue Capitol Starline Set, among others), Australia (**The Beatles Singles Collection Australian 20th Anniversary 1962-1982**), France, and Canada are featured as well. Because couplings vary around the world, these reviews are grouped by song rather than record. Emphasis is placed upon pressings currently in print, as previously mentioned.

An Audiophile's Guide to the Sound of the Fab Four

READING THESE REVIEWS

As previously mentioned, reviews of singles are arranged by song rather than record due to the various couplings issued around the world. Following the listing of the song title is information regarding each pressing reviewed. This information includes country of origin, label, serial number, additional notes (such as the box set the record came in, if it is a picture disc, etc.), and master number.

The master number is as it appears on the surface of the record itself. Because some records have the master number separated into small groups of characters spread around the entire flat area of the disc, it is not always known where to start reading the number. It is therefore recommended that in comparing what is on a disc to what is listed here, the reader try to match all the numbers and letters and not worry if the order is totally correct. Also, any messages found around the label area, such as "Bell Sound" and "Mastered by Capitol," have not been included as part of the master number.

To help make this clear, here is an example of a master number as it appears on a disc:

A-6299_45870_H10_3

The underline character (_) signifies a blank space. The space is equivalent to hitting the space bar on a typewriter, roughly as wide as one character. If two underline characters appear consecutively (__), the blank space is larger than one character width. In fact, it may be an inch long or half the distance around the record. Therefore, if you started reading the above master number from a different starting point in the record you could come up with the master number as follows:

45870_H10_3_A-6299   or   H10_3_A-6299_45870

Therefore, if a record matches the number presented herein but appears to be in a different order, the groups may be rearranged due to where the reading started. (By the way, the above master number is *Strawberry Fields Forever* from the U.S. Blue Starline set by Capitol.)

Following the information about the records themselves is the main body of the review. General sonics are discussed, as well as comparisons among pressings, etc. If label information incorrectly indicates stereo or mono it is also noted. Where appropriate, the review concludes with a ranking of pressings in order of preference, with reasons and notes presented as required.

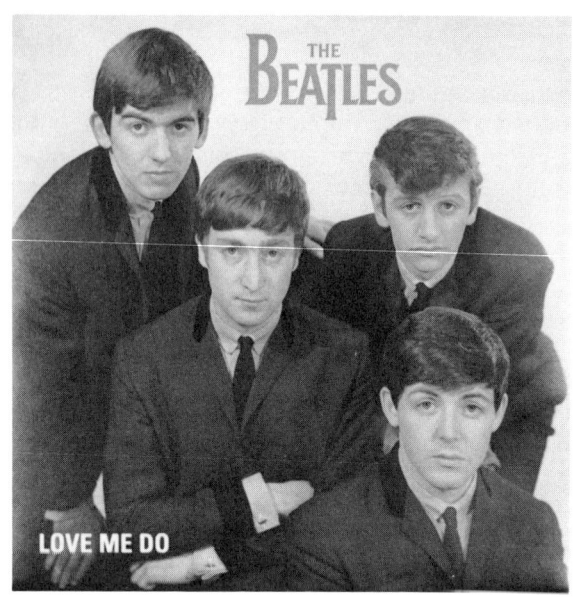

Love Me Do (front)
(England)

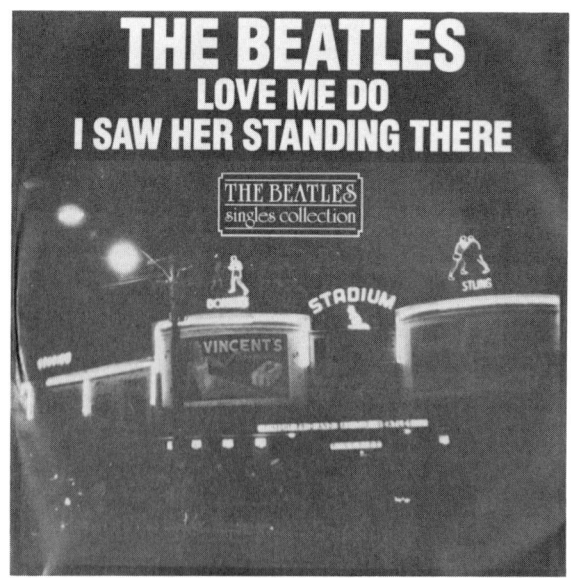

Love Me Do (front)
(Australia)

An Audiophile's Guide to the Sound of the Fab Four

LOVE ME DO

1. (Australia) **The Beatles Singles Collection Australian 20th Anniversary 1962-1982** Parlophone A8105 Master Number A-8105A.
2. (England) **The Beatles Singles Collection** Parlophone (red label) R4949 Master Number 7XCE17144-2.
3. (England) **The Beatles Singles Collection** Parlophone RP4949 Master Number RP4949A PICTURE DISC.
4. (Japan) **The Beatles Singles Collection** Odeon EAS-17311 Master Number 45-R-4949-U-1S.
5. (Japan) **The Beatles Singles Collection** Odeon EAS-17337 Master Number RLP-4949A PICTURE DISC.
6. (US) 1982 edition with yellow/orange swirl label Capitol B-5189 **Stereo** Master Number B-5189-S-45-X45012_G-1.

Note: All pressings say mono or are assumed to be mono unless the label indicates stereo, in which case it is listed above.

These six pressings have two things in common: none are true stereo, and all are bass heavy. The fact that none are true stereo is not a major handicap; the bass heaviness, however, is another story.

It seems as if the 1980s have taken on the weight of the musical world. Each of these recent editions have the lower frequencies (below 100 Hz) so boosted in level as to be grossly over-emphasized. Even if the name Beatles does bring about some connotation of the word B-E-A-T, it was never meant to sound like this. This song (no matter which pressing) only becomes listenable when the bass is reduced in level by 2 to 4 dB from 100 Hz on down.

The six pressings can be divided into two groups: reprocessed stereo and true mono. The U.S. and Australian editions are in reprocessed stereo, while the other four versions are in true mono.

Both the reprocessed stereo editions have boosted highs in the right channel and depressed highs in the left channel. This gives the impression that the tambourine is to the right of center and the over-emphasized bass guitar and bass drum are to the left of center. Because this is accomplished just by adjusting the frequency balance, the images are not stable and the effect is not very satisfying.

Of the true mono editions, not much can be found to distinguish between them. The two picture discs seem to be identical to their black vinyl counterparts. How well they would hold up to repeated playings is not known, although historically it has been shown that picture discs tend to develop noisy playing surfaces.

183

Love Me Do (Side 1)
(England)

Love Me Do (Side 1)
(U.S. 20th Anniversary Edition)

If a choice must be made between the black vinyl issues from England and Japan, the Japanese pressing is very slightly cleaner in spots. Small amounts of sibilant distortion present on the English record are not found on the Japanese version. The difference is so slight, however, as to be unnoticeable without headphones.

In summation, any of the true mono editions is preferable to the two reprocessed stereo versions. Here's the final breakdown:

Ranking:
True Mono Edition
Japanese Black Vinyl
Japanese Picture Disc
(Picture disc editions are not recommended based on possible problems with wear after repeated playings, as previously mentioned.)
English Black Vinyl
English Picture Disc
(Picture disc editions are not recommended based on possible problems with wear after repeated playings, as previously mentioned.)
Reprocessed Stereo Edition
Australian
U.S.
(The Australian edition is preferred to the U.S. version because the bass over-emphasis, although still present, is not as prominent and oppressive.)

NOTE: An identical U.S. pressing (same master number as reviewed here) is available on the purple Capitol label.

P.S. I LOVE YOU

1. (England) **The Beatles Singles Collection** Parlophone (red label) R4949 Master Number 7XCE_17145-2 .
2. (England) **The Beatles Singles Collection** Parlophone RP4949 Master Number RP+4949+B PICTURE DISC.
3. (France) Odeon 2C006-04453 Master Number 4453_A_21_M3_286306.
4. (Japan) **The Beatles Singles Collection** Odeon EAS-17311 Master Number 45-R-4949-B-U_1S.
5. (Japan) **The Beatles Singles** Collection Odeon EAS-17311 Master Num-

P.S. I Love You (back)
(England)

P.S. I Love You (front)
(France)

ber RLP-4949-B PICTURE DISC.
6. (US) 1982 edition with yellow/orange swirl label Capitol B-5189 **Stereo** Master Number B-5189-S-45-X45013 G-1#2.
Note: All pressings say mono or are assumed to be mono unless the label indicates stereo, in which case it is listed above.

In reviewing *P.S. I Love You*, a French pressing was included because this song does not appear in The Beatles Singles Collection Australian 20th Anniversary 1962-1982 boxed set.

As with *Love Me Do*, none of the editions reviewed here are in true stereo. The U.S. and French editions are reprocessed stereo, with boosted highs in the right channel and depressed highs in the left channel. The vocals and percussion appear slightly right of center, while Paul's bass guitar appears to the left of center. Although providing some apparent stereo separation, the sound is also somewhat darkened by this process.

These two editions share another common characteristic: the midrange and upper bass are overbearing. Although this problem is at its worst on the French pressing, both have moments where the sound gets so thick as to almost smother the listener. Neither of these pressings is acceptable for serious listening.

The two English and two Japanese pressings are in true mono. Although by definition lacking separation, they are all less overbearing in the midrange and upper bass. In similar style to *Love Me Do*, the picture disc issues appear to be indistinguishable from their black vinyl counterparts. Further comments are based on the black vinyl pressings.

In a direct comparison of the English and Japanese pressings, and nod must go to the Japanese edition. The English disc has a slight amount of background "hash" not evident on the Japanese record. This makes the Japanese version sound slightly more detailed and clearer from top to bottom. The midrange of the Japanese disc is more natural sounding and not at all overbearing. Although it is only marginally better than the English edition in this regard, it is significantly better than both the U.S. and French versions.

In summation, the Japanese pressing is a slight favorite over the English edition, with the U.S. and French a very distant third and fourth.

Ranking:
    Japanese Black Vinyl
    Japanese Picture Disc
        (Picture disc editions are not recommended based on possible problems with wear after repeated playings.)
    English Black Vinyl

English Picture Disc
(Picture disc editions are not recommended based on possible problems with wear after repeated playings.)
U.S.
(This song, as is also evident with *Love Me Do*, is an example of a misguided attempt to try to squeeze more from a master tape than is actually there. The desire to create a stereo recording from a mono master tape has created not a more satisfying record, but a less satisfying one. These two songs exemplify the fact that mono can sound very good indeed, especially in contrast to reprocessed stereo.)
French
(This song, as is also evident with *Love Me Do*, is an example of a misguided attempt to try to squeeze more from a master tape than is actually there. The desire to create a stereo recording from a mono master tape has created not a more satisfying record, but a less satisfying one. These two songs exemplify the fact that mono can sound very good indeed, especially in contrast to reprocessed stereo.)

NOTE: An identical U.S. Pressing (same master number as reviewed above) is available on the purple Capitol label.

PLEASE PLEASE ME

1. (Australia) **The Beatles Singles Collection Australian 20th Anniversary 1962-1982** Parlophone A8080 Master Number A-8080A.
2. (England) **The Beatles Singles Collection** Parlophone (red label) R4983 Master Number 7XCE17217-3.
3. (Japan) **The Beatles Singles Collection** Odeon EAS-17312 **Stereo** Master Number 7XCE-17217-U_1S.

Note: All pressings say mono or are assumed to be mono unless the label indicates stereo, in which case it is listed above.

Only three pressings are reviewed here due to the lack of a current U.S. single version of this song being in print. Although only the Japanese pressing is identified as being in stereo, the Australian version is also. The English pressing, as well as being in mono, is a different version of the song!

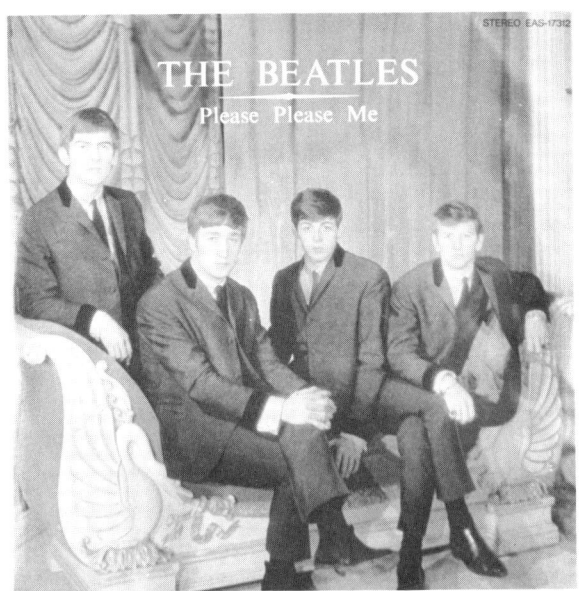

Please Please Me (front)
(Japan)

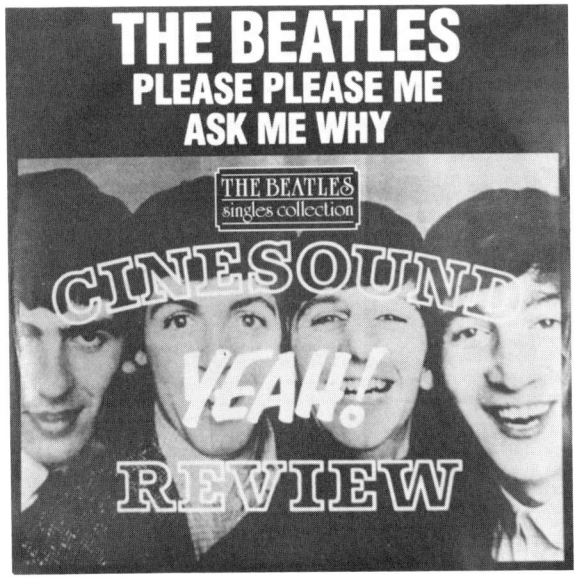

Please Please Me (front)
(Australia)

The stereo versions, which come from the same master tape, have the "mistake" in the background/foreground vocals: "I know *I* never even"/"I know *you* never even" being sung simultaneously by John and Paul. The English version, in mono, has the correct lyrics.

Sonically, the English pressing is quite different than the others. It is cut at a much higher level and lacks the detail and finesse of the stereo pressings. It is definitely a "power" song - loud with strong bass and piercing harmonica. There is a bit of distortion throughout the vocals and the separation between the lead and background locals is blurred; it is hard, at times, to distinguish between them. There also seems to be a slight "veil" or "haze" that separates the listener from the music. It should be noted that, since this song really jumps out from the speakers and grabs you, the above-mentioned negative characteristics are not apparent at first.

Of the stereo pressings, the Japanese edition is slightly smoother and cleaner than the Australian version. While the Australian is less veiled than the English, the Japanese is clear, pristine, and without a trace of veil or haze. The stereo separation (on both discs) provides a distinct separation between the lead and background vocals, and the effect, in conjunction with the "instruments on the left/vocals on the right" stereo spread, makes this less of a "power" song than the English mono edition.

The difference in feeling between the mono and stereo versions of this song makes *Please Please Me* a unique case: two songs rather than one.

In summation, there is enough difference between the stereo and mono versions of this song that a collection would not be complete without both of them.

    Ranking:
        Japanese (Recommended.)
        English (Recommended.)
        Australian
        (The Australian pressing is a notch lower in sonic quality than the Japanese and therefore is ranked last.)

ASK ME WHY

1. (Australia) **The Beatles Singles Collection Australian 20th Anniversary 1962-1982** Parlophone A8080 Master Number A-8080B.
2. (England) **The Beatles Singles Collection** Parlophone (red label) R4983 Master Number 7XCE17218-3.
3. (Japan) **The Beatles Singles Collection** Odeon EAS-17312 **Stereo** Master

Number 7XCE-17218-U-1S.
Note: All pressings say mono or are assumed to be mono unless the label indicates stereo, in which cast it is listed above.

The lack of a U.S. edition currently being in print leaves only these three boxed set editions for review. As with the flip side of these records (*Please Please Me*), the Australian pressing is in stereo although the label and picture cover fail to indicate so.

Sonically the English pressing is quite problematical. Although it has strong bass presentation and up-front vocals, the overall sound is rather harsh. The vocals tend to be slightly distorted in some places and overbearingly harsh in others.

The stereo pressings, although slightly different, are both glorious. The presentation style is words in the right channel, music in the left. This, coupled with a slightly reduced vocal level in comparison to the English version, gives the song a more refined quality (the vocals are less up-front). The instrumentation is more readily discernible, as are the background vocal harmonics, than in the harsh-sounding pressing from England. Both the stereo pressings are slightly reduced in bass level, although this is where the Japanese and Australian versions differ.

The Japanese pressing, although having reduced overall bass output than the English, seems to go slightly deeper into the bass frequencies. This gives a leaner impression, but still presents a firm foundation to the song. The lack of harshness is a pleasure in comparison to the English pressing, contributing to the smooth, refined aura of the song.

The Australian pressing is very similar to the Japanese. Only a slight roll-off at both frequency extremes prevents the Australian from matching the excellence of the Japanese disc. The differences between these two pressings are so slight as to be only noticeable under close scrutiny.

In summation, the overall harshness of the English pressing makes it the least desirable of the three reviewed here, while the sweetness, clarity, and frequency extension of the Japanese pressing make it the favorite.

Ranking:
Japanese
Australian
English

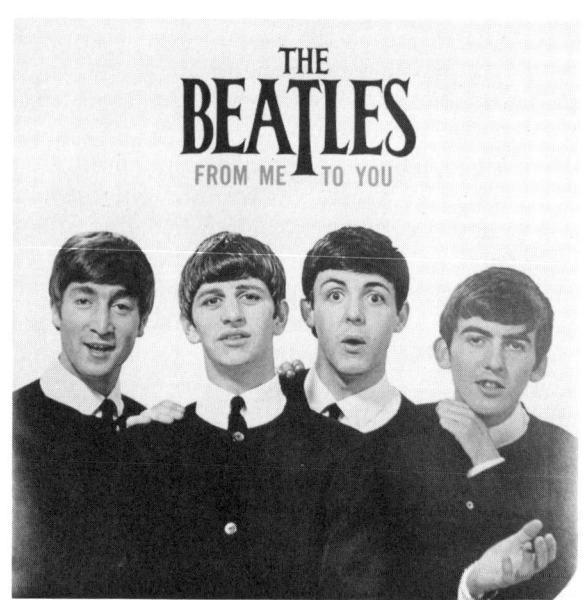

From Me To You (front)
(England)

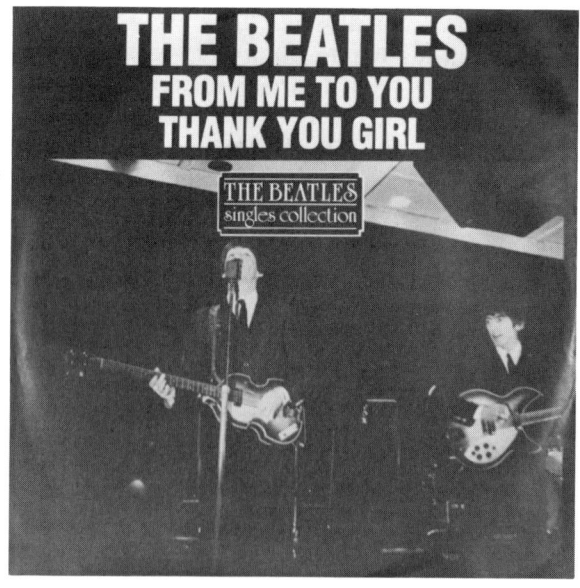

From Me To You (front)
(Australia)

An Audiophile's Guide to the Sound of the Fab Four

FROM ME TO YOU

1. (Australia) **The Beatles Singles Collection Australian 20th Anniversary 1962-1982** Parlophone A8083 Master Number 7XCE17329.
2. (England) **The Beatles Singles Collection** Parlophone R5015 Master Number 7XCE17329-2.
3. (Japan) **The Beatles Singles Collection** Odeon EAS-17313 **Stereo** Master Number 7XCE-17329-U_1S.

Note: All pressings say mono or are assumed to be mono unless the label indicates stereo, in which case it is listed above.

As with *Ask Me Why*, there is not an edition of this song currently in print in the U.S. as a single. Of the three versions reviewed here, only the Japanese pressing is in stereo.

The English pressing, although listenable, is the worst of the three. Paul's bass is barely audible at times, robbing the song of its all-important low end foundation. At the other end of the spectrum the high frequencies are harsh on occasion. Vocals are plagued by distortion throughout the length of the song. These problems are not major when examined individually, but as a whole this disc is unsatisfactory for critical listening.

The Australian pressing is similar to the English in all areas. It is slightly improved in the high end, however, being smoother and less distorted on the vocals. The bass end is only marginally improved - its level still seems a trifle low to be able to balance out the song. All in all this is more listenable than the English, although it still shows faults when closely scrutinized.

The Japanese pressing, any way you look at it, is a gem. It is in stereo, with words in the right channel and music in the left. The bass level is greater than the Australian, just enough to provide a firm foundation to the song without being intrusive or oppressive. The overall presentation is silky smooth without a trace of harshness or distortion. The level of detail in the song is significantly greater than evident on the vocals; it is possible to hear the echo effects added to the vocals and the popping of "P's" whenever the word `keep' is sung.

In summation, the Japanese pressing is far superior to the others, with the Australian being slightly better than the English.

Ranking:
Japanese
Australian
English

Thank You Girl (back)
(Australia)

Thank You Girl (back)
(Japan)

THANK YOU GIRL

1. (Australia) **The Beatles Singles Collection Australian 20th Anniversary 1962-1982** Parlophone A8083 Master Number 7XCE17330.
2. (England) **The Beatles Singles Collection** Parlophone R5015 Master Number 7XCE17330-2.
3. (Japan) **The Beatles Singles Collection** Odeon EAS-17313 **Stereo** Master Number 7XCE-17330-U_1D.

Note: All pressings say mono or are assumed to be mono unless the label indicates stereo, in which cast it is listed above.

This is another song not currently having an American single pressing in print. The three pressings reviewed here actually comprise two different versions of this tune. The Japanese pressing, as well as being in true stereo, contains the harmonica riff ending, whereas the Australian and English pressings, being mono, do not.

The two mono pressings are virtually identical in every respect. Bass is firm and has good extension. Vocals are clean and well presented, without a trace of harshness. Treble is clean and fairly extended; only a slight hint of shimmer is missing from Ringo's cymbals. The only difference between the two mono pressings is a very slight reduction in bass level in the Australian version. This is so slight as to be unnoticeable except in direct comparison to the English edition.

The Japanese pressing, although true stereo, is a sonic mess. The bass is overblown in level and tubby in quality. Vocals are presented amidst an excessive amount of echo. This echo robs the vocals of the clarity that is present on the mono versions. The stereo presentation - words on right and music on left - sounds quite artificial in comparison to the mono pressings. The only appealing feature of the Japanese pressing is the fact that it contains the harmonica riff ending as previously mentioned.

Ranking:
English
Australian (a very close second).
Japanese (a very distant third).

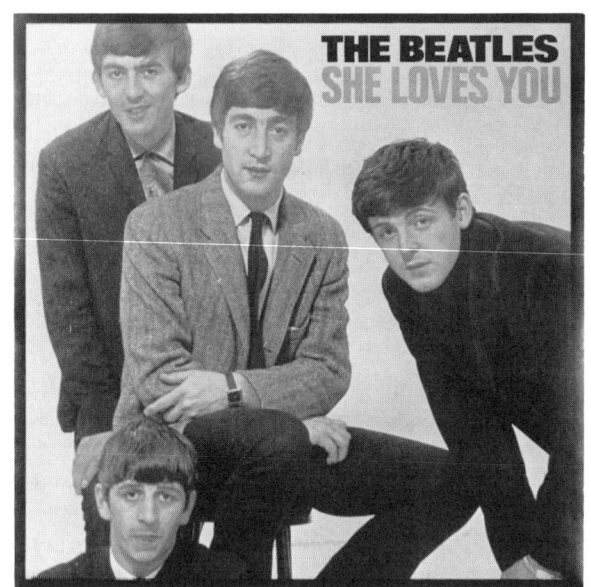

She Loves You (front)
(England)

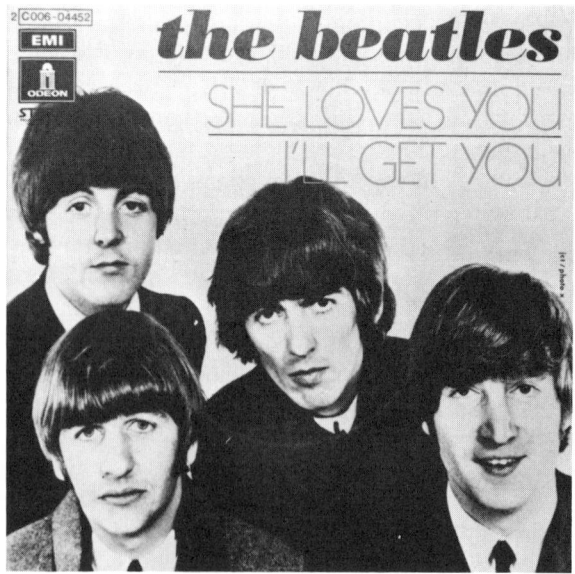

She Loves You (front)
(France)

SHE LOVES YOU

1. (Australia) **The Beatles Singles Collection Australian 20th Anniversary 1962-1982** Parlophone A8093 Master Number 7XCE17395.
2. (England) **The Beatles Singles Collection** Parlophone R5055 Master Number 7XCE17395-2.
3. (France) Odeon 2C006-04452 **Stereo** Master Number M3_290_188_04452_A_21.
4. (Japan) **The Beatles Singles Collection** Odeon EAS-17314 **Stereo** Master Number 7XCE-17395-U-_1S.

Note: All pressings say mono or are assumed to be mono unless the label indicates stereo, in which case it is listed above.

Without an American single version being currently in print, a French pressing has been reviewed here along with the three boxed set editions from Australia, England, and Japan. Of these four versions only the English pressing is in true mono, the others being reprocessed stereo.

More than any other, song *She Loves You* seems to epitomize, at least here in America, the essence of Beatlemania. It is only fitting, then, that the pressing from the Beatles' native England takes the honors as the best-sounding version of this song. This version, in glorious mono, is almost perfect. Vocals are forward and clear, treble is extended, and there is not a trace of harshness to be found. The only slight deviation from perfection occurs in the bass, where the lowest frequencies seem to be recessed and ill-defined at times.

Of the reprocessed stereo versions, the Japanese pressing takes the honors. It is slightly fuller than the English pressing. The right channel has boosted highs and the left channel has boosted bass. It is the reprocessing that creates the sonic problems here, characterized by the slightly too full bass (as previously mentioned) and an over-emphasized high end. Ringo's cymbals are so over-emphasized as to sound like one constant shimmer rather than drumsticks on cymbals. Vocals sound slightly "echoey" and the song has less overall punch than the English version.

The French pressing earns a runner-up position among the reprocessed stereo editions. As well as being cut at a lower level than the Japanese, its bass is slightly fatter and less defined. The vocals are also slightly recessed. In total, however, these problems are not too severe.

The worst of all, by a wide margin, is the Australian pressing. Bass is extremely overprominent and bloated. The highs are so boosted as to be distorted throughout the song. Vocals are distorted and unclear. In a word, this version is terrible.

Ranking:
English
Japanese
French
Australian (a very distant fourth).

I'LL GET YOU

1. (Australia) **The Beatles Singles Collection Australian 20th Anniversary 1962-1982** Parlophone A8093 Master Number 7XCE_17396.
2. (England) **The Beatles Singles Collection** Parlophone R5055 Master Number 7XCE17396-2.
3. (France) Odeon 2C006-04452 **Stereo** Master Number M3_290_189_04452)B_21.
4. (Japan) **The Beatles Singles Collection** Odeon EAS-17314 **Stereo** Master Number 7XCE-17396-U_1S.

Note: All pressings say mono or are assumed to be mono unless the label indicates stereo, in which cast it is listed above.

A French pressing has been reviewed due to the lack of an American pressing currently being in print, along with the three boxed set editions. Although two of the discs are labelled as being in stereo, neither of them are in true stereo.

The English pressing, in mono, is rather difficult to tolerate. The top end of this disc is very harsh-sounding and distorted. Ringo's cymbals lack all definition and sound like a stream of constant "hash" rather than individual strikes by the drumsticks. The vocals are also distorted and "dirty" sounding. The bass end, although fairly clean and well defined, is slightly lacking in weight. This helps to draw the listener's attention to the problematical top end.

In overall sound the French pressing is as bad as the English. The only difference is the reprocessed stereo presentation - bass boost in the left channel, treble boost in the right channel. The high frequencies are harsh and distorted, in similar fashion to the English edition. Again, an almost intolerable pressing.

The Australian pressing, in mono, is better in some aspects than the English and French editions. The treble distortion and hash are gone, making this infinitely more pleasant to hear. However, close listening reveals that this cleaning up of the high end seems to have been accomplished at the expense of high frequency extension. Normally, this reduction in high frequency content would tend to make a song sound "dark" or "closed-in." It does not, in this case, due to the almost total lack of bass response. In fact, the song sounds slightly top-heavy in spite of the reduction in high frequency content.

The best of the four pressings reviewed here is the Japanese. It is in reprocessed stereo, in similar style to the French edition explained earlier. This reprocessing is rather mild in effect, a definite plus for this disc. A heavy hand in reprocessing can lead to unnatural effects, such as instruments wandering across the stereo spread. This is not in evidence on this disc.

This version is fuller sounding than the others. The mid-bass is increased in level and the low bass has greater extension. This provides a firm foundation to the song. At the top end there is not a trace of harshness or distortion, and this was accomplished without sacrificing high frequency response. In general, this as an excellent-sounding disc with good frequency balance and no distortion.

    Ranking:
        Japanese
        Australian
        English
        French

It is interesting to compare the rankings of *I'll Get You* with *She Loves You*. Although these are flip sides, no pressing earns the same rank with both sides of the disc.

I WANT TO HOLD YOUR HAND

1. (Australia) **The Beatles Singles Collection Australian 20th Anniversary 1962-1982** Parlophone A8103 Master Number 7XCE17559.
2. (England) **The Beatles Singles Collection** Parlophone R5084 Master Number 7XCE17559-3.
3. (Japan) **The Beatles Singles Collection** Odeon EAS-17315 **Stereo** Master Number 7XCE-17559-U_1S.
4. (US) Blue Starline Edition Capitol X-6278 (or A-6278) Master Number (A-6278) _45-44771_J-1.
5. (US) 20th Anniversary Edition with yellow/orange swirl label Capitol 5112 Master Number 45-5112-#44771_G-2.
    Note: All pressings say mono or are assumed to be mono unless the label indicates stereo, in which cast it is listed above.

I Want To Hold Your Hand (Side 1)
(U.S. Blue Starline Edition)

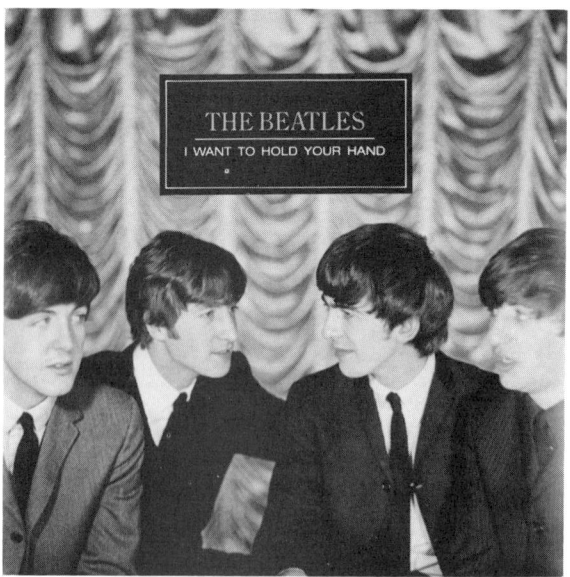

I Want To Hold Your Hand (front)
(England)

I Want To Hold Your Hand (front)
(Australia)

I Want To Hold Your Hand (front)
(U.S. 20th Anniversary Edition)

Two different American pressings are currently available; five different pressings have been reviewed here. The Blue Starline version was released in two different label configurations, one stating stereo and one stating mono. These two labels graced the same mono pressing of the song (see master number given above).

Although only the Japanese pressing states stereo on the label, the Australian pressing, though different, is also in stereo. Both American editions and the English pressing are in mono. The three mono pressings sound very similar, with only minor differences amongst them.

The English pressing can be characterized as lightweight in sound. The bass end of the frequency range is almost totally nonexistent. The high frequencies, as well as dominating the overall sound of the song, suffer from a very slight lack of definition; however, this is only readily apparent when listening via headphones.

The US Blue Starline pressing is difficult to distinguish from the English pressing without concentrated listening effort. Close scrutiny reveals a slightly fuller bass end, and a slightly denser overall sound presentation. This denseness is due to a slight lack of overall definition throughout the song.

The US 20th Anniversary Edition, with the yellow/orange swirl label, is practically identical to the Blue Starline pressing. An extremely small increase in definition in the low and middle frequencies is discernible, although the high end is still somewhat ill-defined. Of the three mono pressings, this, by a slight margin, is the best.

The Japanese pressing, though labelled stereo, is a puzzler. Casual listening gives the impression that this is in reprocessed stereo. The sonic picture appears to be boosted highs in the left channel and muted highs in the right channel. This seems to be consistent with the presentation of other reprocessed stereo pressings of Beatles songs. Careful listening, however, reveals that this disc is actually in true stereo. Vocals are centered, cymbals are to the left, and one of the guitar parts (the smallest one) is to the right. Headphone listening seems to confirm the true stereo presentation, although based on other Beatles recordings from 1963, this is hard to believe. The tell-tale sign of reprocessing, cross-channel leakage, is absent from this pressing. If this is not actually true stereo, it is the best (and most clever) reprocessing available on record.

Looking past the stereo presentation, this edition sounds fuller than the mono pressings. While it still sounds slightly lean and tilted toward the high end, instrumentation is more detailed and cleaner-sounding than on any of the mono pressings.

The Australian pressing, although not labelled stereo, is in fact true stereo. It is the familiar words in the right channel, music in the left channel presentation typical of early Beatles songs. Instrumentation is more detailed than on the mono pressings, but the vocals seem recessed and distorted in spots. This problem is a minor one - just enough to keep this a notch below the Japanese edition in overall sonic quality.

> Ranking:
> Japanese
> Australian
> > (Although the Australian edition is ranked second, it is recommended due to the fact that it is a different true stereo edition than the Japanese pressing.)
>
> US 20th Anniversary Edition
> US Blue Starline Edition
> English

THIS BOY

1. (Australia) **The Beatles Singles Collection Australian 20th Anniversary 1962-1982** Parlophone A8103 Master Number 7XCE_17560-3.
2. (Canada) **The Beatles Forever Singles Collection** Capitol 72144 **Stereo** Master Number 72144_FYCE-17560_2.
3. (England) **The Beatles Singles Collection** Parlophone R5084 Master Number 7XCE17560-4-1-1.
4. (Japan) **The Beatles Singles Collection** Odeon EAS-17315 Master Number 7XCE-17560-U_1S.
   Note: All above say mono or are assumed to be mono unless the label indicates stereo, in which case it is listed above.

This song has never been issued on a single in the US. The Canadian pressing, long known in Beatles collectors' circles as *the* true stereo edition, is reviewed here. The other three versions are not identified as being in stereo, although the Australian pressing is (and true stereo, at that).

The Canadian pressing, being true stereo, has the words in the right channel and the music in the left channel. Sonically, this edition is not very distinguished. The low end is not very strong or well-defined. It is present, but not substantial enough to provide a firm foundation to the song. Vocals sound slightly veiled, as if a curtain is hanging between the listener and John, Paul, and George, and the high end is slightly deficient in "air" and extension.

The Australian pressing is terrible. Vocals are distorted throughout

This Boy (front)
(Canada)

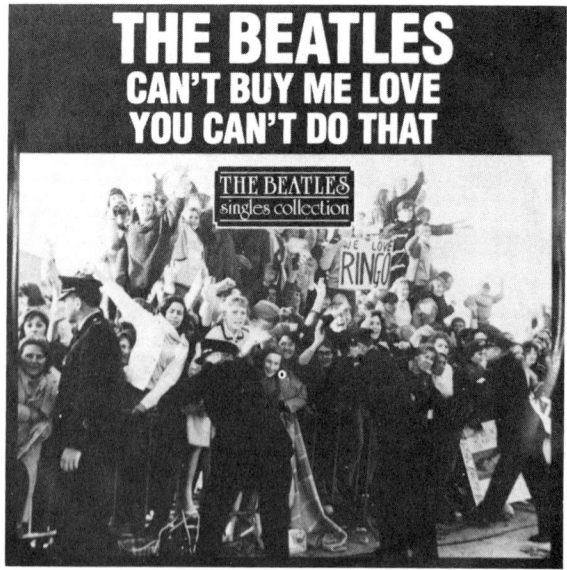

Can't Buy Me Love (front)
(Australia)

the entire song; in places where the vocals are prominent the distortion is so bad as to sound as if the record is a defective pressing. This may in fact be the case, but it is doubtful for two reasons. First, the distortion seems almost totally isolated in the right channel, as if the master tape playback was defective when the lacquer was cut. Second, pressing defects usually effect both sides of a disc. This is certainly not the case here, as *I Want To Hold Your Hand* (the flip side) sounds quite fine.

The mono pressing from Japan, depending on your tolerance for the true stereo style of isolated words and music, may be the sonically best edition of the song reviewed here. Other than a weak low end, this is an excellent-sounding disc. In comparison to the Canadian, this pressing is superior from the midrange through the high end. Treble is very clean and well extended. The top end "air" is present in all of its glory. Vocals are crystal clear - the veil has been lifted. Midrange presence is more apparent due to the finely detailed presentation afforded by this disc. This edition can be summed up as up-front in relation to the recessed sound of the Canadian pressing.

The English pressing, also in mono, in similar in sound to the Japanese. Bass is slightly more in evidence, although at first this may not be apparent. Vocals are slightly less clear, but again, it takes more than one listening session to confirm this point.

    Ranking:
        Canadian
            (This is recommended because it is in true stereo.)
        Japanese
            (Other than a lack of soundstage presentation (by definition of mono) this is sonically better than the Canadian edition.)
        English
        Australian

CAN'T BUY ME LOVE

1. (Australia) **The Beatles Singles Collection Australian 20th Anniversary 1962-1982** Parlophone A8113 Master Number A8113A.
2. (England) **The Beatles Singles Collection** Parlophone R5114 Master Number 7XCE17657-2.
3. (Japan) **The Beatles Singles Collection** Odeon EAS-17316 **Stereo** Master Number 7XCE-17657-U_1S.

4. (US) Blue Starline Edition Capitol A-6279 (or X-6279) **Stereo** Master Number A-6279 44914 H6#1.
Note: All above say mono or are assumed to be mono unless the label indicates stereo, in which case it is listed above.

Of the four versions reviewed here, the US and Japanese pressings are labelled as being in stereo. The US Blue Starline edition is actually mono, and later printings have a different label, which states mono, and a different serial number, with an "X" prefix instead of an "A" prefix. Both Blue Starline printings are actually the same cutting of the song (see master number above).

Although not labelled as such, the Australian pressing is in true stereo, as is the Japanese. The differences between the true stereo and mono editions of this song are so great as to demand treatment separately during the review process. The true stereo pressings will be discussed first.

Upon first listening to the Australian pressing the true stereo presentation is easily recognizable. The majority of the music is confined to the left channel while the words (and small amounts of music) are presented in the right channel. Although this presentation has very clear-sounding vocals, it can be disconcerting at times. To hear voices from the right and the instruments played by the singers from the left is very unrealistic.

Bass is generally lacking weight and is somewhat indistinct, with individual notes on Paul's bass and Ringo's bass drum hard to isolate. The high end is almost totally missing, with Ringo's cymbals only present for brief moments. The missing high frequencies make the music seem to be lacking in overall detail, with most transients seeming blurred. In general, the song has a "polite" sound, and this is somewhat in contrast with the nature of *Can't Buy Me Love*.

The Japanese pressing is very similar to the Australian. Although the highs are still lacking, the overall presentation is somewhat more detailed in nature. The bass frequencies also are slightly stronger, but still lacking in required weight. Again, the sound is "polite," but every so slightly the better of the two stereo editions.

The main difference between the stereo and mono editions, other than the soundstage (by definition), is in the high frequency range. In the English pressing, Ringo's cymbals are evident throughout the song. The high frequencies are so much more apparent as to seem like a different cymbal track was added to the instrumental backing of this song. Vocals are still clear and bass is present but still slightly weaker than it should be. This edition does not sound "polite" as the stereo versions do, and this seems to better express the feeling of *Can't Buy Me Love*.

The US pressing is similar to the English. Ringo's cymbals are even

You Can't Do That (back)
(Australia)

further forward in the mix and slightly louder. Vocals are stronger and overall presence is greater. Bass is almost indistinguishable from the English, although at times it is slightly less forceful. In general, this edition sounds more up-front than the English. It is only in the US pressing that *Can't Buy Me Love* sounds like the "power" song that it really is.

> Ranking:
> **True stereo pressings**
> > Japanese
> > > (Because the stereo and mono pressings are so different, both of these are recommended.)
> > Australian
> **Mono pressings**
> > US
> > > (Because the stereo and mono pressings are so different, both of these are recommended.)
> > English

YOU CAN'T DO THAT

1. (Australia) **The Beatles Singles Collection Australian 20th Anniversary 1962-1982** Parlophone A8113 Master Number A8113B.
2. (England) **The Beatles Singles Collection** Parlophone R5114 Master Number 7XCE17658-2.
3. (Japan) **The Beatles Singles Collection** Odeon EAS-17316 **Stereo** Master Number 7XCE-17658-U-1S.
4. (US) Blue Starline Edition Capitol A-6279 (or X-6279) **Stereo** Master Number A-6279 45-44913 H11.

   Note: All above say mono or are assumed to be mono unless the label indicates stereo, in which case it is listed above.

As with the flip side, *Can't Buy Me Love*, the Australian (although not so labelled) and Japanese pressings are in true stereo. The US Blue Starline edition, although labelled as stereo, is actually mono, as is the English pressing. The US Blue Starline edition was later issued with serial number X-6279 stating mono, but containing the same cutting (see master number above).

Of the true stereo pressings, the Australian is the better of the two. The stereo presentation is as follows: words (in reduced volume) and small amounts of music in the right channel, and words (at full volume) and most of the music in the left channel. The soundstage has most of the music on the left, vocals to the left of center, and small bits of the music to the right. This makes the song sound somewhat slanted toward the left speaker, but the effect is not too severe. The entire frequency range is well presented by the Australian pressing. Bass is full and well defined, and treble is extended into the uppermost octave. The sonic presentation is very strong and powerful.

The Japanese pressing does not measure up to the excellence of the Australian. Although the stereo separation is slightly wider, the frequency balance is quite uneven. The lower midrange is entirely too full and overblown. This makes the vocals somewhat muddy and ill-defined. High frequency extension is limited, robbing the song of the "air" around Ringo's cymbals. In general, this pressing is fat, tubby, and ill-defined. The overblown lower midrange makes the song seem stuffy and oppressive. This pressing is not easy to tolerate.

The English pressing is the better of the two mono editions. Vocals are clear and forward in the mix. Frequency extension is good at both extremes. As with the Australian, this is a very powerful pressing.

The US pressing is not as clean as the English. Vocals are slightly distorted and Ringo's cymbals are not as clear. The bass response is reduced in level and seems weak in spots. Overall this pressing is fair, but it pales in comparison to the excellent English disc.

Ranking:
True stereo pressings
Australian
(Although different in soundstage presentation (of course), these are both outstanding records and are recommended.)
Japanese
Mono pressings
English
(Although different in soundstage presentation (of course), these are both outstanding records and are recommended.)
US

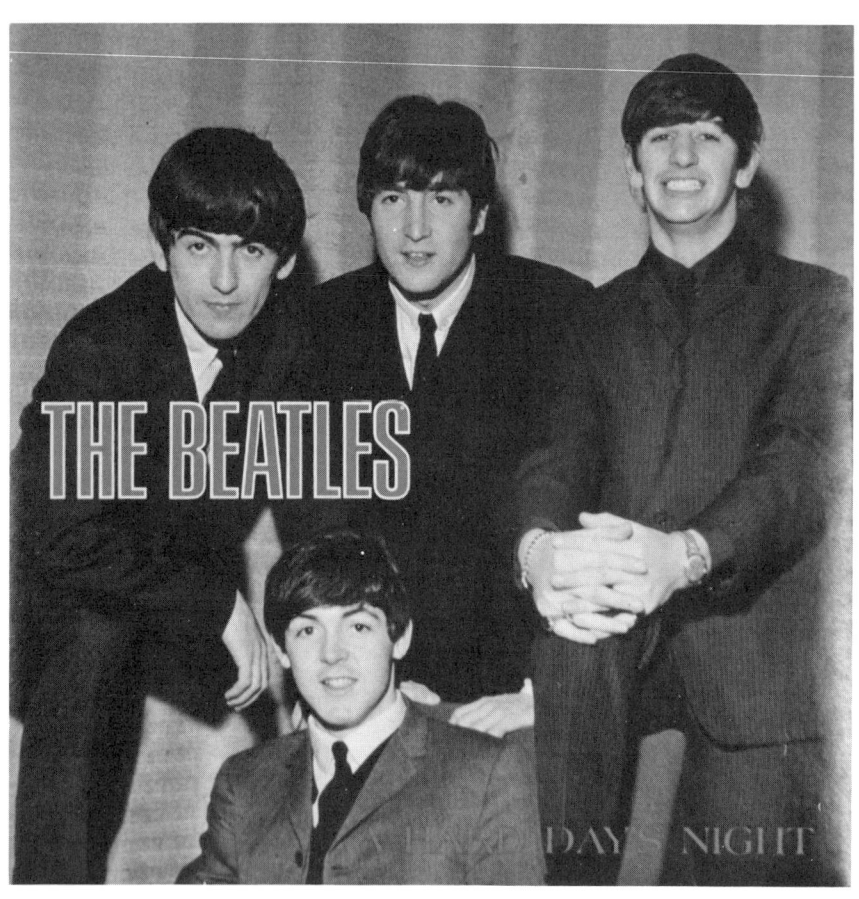

A Hard Day's Night (front)
(Japan)

An Audiophile's Guide to the Sound of the Fab Four

A HARD DAY'S NIGHT

1. (Australia) **The Beatles Singles Collection Australian 20th Anniversary 1962-1982** Parlophone A8123 Master Number A8123A.
2. (England) **The Beatles Singles Collection** Parlophone R5160 Master Number 7XCE17714-2.
3. (Japan) **The Beatles Singles Collection** Odeon EAS-17317 **Stereo** Master Number 7XCE-17714-U_1S.
4. (US) Blue Starline Edition Capitol A-6281 (or X-6281) **Stereo** Master Number A-6281_45035_H6#1.

Note: All above say mono or are assumed to be mono unless the label indicates stereo, in which case it is listed above.

The Japanese and American editions are labelled as being in stereo, although the American edition is mono. Later pressings have a different label, stating mono and using the "X" prefix to the serial number. Both label variations of the US Blue Starline edition of this disc are the same cutting (see master number above). Neither the Australian nor the English pressing is labelled as being in stereo, although the Australian pressing actually is. This song is another example that proves that labels may be deceptive; it's what's in the grooves that counts.

The Japanese pressing is the best of those reviewed here. The stereo presentation has most of the music and vocals in the left channel, and small bits of music and vocals in the right channel. Because the vocals are stronger in the right channel and the music is stronger in the left channel, the soundstage presentation appears to have the music to the left of center (with occasional instrumentation on the right) and vocals to the right of center. This gives a more realistic stereo image than the "hole-in-the-middle" effect that occurs when all of the music is in one channel and all of the words are in the other.

As to the sound, it is very good. Treble is extended and detailed. The midrange is clean and upper bass is full. Low bass is missing, but that is the case with all of the pressings under consideration here. All in all, this is a fine-sounding record.

The Australian pressing, although also in stereo, is not quite as good as the Japanese. The high frequencies are not as extended, robbing Ringo's cymbals of their sheen and definition. The entire song, from top to bottom, sounds rather dense. There is not much distinction among the instruments, and the vocals are not entirely clean.

The English pressing, although in mono, is every bit as good as the Japanese. Other than the obvious difference in soundstage, the two are practically indistinguishable. The US pressing, also in mono, is not as good as the English. The midrange is slightly too full and is a touch overbearing. The high frequencies show small amounts of distortion in various places throughout the song. Vocals are not entirely clear, sounding occasionally recessed and "echoey." Of the four records reviewed here, the US edition is the least desirable.

>   Ranking:
>   Japanese
>   English
>   (This is only ranked second because it is in mono. Actually, since *A Hard Day's Night* was originally released in mono, this is more faithful to the 1964 release than the Japanese pressing; however, since the stereo imagery enhances the overall presentation of the song, the Japanese disc gets the nod in the ranking.)
>   Australian
>   US

THINGS WE SAID TODAY

1. (Australia) **The Beatles Singles Collection Australian 20th Anniversary 1962-1982** Parlophone A8123 Master Number A8123B.
2. (England) **The Beatles Singles Collection** Parlophone R5160 Master Number 7XCE17715-1N.
3. (Japan) **The Beatles Singles Collection** Odeon EAS-17317 **Stereo** Master Number 7XCE-17715-U_1S.
    Note: All above say mono or are assumed to be mono unless the label indicates stereo, in which case it is listed above.

Things We Said Today has never been issued on a single in the US, hence only the three boxed set editions are discussed here. Although only the Japanese is labelled stereo, the Australian pressing is as well.

The stereo presentation is the same as the flip side, *A Hard Day's Night*. Most of the music comes from the left and most of the vocals come from the right. All three versions suffer from a lack of deep bass, although this is not a major problem.

In comparing the two stereo editions, the Japanese is slightly superior to the Australian. Although both are balanced toward the high end, the Japanese pressing has greater extensions at both ends of the frequency range. This results in a slightly fuller, more detailed presentation, especially notice-

I Feel Fine (front)
(Japan)

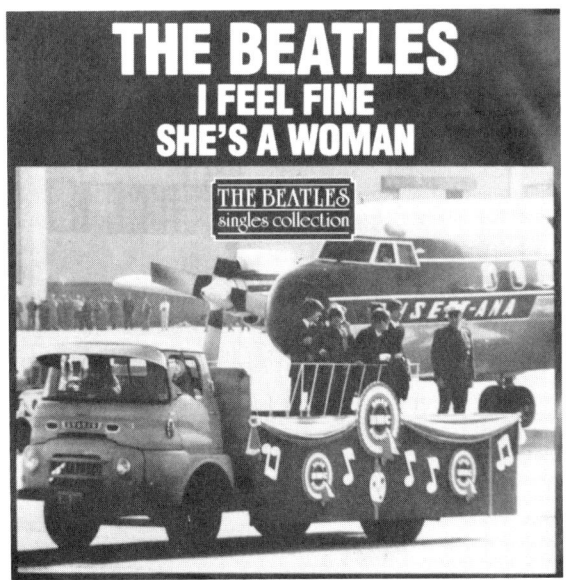

I Feel Fine (front)
(Australia)

able in the sound of the guitar. Both editions sound similar in the vocals, and this is their primary weak spot. Vocals are recessed and bathed in echo, making the voices sound soft and somewhat distant in comparison to the music.

The English pressing, although in mono, is the best of the three reviewed here. This is so for two distinct reasons: the high frequencies are slightly more pronounced, and the vocals are slightly more up-front. Ringo's cymbals are clearer, and the entire song has more presence due to the increased level of the high frequencies. Vocals are free of echo and do not sound recessed. This also adds to the overall presence of the song.

Ranking:
English
Japanese
Australian

I FEEL FINE

1. (Australia) **The Beatles Singles Collection Australian 20th Anniversary 1962-1982** Parlophone A8133 Master Number 7XCE18171.
2. (England) **The Beatles Singles Collection** Parlophone R5200 Master Number 7XCE18171-2.
3. (Japan) **The Beatles Singles Collection** Odeon EAS-17138 **Stereo** Master Number 7XCE-18171-U_1S.
4. (US) Blue Starline Edition Capitol A-6286 (or X-6286) **Stereo** Master Number A-6286_45-45085_H11.

   Note: All above say mono or are assumed to be mono unless the label indicates stereo, in which case it is listed above.

As with many other Australian true stereo pressings, this is not labelled as such. Of the mono pressings, the US edition is the better of the two. The English pressing is extremely harsh-sounding. The high end is significantly too prominent and "hot." The entire disc is lacking in definition; the instrumentation sounds "bunched-up, making it very difficult to distinguish the individual instruments. The bass end of the frequency range is somewhat weak; coupled with the overbright high end this disc is not easy to tolerate if it is played at a volume above background level.

As mentioned elsewhere (see *A Hard Day's Night*), the US Blue Starline edition, although labelled as being in stereo, is not. This pressing is only slightly better than the English. The high end, although still somewhat over-emphasized, is not as piercingly hot. The treble is still slightly harsh-sounding, but the slightly recessed vocals seem to offset this. The bass end is similar in sound to the English, that is, lacking in sufficient weight to balance the song's sound. The overall definition is slightly better than the UK edition, with the instrumentation not sounding as "bunched-up."

The Japanese pressing is by far the better of the stereo editions reviewed here. It is smooth, detailed, and well-extended at both ends of the frequency range. Vocals are up-front without a trace of distortion. Ringo's bass drum can literally be felt - a tribute to the bass presentation. Individual instruments are easily located in space due to the detailed soundstage.

The Australian pressing is not as well-extended at either end of the frequency spectrum. Ringo's bass drum is not in evidence, and his cymbals lack their expected shimmer. Vocals are distorted in some places, and sound somewhat recessed and lacking in "bite" and presence. The overall instrumentation is also not as detailed as the Japanese pressing.

Ranking:
Japanese
Australian
US
English

NOTE: Two identical U.S. pressings (same master number as reviewed here) are available on the purple Starline and on the black-and-rainbow colorband Starline labels from Capitol.

SHE'S A WOMAN

1. (Australia) **The Beatles Singles Collection Australian 20th Anniversary 1962-1982** Parlophone A8133 Master Number 7XCE18172.
2. (England) **The Beatles Singles Collection** Parlophone R5200 Master Number 7XCE18172-2.
3. (Japan) **The Beatles Singles Collection** Odeon EAS-17318 Master Number 7XCE-18172-U_1S.
4. (US) Blue Starline Edition Capitol A-6286 (or X-6286) **Stereo** Master Number A-6286_45-45086_H10#2.
    Note: All above say mono or are assumed to be mono unless the label indicates stereo, in which case it is listed above.

As with the flip side, the Australian pressing of *She's A Woman* is in true stereo, even though its label fails to indicate so. This is a rather rare version of the song, available nowhere else as a single. It is only available as

She's A Woman (back)
(England)

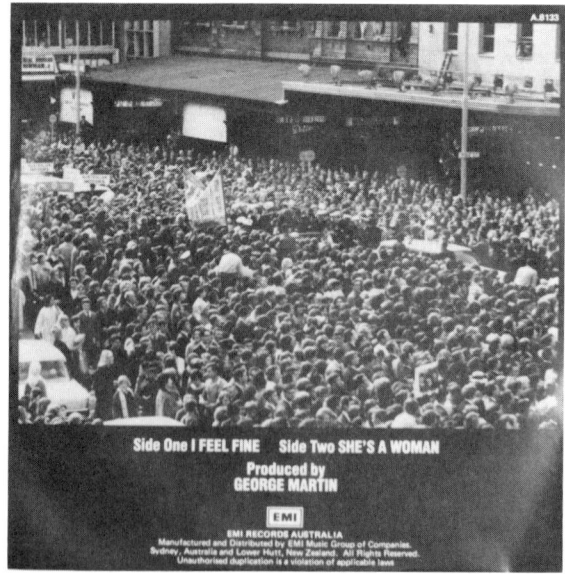

She's A Woman (back)
(Australia)

part of **The Beatles EP** (from **The Beatles EP Collection** boxed set) and in **The Beatles Greatest Vol II** LP from Australia and Singapore.

The stereo presentation is not very exciting, with the right channel consisting mostly of vocals and macacas. The left channel, as well as having vocals, has most of the bass energy and Ringo's cymbals. Sonically, this pressing is somewhat disappointing. It is good, but not as good as it probably should be.

The high frequencies are slightly depressed and not fully extended to the uppermost octave. This results in a mildly "dry" and "closed-in" sound. There seems to be a small dip in frequency response in the lower midrange, because the vocals seem somewhat veiled and recessed. The bass response of the record is weak, with a slight lack of weight evident at the low frequencies.

Each of these problems is minor, and even in combination they do not detract significantly from the overall sound of this record. Close scrutiny only leaves the listener with an unfulfilled feeling, wishing that the potential for sonic greatness had been realized in this pressing.

Of the three mono pressings reviewed here, the Japanese edition is the best. In fact, it is sonically superior to the Australian pressing, exhibiting none of the specific problems previously discussed. The highs are airy and extended, giving this pressing a light and "open" sound. Vocals are up-front and presented without a trace of harshness. The low end is full and deep, without being overblown or fat. The superb sonics of this pressing show that stereo separation is not a requirement in order to have a truly first-rate disc.

The remaining mono pressings, from England and the US, are both inferior to the Japanese edition, although for different reasons. The English version is almost identical to the Japanese, suffering only from a slightly depressed high end similar to the Australian edition. This depression is very minor - so minor as to be only apparent in direct comparison. Other than for the fact that the English pressing is cut at a lower level that the Japanese, these two records are almost identical.

The American pressing, however, is a totally different (and sad) story. This edition is an example of what happens when somebody (it was probably Dave Dexter, Jr., the man who "produced" the Beatles' records in America) goes crazy adding echo. From the opening guitar chords throughout the remainder of the song, the vocal portions are drowned in echo. This totally destroys the song, otherwise ruining a good sonic presentation. Other than a slight harshness in the treble range during Ringo's cymbal playing in the chorus, this is a fine-sounding disc. Even the slight hardness can probably be explained by the fact that this pressing is cut at an extremely high volume.

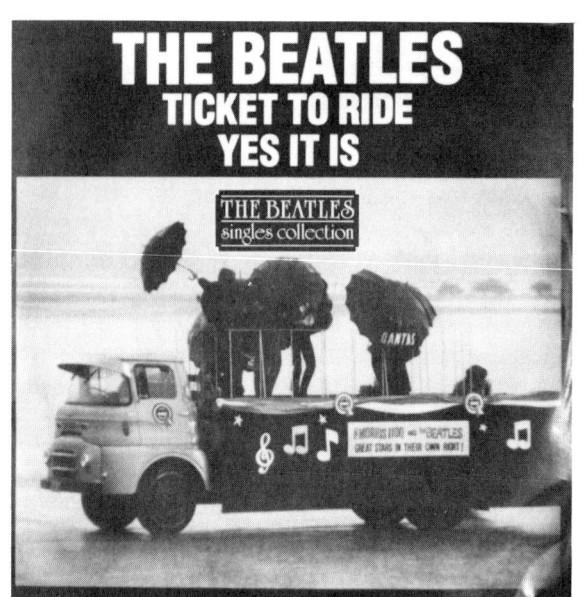

Ticket To Ride (front)
(Australia)

Ticket To Ride (front)
(Japan)

Ranking:
Japanese
Australian
(Although ranked second, this is recommended due to the rarity of the true stereo version of this song.)
English
US

TICKET TO RIDE

1. (Australia) **The Beatles Singles Collection Australian 20th Anniversary 1962-1982** Parlophone A8153 Master Number 7XCE18524.
2. (England) **The Beatles Singles Collection** Parlophone R5265 Master Number 7XCE18524-4.
3. (Japan) **The Beatles Singles Collection** Odeon EAS-17319 **Stereo** Master Number 7XCE-18524-U_1S.
4. (US) Blue Starline Edition Capitol A-6288 (or X-6288) **Stereo** Master Number A-6288_45219_H10#1.

Note: All above say mono or are assumed to be mono unless the label indicates stereo, in which case it is listed above.

The Australian pressing, although not so labelled, is in true stereo, as is the Japanese edition. Of the four versions reviewed here, none stands head and shoulders above the others in terms of sonic quality.

The best of the bunch, although not perfect by any means, is the English pressing. Frequency balance is generally good, with fairly wide extension at both ends of the spectrum. Two small problems exist, both probably caused during the recording/mixing process rather than in the mastering/pressing process. All vocals are presented in a slightly "veiled" manner. Voices never sound as if the singers were singing directly into their microphones, but rather as if a fairly heavy curtain or drape intervened. Also, there is a touch too much echo and/or artificial "air" to the vocals. The second problem involves Ringo's drums. The drum rolls are mixed so far into the background (at such a low level) as to be almost non-existant.

Of the remaining three discs, the Japanese comes closest to matching the English in terms of sonic quality. The stereo separation, while not overly dramatic, does indeed liven-up the presentation as a whole. This is more than offset, however, by the veiling of the vocals. The problem is slightly more exaggerated than on the English disc. Also, the midrange seems to be fat and slightly overblown, a problem that is excruciatingly noticeable when listening at high volume.

Yes It Is (back)
(Australia)

Yes It Is (back)
(England)

The American pressing sounds remarkably like the Japanese. The fact that it is mono relegates it to third place in the ranking.
The Australian pressing is also similar to the Japanese. It shares the problems of veiled vocals and overblown midrange. It does, however, compound things by adding an additional problem. Treble extension is limited in comparison to the other pressings of this song. This is especially noticeable on the tambourine, which sounds too "dark" to be the real thing. This is the only one of the four reviewed here that is totally unsatisfying and difficult to listen to, even if it is in true stereo.

Ranking:
English
Japanese
US
Australian

YES IT IS

1. (Australia) **The Beatles Singles Collection Australian 20th Anniversary 1962-1982** Parlophone A8153 Master Number 7XCE18255.
2. (England) **The Beatles Singles Collection** Parlophone R5265 Master Number 7XCE_18255-2.
3. (Japan) **The Beatles Singles Collection** Odeon EAS-17319 **Stereo** Master Number 7XCE-18255-U_1S.
4. (US) Blue Starline Edition Capitol A-6288 (or X-6288) **Stereo** Master Number A-6288_45220_H10.

Note: All above say mono or are assumed to be mono unless the label indicates stereo, in which case it is listed above.

Yes It Is is the first Beatles single, at least chronologically, not to have a stereo edition reviewed here. No true stereo version of this song yet exists on seven-inch vinyl.

Sonically, this song is a bit different from most other Beatles tunes. It is a very "down" type of song - not musically lively at all. However, some differences exist among the versions reviewed here that influence the "down" feeling presented by the song.

The Australian version is probably the worst, but due to the nature of *Yes It Is* is more than acceptable. The low bass is missing, harmony vocals are veiled, and instrumentation is not very well defined. Only vocals solos and an occasional cymbal have any "air" to them at all. This overall "dark" sound would be unpleasant on *She Loves You*, for example, but here it is

Help! (front)
(Japan)

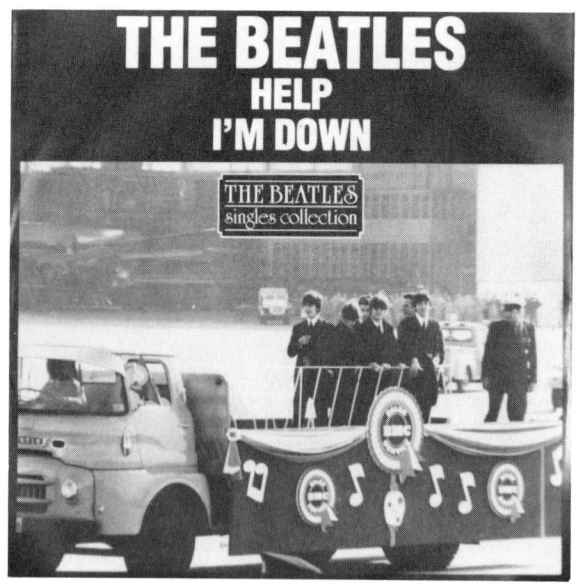

Help! (front)
(Australia)

generally not a problem.

The Japanese pressing, at first blush, seems significantly more "airy" than the Australian edition. This is due to two reasons: slightly better treble extension and small amounts of distortion. This distortion seems omnipresent, although it is actually only noticeable on the vocals. Headphone listening is not recommended, as the closed-in presentation of headphones makes the distortion piercing at times. Since the distortion, at least through speakers, is not a detriment, this edition is slightly favored over the Australian pressing.

The US and English pressings are both much better than the two editions mentioned above. They are very similar in sound - only close scrutiny reveals any differences at all. Both are clean and totally distortion-free. Frequency extension at both ends of the spectrum is improved, although this is the one area that separates the US and English discs. Instruments are well defined, as are the vocals. Vocal definition is apparent on both harmonies and solos. Ringo's cymbals are more "real" than as presented on the Australian or Japanese editions.

The difference between the US and English pressings lies in the fact that the English disc is slightly more extended at both ends of the frequency range. This is almost unnoticeable without headphones; in fact, even with headphones it is very slight.

Ranking:
English
US (a very close second)
Japanese
Australian

NOTE: Two identical U.S. pressings (same master number as reviewed above) area available on the purple Starline and the black-and-rainbow colorband Starline labels from Capitol.

HELP!

1. (Australia) **The Beatles Singles Collection Australian 20th Anniversary 1962-1982** Parlophone A8163 Master Number A8163A.
2. (England) **The Beatles Singles Collection** Parlophone R5305 Master Number 7XCE 18280-4.
3. (Japan) **The Beatles Singles Collection** Odeon EAS-17320 **Stereo** Master Number 7XCE-18280-U_1S.

4. (US) Blue Starline Edition Capitol A-6290 (or X-6290) **Stereo** Master Number A-6290_45-45292_H11.
   Note: All above say mono or are assumed to be mono unless the label indicates stereo, in which case it is listed above.

The Australian edition, as is the case on many other occasions, is in true stereo although not so labelled. Along with the Japanese edition, these two are the stereo pair of the four versions reviewed here.

With *Help!* the differences among these four pressings are not very great. The two mono editions, however, are both slightly superior to the stereo versions. This is actually a case of analyzing tradeoffs, for the gains in imagery afforded by the stereo editions are more than balanced by losses in frequency balance and vocal presentation.

The US edition, by a small margin, is the best of the four reviewed here. The highlight of this pressings is in the vocals. They are up-front and clear, and against the slightly limited frequency range of the recording are very well presented. Both ends of the frequency spectrum are mildly restricted in extension. The treble end is missing the uppermost "air" to the cymbals; however, this is not so apparent as to cause the song to sound dull. Very low bass is absent from this song as well, although enough bass is present, along with an "in-control" midrange, to present a "lean and clean" sound.

The English record is very similar to the American with one exception. The low end is slightly fat and ill-defined, presenting an undercurrent of low frequency garbage. This is not totally overbearing, however, but of enough consequence to make this pressing less desirable than the American.

The Australian pressing, while benefitting from the imagery offered by the true stereo presentation, suffers from a problem with the vocals. The lead vocals are buried in the stereo mix. John's voice is both lower in volume and somewhat "cloudy" in comparison to the mono editions. This pressing suffers from low frequency grunge (as does the English), but is very nicely extended in the high frequencies.

In very uncharacteristic fashion, the Japanese pressing is the worst of the lot, although not by a large margin. It is similar to the Australian edition in that it suffers from recessed vocals. It does not have the ultimate in high frequency extension as does the Australian, and also has one additional flaw that forces it to be ranked last in this group. The midrange is too full - so much so as to be overbearing at times. This is in contrast to the "in-control" midrange of the US disc.

In summation, although the US edition actually does less than the stereo editions, lacking the imagery and frequency extension of the Australian and/or Japanese pressings, it does what it does extremely well!

Ranking:
US
English
Australian
Japanese

I'M DOWN

1. (Australia) **The Beatles Singles Collection Australian 20th Anniversary 1962-1982** Parlophone A8163 Master Number A8163B.
2. (England) **The Beatles Singles Collection** Parlophone R5305 Master Number 7XCE-18281-U_1S.
3. (Japan) **The Beatles Singles Collection** Odeon EAS-17320 **Stereo** Master Number 7XCE-18281-U_1S.
4. (US) Blue Starline Edition Capitol A-6290 (or X-6290) **Stereo** Master Number A-6290_45-45293 _H11.
   Note: All above say mono or are assumed to be mono unless the label indicates stereo, in which case it is listed above.

Although the US Blue Starline Edition is labelled as being in stereo, it is not. Conversely, the Australian version, while not so labelled, is in stereo. The four versions reviewed here will be discussed in pairs, stereo, and mono.

The Japanese version, in true stereo, is a fine-sounding record. Instrumentation is mainly presented in the left channel, with vocals generally centered between the speakers. The right channel, while containing mostly vocals, also has an occasional guitar as well. Frequency balance is good, with both ends of the spectrum well extended. The treble end, although reaching the highest frequencies, is very slightly depressed in level. Vocals are clear and up-front.

The Australian pressing, also in true stereo, is almost indistinguishable from the Japanese. The only differences, and these are slight, occur in the bass and the vocals. The very lowest frequencies are missing, and the low bass that is present is slightly less defined than on the Japanese record. The vocals, although clear, are reduced in level and seem recessed in comparison to the Japanese pressing.

The English pressing, in mono, sounds very different from the true stereo pressings. Frequency balance is tipped toward the high end, giving this disc a "sharp" sound quality. Bass is thinner than on the stereo editions, and treble is more prominent. Although the overall sound is less

I'm Down (Side 1)
(U.S. Blue Starline Edition)

We Can Work It Out (front)
(England)

detailed than in the stereo versions, this is a fairly good-sounding record.

The US Blue Starline edition is the best of the four pressings reviewed here. Its bass presentation is stronger and further extended into the low frequencies than the English pressing. Transient response is outstanding, keeping the "sharp" sound to the song without tilting the frequency balance toward the high end. Although this pressing is not as detailed in its instrumentation, and obviously lacking in soundstage presentation in comparison to the stereo editions, it is quite powerful in presentation.

In summation, the US Blue Starline edition is the favorite pressing of the four reviewed here. Because the true stereo editions of this song are so rare, the Japanese pressing (as the better of the two) is also recommended in order to complete an entire collection.

> Ranking:
> US
> (Both of these are recommended.)
> Japanese
> (Both of these are recommended.)
> English
> (This is only very slightly inferior to its respected recommended pressing.)
> Australian
> (This is only very slightly inferior to its respected recommended pressing.)

WE CAN WORK IT OUT

1. (Australia) **The Beatles Singles Collection Australian 20th Anniversary 1962-1982** Parlophone A8183 Master Number A8183A.
2. (England) **The Beatles Singles Collection** Parlophone R5389 Master Number 7XCE_18341-6.
3. (Japan) **The Beatles Singles Collection** Odeon EAS-17321 **Stereo** Master Number 7XCE-18341-U_1S.
4. (US) Blue Starline Edition Capitol A-6293 (or X-6293) **Stereo** Master Number A-6286_45-45377_J11#2.
   Note: All above say mono or are assumed to be mono unless the label indicates stereo, in which case it is listed above.

The Australian pressing, although not so labelled, is in true stereo, while the US Blue Starline edition, contrary to its label, is in mono. The four discs reviewed here will be discussed in pairs, stereo and mono.

The stereo presentation of the Australian pressing features Paul's lead vocal in the right channel, guitars, drums, and tambourine in the left channel, and organ centered between the speakers. Sonically, this record is good, but it is the least desirable of the pressings reviewed here. Paul's lead vocals are slightly muffled and not presented forward in the mix. The high frequencies are well presented, exemplified by the act that the tambourine is sharp and up-front. The low frequencies, however, are a problem. Bass is present, but it is neither well-extended nor well-defined. It is possible to sense, but not distinguish, the mallet of Ringo's bass drum. The expected transient thump of the bass drum is missing. This pressing does not sound thin, just slightly "wrong" at the low end.

The Japanese pressing shares the same soundstage presentation as the Australian. Paul's vocals are still slightly muffled, and also have a small amount of echo added to them. This echo is mild and not oppressive, but is definitely a detracting addition to the song. Where this pressing really shines is in its extended frequency response at both ends of the spectrum. In the treble region, the tambourine displays a nice metallic edge (as it would in a live performance) and the guitar possesses the proper amount of percussive "bite." In the bass region, Ringo's bass drum is very well presented. The whack of the mallet is readily discernible, giving this edition a firm bass foundation. As good as this pressing is, however, it is not the best of the group.

Top sonic honors for *We Can Work It Out* go to the English pressing. Although in mono, this is an excellent-sounding disc. The top end is very well extended and defined. Bass is good, albeit slightly less prominent than on the Japanese disc, but better than on the Australian. Midrange is full, giving this song body and substance, and making the stereo pressings sound thin in comparison. Where this edition really shines is in its presentation of the vocals. First of all, the echo of the Japanese pressing is gone. Secondly, Paul's voice is clear and forward in the mix - a great improvement in comparison to the slightly muffled and recessed vocals of both the Australian and Japanese discs. This pressing is an example of monophonic sound at its best.

Not much can be said about the US Blue Starline edition. It is very similar in sound to the English pressing, but not quite as good. This is because the overall sound is slightly thin, a quality that is very hard to describe accurately. The music does not sound lightweight or top-heavy, but it does sound as if you can "see" through it. This is not a major problem, though.

In summation, all of these pressings are good; it is only through close scrutiny that differences become apparent.

An Audiophile's Guide to the Sound of the Fab Four

Ranking:
English
Japanese
US
Australian

DAY TRIPPER

1. (Australia) **The Beatles Singles Collection Australian 20th Anniversary 1962-1982** Parlophone A8183 Master Number A8183B.
2. (England) **The Beatles Singles Collection** Parlophone R5389 Master Number 7XCE_18342-1.
3. (Japan) **The Beatles Singles Collection** Odeon EAS-17321 **Stereo** Master Number 7XCE-18342U-_1S_2.
4. (US) Blue Starline Edition Capitol A-6293 (or X-6293) **Stereo** Master Number A-6293_45_45378_P15#2.
    Note: All above say mono or are assumed to be mono unless the label indicates stereo, in which case it is listed above.

As with the flip side, *We Can Work It Out*, the Australian and Japanese pressings of *Day Tripper* are in true stereo, while the English and US pressings are in mono. These four editions, other than in soundstage presentation, sound very similar.

The Australian edition presents the same stereo imagery as the Japanese. One guitar is in each of the channels (especially noticeable in the song's beginning), Ringo's drums are in the left, and the tambourine and the vocals are in the right. Frequency balance is good, with both treble and bass fairly well extended. The only minor flaw in this disc is the fact that the vocals are slightly recessed in the mix and lacking in clarity.

The Japanese pressing has much in common with the Australian. Vocals are still recessed and lacking in clarity. It is in the area of frequency response that makes this record superior. Treble is further extended into the uppermost octave, giving this version a slightly more lively sound. Midrange and bass are also more powerful, balancing the extended treble with a full rich sound.

The English pressing is in one sense better, but in another worse than the Japanese. It shares the excellent frequency response at both ends of the spectrum. It is better in its vocal presentation, having the voices more forward in the mix. It is worse due to small amounts of distortion in the vocal presentation. It is this distortion that mars an otherwise almost perfect disc.

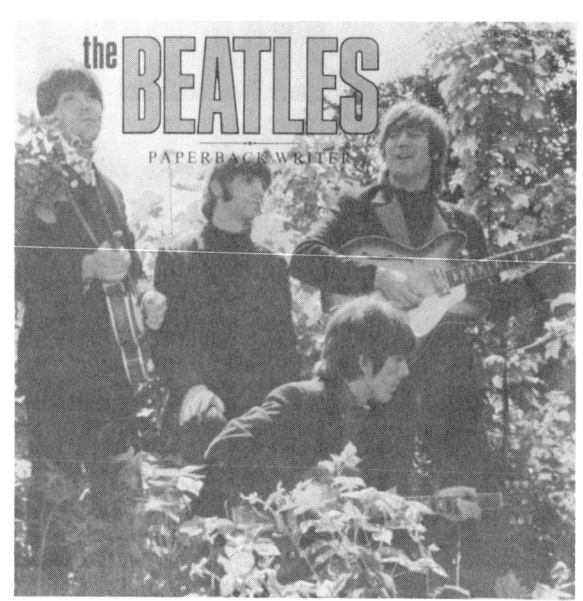

Paperback Writer (front)
(Japan)

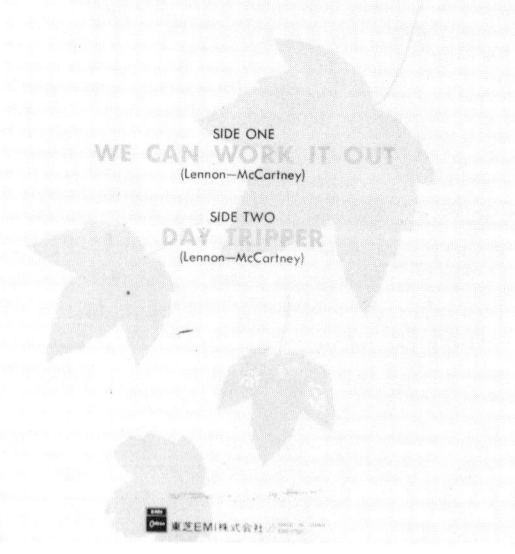

Day Tripper (back)
(Japan)

The US edition, is, by a small margin, the worst of the four reviewed here. It is remarkably similar to the English; its downfall is the presence of distortion on the guitar parts as well as in the vocals.

Ranking:
Japanese
Australian
English
US

It is interesting to note that other than for the distortion problems, the two mono pressings would be the favorites here. This shows that the soundstage improvements offered by stereo pressings do not outweigh the factors of frequency response and vocal clarity.

PAPERBACK WRITER

1. (Australia) **The Beatles Singles Collection Australian 20th Anniversary 1962-1982** Parlophone A8203 Master Number A8203A.
2. (England) **The Beatles Singles Collection** Parlophone R5452 Master Number 7XCE_18380-4.
3. (Japan) **The Beatles Singles Collection** Odeon EAS-17322 **Stereo** Master Number 7XCE-18380-U_1S_3.
4. (US) Blue Starline Edition Capitol A-6292 (or X-6296) **Stereo** Master Number A-6296_45-X45493_J-1.
   Note: All above say mono or are assumed to be mono unless the label indicates stereo, in which case it is listed above.

Of the four discs reviewed here, two are mis-labelled. The Australian pressing is in true stereo, while the US Blue Starline edition is in mono.

The Australian pressing, in true stereo, has the lead vocals to the right of center, backing vocals totally in the right channel, most of the music in the left channel, and Paul's bass to the right of center. This stereo imagery, although presenting something of a "hole in the middle," is at least realistic in the sense that Paul's lead vocals and bass guitar share the same position (to the right of center). This is in contrast to the unacceptable imaging of *I Should Have Known Better*, in which John plays instruments in both the far right and far left positions.

This is a fairly good-sounding record, although it does not sound as fine as the others. High-frequency information is very slightly reduced in level, making the treble sound a trifle less "sharp" than it should. Paul's bass guitar is lacking in definition, sounding bloated and indistinct at times. Solo vocals are forward and clear, but background vocals are too up-front. The "Frere Jacques" chorus is at times too loud and obtrusive.

The Japanese disc presents the same stereo image as the Australian. It is better, however, in its rendition of information at both extremes of the frequency spectrum. Treble is more extended, adding "bite" and definition to the guitar and drums. Bass is fuller and slightly more defined, adding weight and body to the song. Background vocals are also reduced in level, keeping them more in the background where they should be. This is a fine-sounding disc, although something about it doesn't sound quite right. What is wrong is not apparent until a comparison is made with the mono pressings.

The US pressing, in mono, is the best of the four reviewed here. It is significantly more forceful in its presentation than the stereo editions, making this a "power" song that grabs the listener and commands attention. Frequency response is wide and instruments are well defined. Lead vocals are forward and clear. The music is louder in comparison to the words than in the stereo discs, adding to the weight and body of the song. This disc just sounds right.

The English pressing is similar to the US, but has a small problem in the bass. At times the low frequencies seem to drop out, making this disc seem lightweight in spots and uneven overall. This is not a major problem, but in comparison to the excellent US pressing, this just doesn't measure up.

>Ranking:
>US
>>(Neither of these discs can be faulted sonically; it is only the stylistic difference that earns the US disc the higher rating. Because tastes do differ, both pressings are recommended.)
>
>Japanese
>>(Neither of these discs can be faulted sonically; it is only the stylistic difference that earns the US disc the higher rating. Because tastes do differ, both pressings are recommended.)
>
>English
>Australian

NOTE: Two identical U.S. pressings (same master number as reviewed above) area available on the purple Starline and the black-and-rainbow colorband Starline labels from Capitol.

An Audiophile's Guide to the Sound of the Fab Four

RAIN

1. (Australia) **The Beatles Singles Collection Australian 20th Anniversary 1962-1982** Parlophone A8203 Master Number A8203B.
2. (England) **The Beatles Singles Collection** Parlophone R5452 Master Number 7XCE-18381-4.
3. (Japan) **The Beatles Singles Collection** Odeon EAS-17322 **Stereo** Master Number 7XCE-18381-U_1S_1.
4. (US) Blue Starline Edition Capitol A-6296 (or X-6296) **Stereo** Master Number A-6296_45-X45449-J1.

Note: All above say mono or are assumed to be mono unless the label indicates stereo, in which case it is listed above.

As with the flip side, *Paperback Writer*, the Australian and Japanese pressings are in true stereo, while the English and US versions are in mono. The true stereo presentations feature John's lead vocal on the left, background vocals on the right, most of the instruments on the left, Paul's bass guitar to the right of center, and tambourine on the right.

The Australian pressing is, by a small margin, the least desirable of the stereo editions. It is plagued by an extremely fat and overblown bass. Paul's bass guitar is totally lacking in definition, sending waves of low frequency energy at the listener. Individual bass notes are almost indistinguishable beneath the smothering blanket of low frequencies. Treble extension is slightly curtailed, making the top octave sound dull and "slow." The lead vocal is also somewhat far back in the mix. When taken in total, these problems make this disc unlistenable at anything above whisper-quiet levels.

The Japanese pressing is slightly better than the Australian. Treble is further extended, making the tambourine in the right channel sound more "alive" and realistic. This increase in high frequency content removes the "slow" feeling imparted by the Australian pressing. Vocals are slightly further forward in the mix, making John's voice float above the music. The bass on this disc is still a problem, however. Low frequency content, although not as strong as on the Australian pressing, is still overbearing. This record can be enjoyed at levels above a whisper, but at anything approaching realistic levels the listener will be bowled over by the low-frequency energy.

The English pressing, in mono, shares the bass problems of the Australian record. John's lead vocal is further forward in the mix, but it is also slightly distorted in places. This distortion causes this pressing to be ranked last among the four reviewed here.

The US Blue Starline edition has both positive and negative points. On the negative side, treble extension is not as good as the Japanese pressing, and John's vocals are not as far forward in the mix as they are on the

Yellow Submarine (front)
(England)

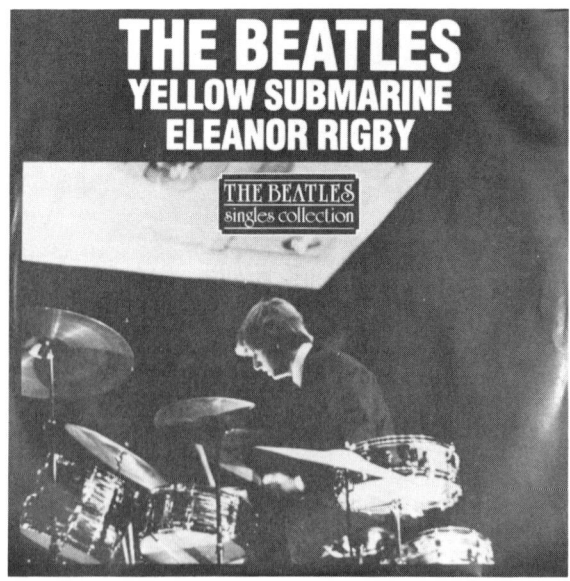

Yellow Submarine (front)
(Australia)

English edition. On the positive side, this is the only edition of *Rain* that is not plagued by bass problems. This is a pleasure in comparison to the other three pressings. Only the US record can be enjoyed at realistic volume levels without the listener being buried in bass. Although this pressing is far from perfect, it is the best of the bunch.

Ranking:
US
Japanese
Australian
English

NOTE: Two identical U.S. pressings (same master number as reviewed above) area available on the purple Starline and the black-and-rainbow colorband Starline labels from Capitol.

YELLOW SUBMARINE

1. (Australia) **The Beatles Singles Collection Australian 20th Anniversary 1962-1982** Parlophone A8213 Master Number 7XCE18396 _7XAPA1172.
2. (England) **The Beatles Singles Collection** Parlophone R5493 Master Number 7XCE_18396-3.
3. (Japan) **The Beatles Singles Collection** Odeon EAS-17323 **Stereo** Master Number 7XCE-18396-U_1S_1.
4. (US) Blue Starline Edition Capitol A-6297 (or X-6297) **Stereo** Master Number A-6297_45619_H7#4.
   Note: All above say mono or are assumed to be mono unless the label indicates stereo, in which case it is listed above.

Although the US Blue Starline edition is labelled as being in stereo, it is not. These four records comprise two different versions of the song, and believe it or not, it is not the stereo presentation of the Japanese pressing that differentiates the two versions. The background vocal track is different in the two versions, and this leads to the conclusion that two entirely different performances have been issued as singles.

To differentiate the versions, pay close attention to the middle of the song where Ringo's lead vocals are repeated in the background by John. Version 1, present on the Australian and US pressings, is detectable by the fact that John's background repetition vocals start on the line "as we live a life of ease," where he echoes "a life of ease." Version 2, present on the

English and Japanese editions, starts the background repetition vocals *one line later*, on the line "everyone of us has all we need," where John echoes "all we need." Sonically, the Australian pressing, although fair, is the worst of the bunch. High-frequency presentation is restricted in extension, making this edition sound somewhat "dark" in color. Low-frequency response is boosted, making Ringo's bass drum sound too loud in relation to the other instruments. This bass boost also tends to make the lead vocals sound "thick" in places. When more than one voice is present simultaneously, distortion is also evident. This stops at the conclusion of one chorus and resumes at the start of the next one.

The English edition is similar in overall sound to the Australian, but slightly better. The improvement lies in the high frequencies, which show better extension in the top octave. Some of the characteristic darkness of the Australian pressing has been removed here, although the treble is still not as strong as it should be. Low frequencies are still too prominent on this record, leading to the same "thick" sound on vocals. Chorus distortion is also still in evidence here. In all, this is an improvement over the Australian edition, but not a great one.

The Japanese pressing, in true stereo, has the vocals exclusively in the right channel. The majority of the instrumentation is in the left channel, but some leakage makes the music audible behind the voice in "right only" listening. This edition is much better than the two mentioned above; the improvement lies in the presentation of the vocals. Lead vocals are forward in the mix and without the "thickness" that characterizes the other two pressings. Choral vocals are slightly veiled, but free of distortion. A definite improvement!

Treble is again very slightly depressed in extension, and Ringo's bass drum is still too prominent, but the improvement in vocal presentation makes these problems seem minor. The "darkness" has been removed from this pressing, making this record quite enjoyable. In fact, personal preferences being what they are, this may be some listeners' favorite of the four reviewed here. Those who relish the "thump" of the bass drum will love this issue.

The US Blue Starline edition is, for all intents and purposes, flawless. Treble is further extended than all the other pressings, providing just the correct amount of "air" at the top of the frequency range. Bass response has been reduced to manageable levels, removing the over-prominent "thump" of Ringo's bass drum. This song sounds clean and "open" from top to bottom, free of any problems with distortion. In comparison to the others it sounds "lightweight" at the bottom, which will probably lead some listeners to prefer the Japanese edition. It is, mind you, a well-balanced disc, and a joy to hear!

An Audiophile's Guide to the Sound of the Fab Four

Ranking:
US
(Because these two pressings contain different versions of this song, both are recommended for those who desire a complete collection.)
Japanese
(Because these two pressings contain different versions of this song, both are recommended for those who desire a complete collection.)
English
Australian

ELEANOR RIGBY

1. (Australia) **The Beatles Singles Collection Australian 20th Anniversary 1962-1982** Parlophone A8213 Master Number 7XCE18395 7XAPA1173.
2. (England) **The Beatles Singles Collection** Parlophone R5493 Master Number 7XCE_18395-3.
3. (Japan) **The Beatles Singles Collection** Odeon EAS-17323 **Stereo** Master Number 7XCE-18395-U_1S_3.
4. (US) Blue Starline Edition Capitol A-6297 (or X-6297) **Stereo** Master Number A-6297_45-45616_H1.

Note: All above say mono or are assumed to be mono unless the label indicates stereo, in which case it is listed above.

Of the four records reviewed here, only the US Blue Starline edition is incorrectly labelled, being in mono rather than stereo. The Japanese pressing, in stereo, is substantially different than the mono editions, and will be discussed first.

The soundstage presentation of the Japanese edition is very strange, to say the least. At the outset, and throughout most of the song, this disc is the familiar "words on right, music on left" style that characterizes many early Beatles records. However, when the chorus is sung ("Aah, look at all the lonely people....") Paul's voice appears in both channels, with the left channel singing being slightly different than the right. The harmony vocals also appear on the left channel, giving this song a "ping-pong" quality that is rather unnerving. While the instruments remain planted firmly in their positions, the vocals bounce back and forth in willy-nilly style.

Stereo effects aside, this pressing is sonically first-rate. Vocals are forward and distinct from the instrumentation. High frequencies are ex-

Eleanor Rigby (back)
(Japan)

tended, providing an "airy" quality to the strings. When the cellos play in their lower registers the sound is full-bodied without being overly heavy.

Of the mono pressings, the English is the worst of the three. Vocals are strained and distorted at times. High frequencies are reduced in level, making the strings sound "dark" and lifeless. The midrange sounds thick and overblown in spots, especially during the chorus. This pressing is listenable, but only at reduced volume level, when the sonic problems are not overbearing.

The Australian pressing, also in mono, is not very different from the English. High frequencies are slightly more extended, giving the "air" and life back to the strings. Vocals, however, are still strained and distorted, and the midrange remains thick and overblown. While this record is slightly better than the English pressing, it still does not fare well at anything approaching realistic listening levels.

The US Blue Starline edition is the best of the mono pressings. It suffers from absolutely no problems whatsoever! High frequencies are extended into the uppermost octave, and strings are full-bodied in their lower registers. Vocals are sweet-sounding and float forward of the instrumentation without a trace of strain or distortion.

In summation, the Japanese and US Blue Starline pressings are the cream of this crop. For those who desire a complete singles collection, both are recommended. Otherwise, it is a personal choice as to whether the "ping-pong" vocals of the Japanese edition detract from its overall quality.

> Ranking:
> US
> (Sonically these are both outstanding and differ only in soundstage presentation.)
> Japanese
> (Sonically these are both outstanding and differ only in soundstage presentation.)
> Australian
> English

NOTE: Two identical U.S. pressings (same master number as reviewed above) area available on the purple Starline and the black-and-rainbow colorband Starline labels from Capitol.

STRAWBERRY FIELDS FOREVER

1. (Australia) **The Beatles Singles Collection Australian 20th Anniversary 1962-1982** Parlophone A8243 Master Number 7XAPA1274-2.
2. (England) **The Beatles Singles Collection** Parlophone R5570 Master Number 7XCE_18415-4.
3. (Japan) **The Beatles Singles Collection** Odeon EAS-17324 **Stereo** Master Number 7XCE-18415-U_1S_1.
4. (US) Blue Starline Edition Capitol A-6299 (or X-6299) **Stereo** Master Number A-6299_45870_H10#3.
    Note: All above say mono or are assumed to be mono unless the label indicates stereo, in which case it is listed above.

The US Blue Starline edition, although labelled stereo, is actually in mono. Sonic quality of these records ranges from fair to excellent, and they will be discussed in that order below.

The Australian pressing, while being fair-sounding, is the worst of the four reviewed here. It suffers from three problems, only one of which, however, is of major consequence. In terms of frequency response, both ends of the spectrum are imperfect. The uppermost treble is very slightly reduced in level, robbing Ringo's cymbals of their ultimate "air" and "sheen." The lowest frequencies suffer from a similar problem, also being reduced in level. This only occurs after the first minute or so of the song, leaving the final three minutes sounding thin and lightweight.

The major problem, however, is one of distortion. The upper registers on John's vocals, as well as guitars and horns, are distorted at various times throughout the song. This lends a harshness to the overall impression presented by the song. This prevents realistic listening levels from being enjoyed with this pressing.

The English pressing solves two of the three problems encountered on the Australian. Frequency response at the low end of the spectrum is improved, with the bass guitar and bass drum providing the proper sonic foundation to the music. Distortion is absent, removing the harshness from the song. The only deviation from excellence is evident on Ringo's cymbals, which still lack the realistic "air" that would be present in a live performance.

The US Blue Starline edition is the best of the mono pressings. High-frequency response is airy and extended, and well balanced by the firm low end. The upper midrange and John's vocals are forward and prominent without being overbearing. This disc sounds very "alive" - it reaches out and demands the attention of the listener. It can certainly be enjoyed at realistic listening levels.

Strawberry Fields Forever (front)
(England)

Penny Lane (back)
(England)

As good as the US pressing is, it pales in comparison to the Japanese edition. The Japanese pressing is, in a word, perfect! The stereo presentation is sensible and rock solid. Drums are to the left, John's vocal is right of center, and strings and most guitar work are to the right. Instrumental definition is razor-sharp, bringing the maracas in the left channel to a noticeable place in the mix (the mono editions leave them almost inaudible). Transient response is quick and provides plenty of "bite" to the guitars; this is especially evident on the nine-note, sliding-right-to-left guitar riff occurring between the words "Strawberry Fields forever" and "No one I think is in my tree...."

While presenting a very extended, well-defined, transiently quick frequency range, this song still sounds silky smooth and unstrained at all times. The listener is whisked away into the world of John Lennon's childhood.

>Ranking:
>Japanese
>US
>>(Although not as superb as the Japanese, this is excellent nonetheless. It is recommended for those who desire a complete collection or would rather have this song in mono as it was originally released.
>English
>Australian

PENNY LANE

1. (Australia) **The Beatles Singles Collection Australian 20th Anniversary 1962-1982** Parlophone A8243 Master Number 7XAPA1275-2.
2. (England) **The Beatles Singles Collection** Parlophone R5570 Master Number 7XCE_18416-4.
3. (Japan) **The Beatles Singles Collection** Odeon EAS-17324 **Stereo** Master Number 7XCE-18416-U_1S_3.
4. (US) Blue Starline Edition Capitol A-6299 (or X-6299) **Stereo** Master Number (A-6299)_45-45871_J-11.

   Note: All above say mono or are assumed to be mono unless the label says stereo, in which case it is listed above.

As with the flip side, *Strawberry Fields Forever*, only the Japanese edition of *Penny Lane* is in stereo. Of the three mono pressings reviewed here, the Australian is by far the worst of the group.

The Australian edition has very little to offer the listener in the way of quality sound. Vocals are distorted intermittently throughout the song. The low bass is missing, making this pressing sound thin and lightweight. The uppermost treble is slightly depressed, robbing the song of "air" and making it sound duller than life. Transient response is too slow, making the horns lack their characteristic "bite." In total these problems destroy the listenability of the song.

The English pressing is very similar to the Australian. It shares all of the above-mentioned problems but one. The vocal distortion, previously a major detriment, is absent. The remaining problems do not totally ruin the song; in fact, this can best be characterized as lightweight and slightly dull. It is perfectly listenable at any volume level - the slight dullness helps makes this tolerable even at extremely loud levels. All is not well, however, and this edition does not sound quite right due to the remaining problems.

The US Blue Starline edition is the best of the mono versions of this song. It still suffers from the transient response and high-end problems mentioned above, but its low end is full and firm. This pressing does not sound lightweight and is actually quite good. The remaining problems are rather inconspicuous during normal listening; close scrutiny and headphones will reveal the imperfections, however minor they are.

The Japanese pressing, in stereo, is outstanding! Bass is full and firm, treble is very well extended. Transients have snap, the horns have their realistic "bite." The stereo presentation is stable and logical; vocals and bass guitar are centered between the speakers, trumpets are in both channels, the fire bell is in the left channel, and the piccolo trumpet is on the right (until the end of the song when it moves to the left).

This song is full, sweet, airy, and alive. It is a significant improvement over the mono editions.

>   Rankings:
>   Japanese
>   US
>   English
>   Australian

NOTE: Two identical U.S. pressings (same master numbers as reviewed above) are available on the purple Starline and black-and-rainbow colorband Starline labels from Capitol.

All You Need Is Love (front)
(Australia)

All You Need Is Love (front)
(England)

ALL YOU NEED IS LOVE

1. (Australia) **The Beatles Singles Collection Australian 20th Anniversary 1962-1982** Parlophone A8263 Master Number 7XCE18425_7XAPA _1359-2.
2. (England) **The Beatles Singles Collection** Parlophone R5620 Master Number 7XCE_18425-3.
3. (Japan) **The Beatles Singles Collection** Odeon EAS-17325 **Stereo** Master Number 7XCE-18425-U_1S_1.
4. (US) Blue Starline Edition Capitol A-6300 (or X-6300) **Stereo** Master Number A-6300_46048_H10#3.
   Note: All above say mono or are assumed to be mono unless the label states stereo, in which case it is listed above.

The Japanese pressing is the only one of the four reviewed here that is in stereo. As with all of the US Blue Starline Capitol editions, this one is incorrectly labelled.

The Australian pressing, in mono, is not up to the fine standards of the other three. It suffers from a lack of weight in the lowest frequencies, causing a reduction of impact of Paul's bass guitar and Ringo's bass drum. Instruments are not individually defined, leaving this edition sounding somewhat "dense." Its most distracting problem, however, lies in the area of vocals. John's lead vocal is distorted in various places, adding a harshness to the sound that is very unpleasant.

The English pressing, also in mono, is slightly better than the Australian. Bass is fuller, allowing Paul and Ringo to be heard with greater impact among the still dense-sounding instrumentation. The real improvement lies in the fact that the vocal distortion is gone, although some strain remains. While not sounding harsh, John's presentation just doesn't sound right. The strain is more readily apparent as the listener increases playback volume levels, but doesn't become intrusive into the enjoyment of the song until rather loud levels are reached.

The US Blue Starline edition is the best of the mono pressings. Vocals are strain-free and a pleasure to enjoy. High-frequency information is extended into the uppermost octave, providing detail to the string instruments not present in the other mono discs. The only deviation from perfection is the denseness of the overall instrumental presentation, creating a "wall of sound" effect rather than an illusion of individual instruments playing in your listening room. This is a fine-sounding record, topped only by the exquisite stereo sound of the Japanese pressing.

In terms of frequency response, the Japanese edition is outstanding. Bass if full and very well defined, allowing individual notes from Paul's bass to stand out below the other instruments. The high end is delicately extended into the highest registers, providing the "bite" and "air" required by the horns. The soundstage presentation features John's lead vocal and Paul's bass guitar centered between the speakers, horns evenly divided between the speakers (some are left, some are right, rather than all being centered in between), and strings mostly on the right. This firmly placed image provides physical space among the instruments - a stark contrast to the dense "wall of sound" presentation of the three mono discs.

As a combination, wide frequency response and stable stereo image make this a great record.

>		Ranking:
>			Japanese
>			US
>			English
>			Australian

BABY, YOU'RE A RICH MAN

1. (Australia) **The Beatles Singles Collection Australian 20th Anniversary 1962-1982** Parlophone A8263 Master Number 7XCE18426 _7XAPA1360-2.
2. (England) **The Beatles Singles Collection** Parlophone R5620 Master Number 7XCE_184263.
3. (Japan) **The Beatles Singles Collection** Odeon EAS-17325 **Stereo** Master Number 7XCE-18426-U_1S_1.
4. (US) Blue Starline Edition Capitol A-6300 (or X-6300) **Stereo** Master Number A-6300_46047_H10#3.

>	Note: All above say mono or are assumed to be mono unless the label states stereo, in which case it is listed above.

Although the Japanese record is the only one of the four reviewed here that is in stereo, it is actually reprocessed, rather than true stereo.

Of the three mono pressings, the Australian is ranked last. It is, however, a good-sounding record, having only two small problem areas. The upper regions of the frequency range are reduced in level, leaving the maracas sounding dull and lifeless. Choral vocals are slightly distorted, creating harsh spots during the singing of "Baby you're a rich man too...." The vocal distortion, because it only occurs in a few places, does not greatly detract from the listener's enjoyment. On the positive side, this pressing

Baby, You're A Rich Man (back)
(Japan)

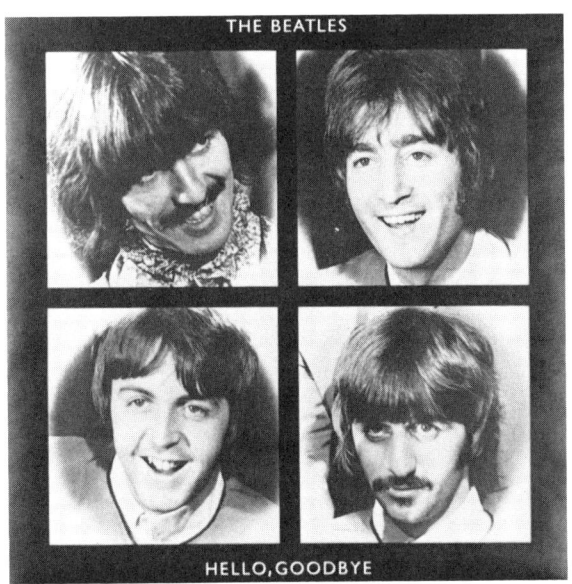

Hello Goodbye (front)
(England)

possesses a great low end, allowing Paul's bass guitar to go down to the lowest regions with force and power. As long as the volume level is kept reasonable this is a thoroughly enjoyable pressing.

The US Blue Starline edition is very similar to the Australian. It differs only at both ends of the frequency spectrum, being better at one and worse at the other. In the low frequencies, this pressing is not as full or powerful. It is not overly lightweight, just slightly thin-sounding. At the high end, this record is further extended, providing the "air" to make the maracas sound real. Because the high end plays a more prominent part than the low end in *Baby, You're a Rich Man*, this is preferred over the Australian edition.

The English pressing is the best of the mono editions. It is similar to the US pressing at both ends of the frequency range. Its strength lies in its vocal presentation, which is forward and free of distortion. The lack of distortion allows this song to be enjoyed at realistic listening levels. The forward presentation of the voice "loosens-up" the overall presentation of the song, which at times sounds dense in both the Australian and English pressings. In all, this is an excellent record!

The Japanese pressing, in reprocessed stereo, is a mixed bag. Its frequency range is very good, being almost identical to that of the English edition. The stereo reprocessing, however, is somewhat troublesome. The left channel has boosted bass and reduced treble and the right channel has reduced bass and boosted treble. This presents an image that is unstable and unsatisfying. Instruments seem to drift from side to side as they play, based upon whether they are producing bass or treble range music. It is this image drift that makes this pressing a close runner-up to the English for overall honors on this song.

    Ranking:
        English
        Japanese
        US
        Australian

NOTE: An identical U.S. pressings (same master number as reviewed above) is available on the purple Capitol label.

An Audiophile's Guide to the Sound of the Fab Four

HELLO GOODBYE

1. (Australia) **The Beatles Singles Collection Australian 20th Anniversary 1962-1982** Parlophone A8273 Master Number 45-7XCE18433 _7XAPA1427.
2. (England) **The Beatles Singles Collection** Parlophone R5655 Master Number 7XCE_18433-1.
3. (Japan) **The Beatles Singles Collection** Odeon EAS-17326 **Stereo** Master Number 7XCE-18433-U_2S.
4. (US) Purple Capitol 2056 Master Number S45-46160-G21.
   Note: All above say mono or are assumed to be mono unless the label states stereo, in which case it is listed above.

Of the four editions of *Hello Goodbye*, the Japanese pressing is the only one in stereo. It is also the best sounding record of the bunch.

In frequency response, the Japanese pressing is well balanced and extended at both ends of the spectrum. Cymbals have their realistic "air" and "shimmer," and electric guitars possess transient "bite." Bass is well defined, allowing individual notes from Paul's bass to be recognized under the other instrumentation.

The stereo presentation is both wide and stable. Ringo's drums, along with the maracas, appear on the left. Paul's bass is on the right, as well as guitars and background strings. Lead vocals appear centered between the speakers, with background voices being on the right.

The only deviation from absolute perfection occurs in the lead vocals. Paul's voice is unclear and too far back in the mix. It sounds as if a heavy curtain is rounding out and slightly muffling the normal vocal transients present in a live performance. This is not a major problem, only mildly annoying.

Of the mono pressings, the US edition is the best. In frequency response it possesses the balance and extension of the Japanese pressing. It is not as precisely detailed in its instrumentation, however, and this is due to the fact that it is not in stereo. The point source presentation (by definition of mono) makes this song sound slightly bunched-up. This is only a detriment to the US pressing in direct comparison to the Japanese; this is an excellent-sounding mono record.

The English pressing, while not being quite as good as the American, is also very fine. It differs from the American in bass response only, where it is neither as defined nor as well extended. Individual notes from Paul's bass lack transient attack and weight; they are "rounder" at the edges and "thinner" in body than they should be. The overall impression is not

Hello Goodbye (Side 1)
(U.S. Purple Capitol Edition)

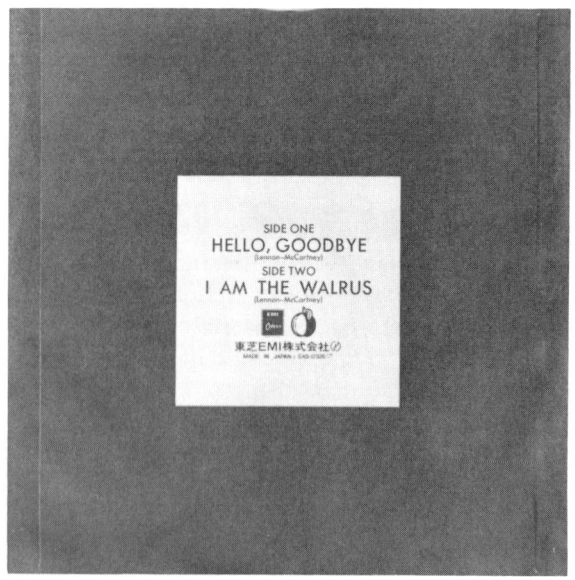

I Am The Walrus (back)
(Japan)

that the song is lightweight, just slightly tipped toward the upper frequencies.
   The Australian pressing is the least desirable of the four reviewed here. As well as sharing the veiled and recessed vocals with all the other pressings, it has problems at both ends of the frequency spectrum. The bass response is even less defined and extended than the English pressing, leaving this edition sounding very lightweight. The highest frequencies are not as extended as they should be, robbing the cymbals of their lifelike metallic "shimmer." Of the four pressings of *Hello Goodbye*, only this record is so significantly troubled as to be difficult to enjoy.

   Ranking:
   Japan
   US
   England
   Australia

I AM THE WALRUS

1. (Australia) **The Beatles Singles Collection Australian 20th Anniversary 1962-1982** Parlophone A8273 Master Number 45-7XCE18434 _7XAPA1428.
2. (England) **The Beatles Singles Collection** Parlophone R5655 Master Number 7XCE_18434-1.
3. (Japan) **The Beatles Singles Collection** Odeon EAS-17326 **Stereo** Master Number 7XCE-18434-U_1S.
4. (US) Purple Capitol 2056 Master Number S45-46161-G21.
   Note: All above say mono or are assumed to be mono unless the label says stereo, in which case it is listed above.

   Each of the four editions of *I Am The Walrus* is quite enjoyable; it is only the excellence of the Japanese pressing that makes the mono records pale in comparison.
   The English pressing is the best of the monos. Its frequency response is very extended - from the subterranean lows at one end to the sweet airy highs at the other. It is a very clean-sounding record, other than some minor distortion on John's lead vocal. This vocal is also not very far forward in the mix, making it blend with the instrumentation at times. The only problem with this record, and it plagues all the mono editions, is the overall denseness of sound. There is an awful lot going on in this song, and the

bunched-up-in-the-center presentation (by definition of mono) makes it difficult for the listener to focus attention on individual instruments.

The Australian pressing is very similar to the English. Its differences lie at both ends of the frequency range, where definition is not quite precise. Low frequency information is present, but not easily recognizable as individual notes. Transient response, when drumstick meets cymbal or tambourine shakes, is slightly rounded or softened. In total, the problems at both ends of the spectrum barely detract from this edition, and only in comparison to the English are they noticeable.

The American edition is the worst of the monos, although it is still very listenable. At the bass end there is a distinct lack of extension, leaving this pressing sounding lightweight in comparison to the others. Instead of creating an overly thin sound, this bass problem serves to lessen the denseness of the overall presentation. While some listeners may prefer this edition, it must be rated last due to the lack of bass information.

The Japanese disc is, in a word, great! John's lead vocal is very far forward and crystal clear. It is so clear, in fact, that in the line "...pretty little policemen...." it is possible to hear him popping his p's. Instrumentation is very well defined throughout the entire frequency range, treble is airy and extended, and bass is deep and powerful.

The stereo presentation is very stable and precise in placement of instruments. The left channel contains the tambourine and part of Ringo's drum set, the remainder of which is spread to the center area between the speakers. The strings and horns appear in the right channel, and John's lead vocals stand forward of the music between the speakers. At the line "Sitting in an English garden...." John's voice moves back into the mix and over to the right channel, where it remains through the conclusion of the song.

In comparison to the mono editions, the Japanese pressing is significantly more detailed and less dense. The stereo imaging allows more information to reach the listener by providing air and space among the instruments. Its frequency response is well balanced and very wide.

All in all, a perfect record!

Ranking:
    Japan
    England
    Australia
    US

An Audiophile's Guide to the Sound of the Fab Four

LADY MADONNA

1. (Australia) **The Beatles Singles Collection Australian 20th Anniversary 1962-1982** Parlophone A8293 Master Number 7XCE18438 _7XAPA1471.
2. (England) **The Beatles Singles Collection** Parlophone R5675 Master Number 7XCE_18438-5.
3. (Japan) **The Beatles Singles Collection** Odeon EAS-17327 **Stereo** Master Number 7XCE-18438-U_1S.
4. (US) Rainbow Colorband Edition Capitol 2138 Master Number 45-46256-J14.
   Note: All above say mono or are assumed to be mono unless the label says stereo, in which case it is listed above.

Of the four versions of *Lady Madonna* reviewed here, only the Japanese pressing is in stereo. It is also, by the way, the best of the bunch. The records will be discussed below in order from worst to best.

The Australian pressing, although ranked last, is a good-sounding record. The presentation is clean and totally free of distortion. The low end is slightly weak and ill-defined, however. Individual notes on Paul's bass guitar and Ringo's bass drum are buried in the mix and difficult to distinguish. The presentation can best be described as "dense."

At the other end of the frequency spectrum, the highest octave is not as extended and strong as it should be. Ringo's cymbals are missing their characteristic "shimmer" and the horns lack their realistic "bite." This leaves the overall presentation sounding a trifle bit dark and duller than life.

The English pressing is very similar to the Australian. Its high end is identical in the fact that it is not extended or as strong as it should be. Instrumentation is also dense-sounding. The difference occurs in the low frequencies, which are fuller and further extended. This provides a firm foundation to the song, albeit an ill-defined one.

The US record is the best of the three mono recordings. Its low end presentation falls in between those of the other two, being stronger than the Australian but slightly weaker than the English. Its claim to distinction, however, is in the upper registers, which are strong and fully extended. Cymbals "shimmer" as expected, and the horns possess their characteristic "bite."

The high end presentation of this pressing helps to remove some of the denseness of instrumentation that plagues both the Australian and English editions. This is a fine-sounding record - definitely first-rate.

The Japanese pressing is even better than the American. It combines the excellent high-frequency presentation with a firm low end (similar

Lady Madonna (front)
(Japan)

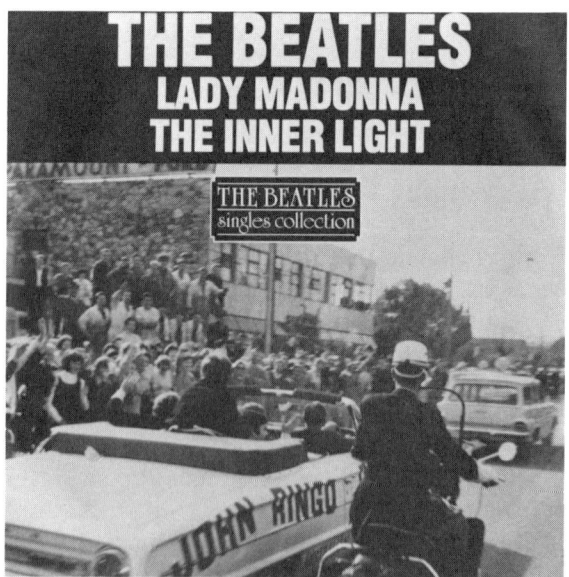

Lady Madonna (front)
(Australia)

to the English) and a fine stereo presentation.

Paul's piano appears, with most of the drums, to the left; horns and vocals are centered; and Ringo's bass drum and cymbals and George's, John's, and Paul's guitars are on the right. This presentation provides "space" around the instruments, so that this pressing sounds just as if the Beatles were playing in your listening room. Close scrutiny, however, does reveal the fact that the four Beatles could not perform this live as it is presented on this disc. Paul plays two instruments, piano and bass guitar, which are presented in different channels. To recreate this live, the piano would have to be to the left of the stage and the bass guitar speaker to the right of the stage. Even if Paul could play the bass and piano at once, no sound man worth his salt would every create a stage sound system like that.

Even with his "incorrect" stereo presentation, this is a great-sounding record!

Ranking:
Japanese
US
English
Australian

THE INNER LIGHT

1. (Australia) **The Beatles Singles Collection Australian 20th Anniversary 1962-1982** Parlophone A8293 Master Number 7XCE18439 _7XAPA1273.
2. (England) **The Beatles Singles Collection** Parlophone R5675 Master Number 7XCE_ 18439-3.
3. (Japan) **The Beatles Singles Collection** Odeon EAS-17327 **Stereo** Master Number 7XCE-18439-U_1S.
4. (US) Rainbow Colorband Edition Capitol 2138 Master Number 45-X46257-F10.

Note: All above say mono or are assumed to be mono unless the label says stereo, in which case it is listed above.

In contrast to the flip side, *Lady Madonna*, all four versions of *The Inner Light* are in mono. This is, in fact, one of the few currently available Beatles singles having that distinction.

All four editions of this song sound very good, with only minor differences among them. The Australian pressing, by a small margin, is the worst of those reviewed here. Its strength is in the high frequencies - the sitar is transiently sharp and clear. Its problems, however, are found in the vocals and the bass. George's lead vocals are slightly recessed in relation to the sitar and rather "echoey." It is as if too much artifical reverb had been added, making the vocals "fatter" and "mushier" than real life. The bass problems are evident on the drum (probably a tabla) being played in the background. The transient impact of the hand on the drum is totally absent, leaving the drum sounding very indistinct and lacking in definition.

In comparison to the Australian edition, the US pressing is slightly better in its presentation of both the vocals and the drums. Although still slightly "echoey," George's voice is further forward in the mix and slightly clearer. The transient impact of the drum is slightly better, although still not as it should be.

The English and Japanese pressings, at least with a good tracking cartridge and turntable, are indistinguishable. Both also solve the problems inherent in the two previously reviewed pressings. George's voice is not bathed in echo and is forward in the mix. The drum, although still in the background, has the required transient snap to make it sound as if it was actually a hand slapping a drum. These two factors make these pressings sound leaner and cleaner than either the Australian or American disc.

A note of caution is in order. The English pressing is cut at a significantly higher (louder) level than the Japanese disc. Any audio system with tracking problems may have difficulty cleanly reproducing this disc, leading to distortion and strain in the high frequencies.

Rankings:
    Japan
        (These are both recommended, keeping in mind the potential problems with the English disc.)
    England
        (These are both recommended, keeping in mind the potential problems with the English disc.)
    US
    Australia

HEY JUDE

1. (Australia) **The Beatles Singles Collection Australian 20th Anniversary 1962-1982** Parlophone A8493 Master Number 7XCE_21185-1.
2. (England) **The Beatles Singles Collection** Parlophone R5722 Master Number 7XCE_21185-2.
3. (Japan) **The Beatles Singles Collection** Odeon EAS-17328 **Stereo** Master Number 7XCE-21185-U_1S_2.
4. (US) Rainbow Colorband Edition Capitol 2276 Master Number S45-46434-G11.

Note: All above say mono or are assumed to be mono unless the label says stereo, in which case it is listed above.

Of all the Beatles' great singles, *Hey Jude* is the best-selling. It is only fitting, then, that it also would be great-sounding. These four pressings do not disappoint in that regard. As with *Revolution*, the flip side, only the Japanese edition is in stereo.

The Australian pressing is the least desirable of those reviewed here, but it is only in direct comparison with the others that its faults become more than just barely noticeable. At first blush this record sounds just about perfect. Paul's piano, especially while it is the only instrument playing, sounds slightly lightweight in its presentation, and the "woodiness" or fullness of the lower strings is missing. This thinness is not so prevalent as to make the piano sound "tinny," just lighter than life. At the other end of the spectrum, Ringo's instruments are not quite right, either. Both the tambourine and cymbals sound duller or softer than they should. Rather than sounding sharp and crisp, they seem as if the metallic edge is missing. The effect is as though a cotton curtain or veil were separating these instruments from the listener.

Even with these faults, the Australian pressing is a very fine-sounding record. The English and American mono pressings, however, are superior. As well as providing some fullness to the piano, the metallic edge is restored to the cymbals and tambourine. These two records are virtually indistinguishable, other than for a small difference in overall cutting level. They are both examples of monophonic sound at its best.

The Japanese pressing, in stereo, is different than the US and English editions at both ends of the frequency spectrum. At the top, this record lacks the metallic edge characteristic of the "live in your listening room" sound. At the bottom, it is both fuller and further extended into the low frequencies. The piano's wood body resonates and sounds real; the bass guitar's individual notes are easily distinguishable.

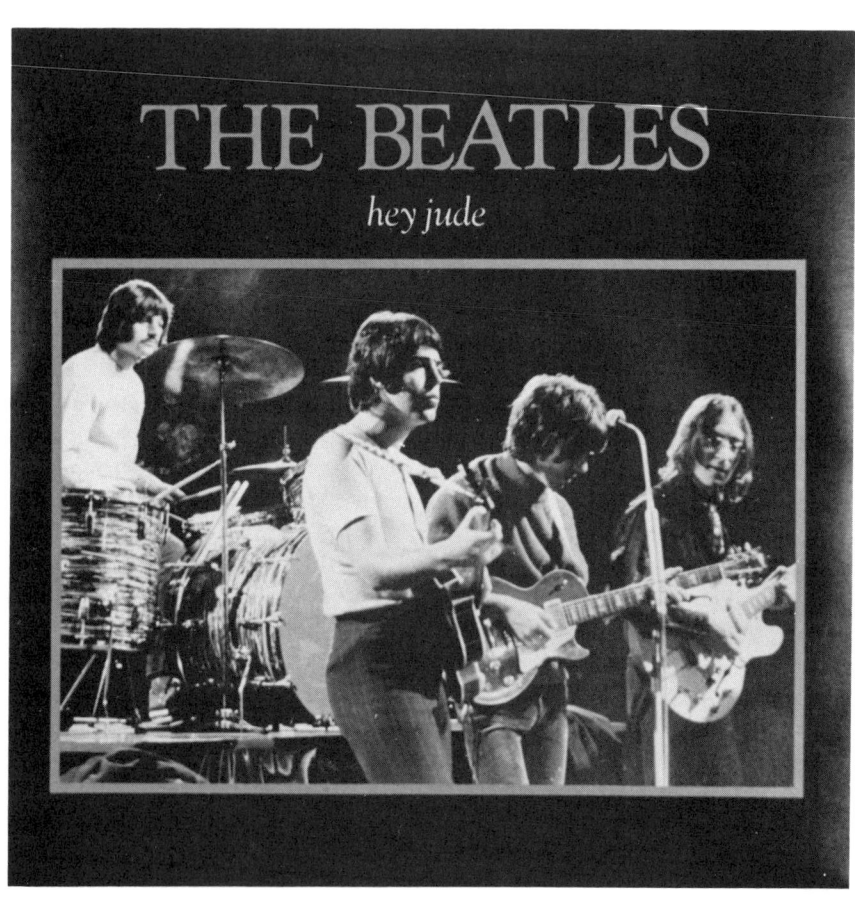

Hey Jude (front)
(England)

The stereo image is wide and rock solid. Both Paul's lead and John and George's background vocals are centered between the speakers. The piano is on the right, the drums are on the left. The bass guitar is also on the right, and the remaining guitar is on the left. This stable image presents a very detailed soundstage, allowing every nuance to be readily apparent to the listener. The lack of utmost extension into the highest frequencies is by no means a major problem; in fact it is almost totally obscured by the excellence displayed in other areas.

   Ranking:
   England (Recommended.)
   US (Recommended.)
   Japan (Recommended.)
   Australia

REVOLUTION

1. (Australia) **The Beatles Singles Collection Australian 20th Anniversary 1962-1982** Parlophone A8493 Master Number 7XCE_21186-1.
2. (England) **The Beatles Singles Collection** Parlophone R5772 Master Number 7XCE_21186-2.
3. (Japan) **The Beatles Singles Collection** Odeon EAS-17328 **Stereo** Master Number 7XCE-21186-U_1S.
4. (US) Rainbow Colorband Edition Capitol 2276 Master Number 45-X46435-W13.
   Note: All above say mono or are assumed to be mono unless the label says stereo, in which case it is listed above.

Of the pressings reviewed here only the Japanese is in stereo, and this fact makes it so significantly different from the other three that it must be considered a separate song. Due to this the mono editions will be discussed first.

The Australian pressing, while suffering from three distinct problems, is not a bad-sounding record. In discussing the problems from top to bottom, the uppermost treble is slightly depressed in level. Ringo's cymbals are missing the "air" and "sheen" that would be present were he playing live in your listening room. John's vocals are slightly recessed and veiled in their presentation. It sounds as if a curtain were hanging between John and the listener, softening the transients and slightly thickening his voice. In the low frequencies, both Ringo's bass drum and Paul's bass are lacking in weight and are very ill-defined. When low frequency information is present, it

Revolution (back)
(Australia)

seems to be a wave of bass energy rather than individual notes or sounds from the bass instruments. These problems are not severe, and this pressing does capture the power and emotion of *Revolution* as John intended.

The US pressing is very similar in sound to the Australian. The only difference occurs at the highest frequencies, which are more extended and lifelike. Ringo's cymbals are reproduced with their "air" and "sheen" intact, bringing his drum kit into your listening room. The vocal and bass problems previously discussed about the Australian pressing are also in evidence here.

The English edition is the best of the mono pressings. While sharing the extended high frequency response, bass presentation is also improved. Although still being somewhat indistinct, it is significantly more forceful. This pressing has the bass power to match the searing guitars.

Before discussing the Japanese pressing, the common characteristics of the mono editions must be discussed. Each of these records conveys the power and strength of John's *Revolution*. The piercing sound of the guitars reinforce the urgency of the message of the song. Although distortion is only present where intended (in the guitar), this song sounds as if it were straining to remain under control. The overall sonic impression is that all hell is about to break loose. This is very fitting, since that is a good description of what actually happens during a revolution.

The Japanese pressing is quite a different story in comparison to the others. The sonic portrait of this version becomes apparent when the opening guitar breaks the silence from the far right of the stereo spread. Ringo's drums appear in the far left, and John's vocal comes in just to the left of center. Paul's bass, and the second guitar, are centered between the speakers.

This presentation adds a significant amount of definition to the instruments not found on the mono pressings. John's voice is also forward in the mix and free of the "veils" previously mentioned. This stereo edition is a finely detailed sonic gem. It does, however, lack the sonic power and urgency that is characteristic of the other editions. The "about to break loose" quality is missing, robbing the stereo version of an important part of John's message. It is due to this fact that a personal decision must be made: is the detailed sonic beauty of the Japanese edition preferred over the power and urgency of the English pressing?

Ranking:
Japan (Both are recommended.)
England (Both are recommended.)
US
Australia

GET BACK

1. (Australia) **The Beatles Singles Collection Australian 20th Anniversary 1962-1982** Parlophone A8763 Master Number 7XCE__ 21296__ A _7XAPA1689.
2. (England) **The Beatles Singles Collection** Apple R5777 Master Number 7XCE_21296-1.
3. (Japan) **The Beatles Singles Collection** Odeon EAS-17329 **Stereo** Master Number 7XCE-21296-U_1S.
4. (US) Rainbow Colorband Edition Capitol 2490 **Stereo** Master Number S45-X46843_-_2490_W11_#1.

   Note: All above say mono or are assumed to be mono unless the label says stereo, in which case it is listed above.

Of the four pressings, of *Get Back*, only the Australian edition is less than listenable. These discs will be discussed in order from best to worst.

The Japanese record is nothing short of perfect. Its frequency response is well balanced and extended in both the bass and treble. Its presentation of the instruments is very detailed and razor-sharp. The stereo spread, while not being very wide, is very realistic. The image created is that of the Beatles and Billy Preston in stage formation performing in your listening room. Paul's bass guitar and vocals are centered between the speakers, as is Billy Preston's keyboard. Ringo's drum set is behind Paul and Billy and spread from right of center to left of center. John and George's guitars appear, one each, on the right and left.

The English pressing is only slightly less desirable than the Japanese. It shares the outstanding frequency response mentioned above. It only is ranked second due to the fact that it is in mono and does not have the detailed instrumental presentation of the stereo edition. The lack of imaging is only a hinderance in direct comparison with the Japanese record; this is a wonderful record.

The US stereo pressing is third best of those reviewed here. While it shares the excellent imaging of the Japanese, it does not share the excellent frequency response. The midrange is too pronounced at times, giving the song a "thick" sound in many places. This does not totally ruin the song, however, and this is definitely a listenable pressing.

The Australian edition suffers from three problems which, in total, make this pressing rather intolerable. The midrange is similar to the American only worse. The song sounds too thick throughout its entire length, becoming overbearing at times. The high frequencies are plagued with dis-

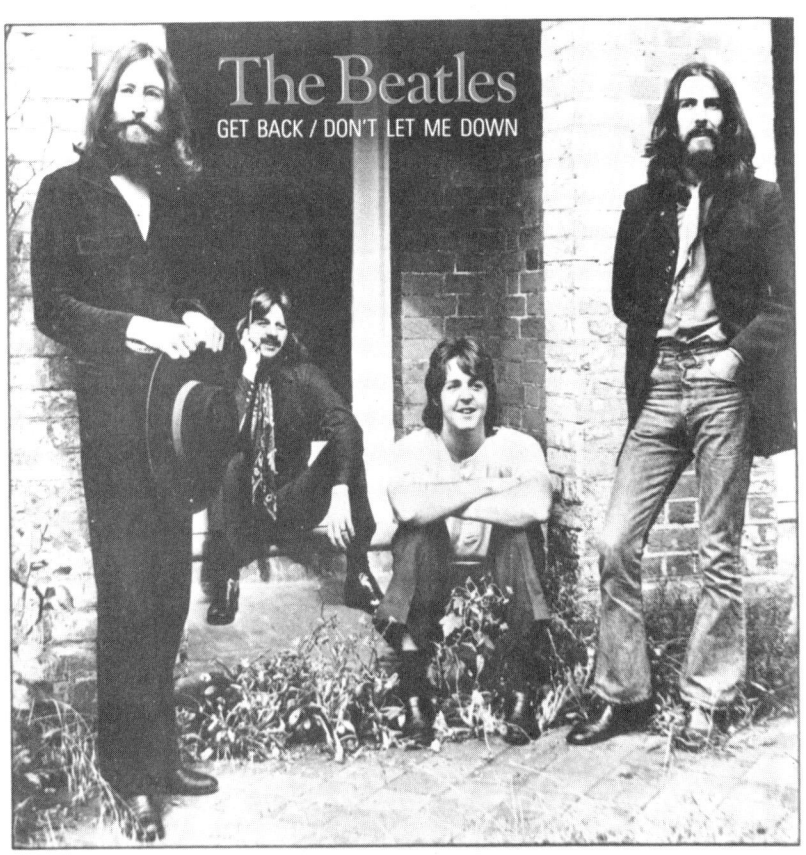

Get Back (front)
(England)

| LISTENING TO THE BEATLES

tortion in places, creating a harsh sound above the thick midrange. The instrumentation is not detailed in its presentation, due to a lack of transient speed up and down the frequency spectrum. All in all, these problems make this record a real chore to endure.

Ranking:
    Japan
    England
    US
    Australia

DON'T LET ME DOWN

1. (Australia) **The Beatles Singles Collection Australian 20th Anniversary 1962-1982** Parlophone A8763 Master Number 7XCE21297_ A _7XAPA1690..
2. (England) **The Beatles Singles Collection** Apple R5777 Master Number 7XCE_21297_-1U.
3. (Japan) **The Beatles Singles Collection** Odeon EAS-17329 **Stereo** Master Number 7XCE-21297-U_ 1S_3.
4. (US) Rainbow Colorband Edition Capitol 2490 **Stereo** Master Number S45_X46844-2-2490_W14_#1.

    Note: All above say mono or are assumed to be mono unless the label says stereo, in which case it is listed above.

    As with the flip side, *Get Back*, two of the four versions of *Don't Let Me Down* are in stereo. And, similarly, three of the four editions are quite good, with only the Australian pressing being below par.
    The Japanese pressing is superior to the others in one or both of the following areas: frequency response and stereo imaging. In terms of frequency response, this disc is first-rate. The presentation is very extended and well balanced, providing power and fullness at the low end and "air" and "shimmer" at the high end. In terms of stereo imaging, Ringo's drums are spread across the soundstage, Paul's bass guitar is in the center, John and George's guitars are left and right, and the vocals are centered. This allows each instrument to occupy its own space in the listener's room, resulting in a very detailed, lifelike sound.
    The English edition is the second best of those reviewed here. It shares the excellent frequency response of the Japanese pressing, beautifully presenting the sonic spectrum from top to bottom. The instrumentation is

not as detailed as the Japanese edition, due to the nature of monophonic sound. This record is so good, however, that the lack of stereo imaging would go unnoticed other than in direct comparison with the US or Japanese pressings.

The US pressing is the third best edition of *Don't Let Me Down*. While it presents the imaging and detailed instrumentation of the Japanese, it has minor problems at both ends of the frequency spectrum. At the high end, extension is slightly limited, robbing Ringo's cymbals of their expected "air" and "shimmer." The song sounds vaguely "closed-in" because of this. At the bottom end, the overall level of the bass has been reduced, leaving this record sounding lightweight and tilted toward the high end. Actually, this lack of bass weight, while being a problem, helps to make this disc listenable. Had the bass response been as full as expected, the lack of high frequency extension would have made this record overbearingly "dark" and "thick" sounding.

The Australian pressing is the only one reviewed here that is not enjoyable. Its treble response is similar to that of the American pressing. In addition to this problem, the vocals suffer from distortion in many places. This record sounds both harsh and "closed-in" at the same time. It is definitely the worst edition of *Don't Let Me Down*.

Ranking:
Japan
England
US
Australia

THE BALLAD OF JOHN AND YOKO

1. (Australia) **The Beatles Singles Collection Australian 20th Anniversary 1962-1982** Parlophone A8793 Master Number 7XCE-21307.
2. (England) **The Beatles Singles Collection** Apple R5786 Master Number 7XCE 21306 - 1U.
3. (Japan) **The Beatles Singles Collection** Odeon EAS-17330 **Stereo** Master Number 7XCE-21306-U_1S.
4. (US) Purple Capitol 2531 Master Number S45 X46865-W11.

Note: All above say mono or are assumed to be mono unless the label says stereo, in which case it is listed above.

Although not mentioned on the label, the English pressing is in stereo, making this the first single from England to bear this distinction.

The Ballad Of John And Yoko (Side 1)
(U.S. Rainbow Swirl Edition)

These four records are very similar in sound, the major identifying element being the lack of imaging of the mono Australian edition.

In terms of frequency response the three stereo records are identical. All possess wide, well balanced sound featuring full bass and airy, extended treble. The stereo presentation has the lead vocals and bass guitar in the center, drums spread across the soundstage, one guitar each in the right and left, the maracas in the left, and the piano in the far right.

The only distinguishing characteristic among the stereo pressings is a very slight amount of harshness in the treble region of the US pressing. This is almost unnoticeable without headphones, where it becomes somewhat more apparent. This problem, although extremely minor, is enough to drop the US edition a notch in the ranking of these versions of *The Ballad of John and Yoko*.

The Australian record, while also being very good, must be considered the least desirable of all because it is in mono. Its presentation is, naturally, "bunched-up" in comparison with the others. It also has a minor problem with the presentation of high-frequency information. The uppermost treble is ever so slightly reduced in level, making the maracas sound darker than life. This problem is also one that is more readily discernible through headphones.

The Ballad of John and Yoko is one of the rare Beatles singles where a listener would be more than satisfied with any of the four pressing reviewed here.

> Ranking:
> England
> (These are virtually indistinguishable and are both recommended as being equally desirable.)
> Japan
> (These are virtually indistinguishable and are both recommended as being equally desirable.)
> US
> Australia

OLD BROWN SHOE

1. (Australia) **The Beatles Singles Collection Australian 20th Anniversary 1962-1982** Parlophone A8793 Master Number 7XCE-_21307-2.
2. (England) **The Beatles Singles Collection** Apple R5786 Master Number 7YCE_21307-2.
3. (Japan) **The Beatles Singles Collection** Odeon EAS-17330 **Stereo** Master

Old Brown Shoe (back)
(Australia)

Number 7XCE-21307-U_1S_2.
4. (US) Purple Capitol 2531 Master Number S45-X-46866-W11.
Note: All above say mono or are assumed to be mono unless the label says stereo, in which case it is listed above.

As with the flip side, *The Ballad of John And Yoko*, the English pressing of *Old Brown Shoe* is in stereo although it is not so labelled. This song is a listener's dream come true, as each version reviewed here is outstanding.

The Australian record is the only mono record here, and it is for this reason that it is the least attractive of the four editions. The frequency response of this edition is well balanced and wide, although the lowest bass frequencies are slightly reduced in level. Instrumental detail is very good, giving this edition a "lean and clean" sound. It is not at all lightweight or tilted toward the high end, just not as full-sounding as it could be.

The US stereo pressing is similar in frequency balance to the Australian. It is preferred, however, due to its stereo presentation. George's vocals are centered between the speakers and Ringo's drums are spread across the soundstage. The piano appears in the far right and the guitar is in the left, as is the organ at the song's conclusion. This is an outstanding record, with rock solid, believable imaging and good frequency response.

The English edition is even better than the American by a small margin. While sharing the outstanding soundstage presentation, this disc's frequency response is slightly better at the low end of the spectrum. Bass is fuller than the Australian and American pressings, giving this record a firmer sound. It is not so full as to make it bottom heavy, just solid and "punchy." This record is so good that it reveals the leanness of the editions previously discussed, a fact that would go unnoticed without direct comparison.

The Japanese record is the best of the four reviewed here. It is just about as perfect as could be. To aptly describe it, take the English pressing and ever so slightly extend the high frequency response and minutely increase its level. The song takes on a sparkle and liveliness that the listener didn't know was missing from the English pressing. This record is almost so good as to not need description.

Ranking:
Japan
England
US
Australia

NOTE: All of these discs are, at a minimum, very good. It is impossible to make a mistake with *Old Brown Shoe.*

SOMETHING

1. (Australia) **The Beatles Singles Collection Australian 20th Anniversary 1962-1982** Parlophone A8943 Master Number 7XAPA1795-2 _YEX749-2_S1B2_A8943.
2. (England) **The Beatles Singles Collection** Parlophone R5811 Master Number 7YCE_21369-1U.
3. (Japan) **The Beatles Singles Collection** Odeon EAS-17332 **Stereo** Master Number 7YCE-21369-U_1S_2.
4. (US) Rainbow Colorband Edition Capitol 2654 Master Number 45-X-46992-2654-1-1_#3.

Note: All above say mono or are assumed to be mono unless the label says stereo, in which case it is listed above.

In similar fashion to the previous single, *The Ballad Of John And Yoko/Old Brown Shoe,* the English pressing of *Something* is in stereo. The four versions of this song will be discussed here in order from best to worst.

The Japanese edition is, as has been the case for many of the other singles, the best of the lot. Its stereo presentation is wide and stable, featuring George's lead vocal in the center, Paul's bass guitar in the right channel, Ringo's drums centered behind the vocals, guitars one each in the left and center, and the organ in the left. Instrumental definition is razor-sharp, allowing the organ, for example, to be easily distinguished even though it is rather buried in the mix. Frequency response is exemplary, presenting the fullness and transient impact of Paul's bass in perfect juxtaposition to Ringo's shimmering cymbals. This record is extremely clean and totally free of distortion, a problem that plagues the other stereo editions.

The Australian pressing, although in mono, is the second best of the group. While being a fine-sounding record, it actually earns its high ranking due to problems with the English and American pressings. Frequency response of the Australian record is slightly inferior to that of the Japanese, suffering from a minor reduction in both treble extension and bass level. The reduction in treble extension leaves Ringo's cymbals slightly lacking in "air" and "shimmer," while the reduced bass level removes some of the firm bottom provided by Paul's bass guitar. Since these two problems occur at opposite ends of the frequency spectrum and are of a similar nature (both being reduction rather than one being reduction and one being boost), the song still sounds very well balanced. The presentation is also extremely clean and distortion-free; this is a fine-sounding pressing that can only be

Something (front)
(England)

Come Together (back)
(England)

faulted in direct comparison with the Japanese.

The English pressing shares the frequency response and stereo imaging of the Japanese. It must be ranked third due to small amounts of distortion present when the record's cutting level gets high during the song's chorus. This is not a major annoyance, just enough to drop it a notch below the clean Australian pressing.

The US edition is the worst of all-reviewed here and borders on being unlistenable. At a minimum it can be considered fatiguing to the listener. Its frequency response is similar to the Australian pressing, being reduced at both ends of the spectrum. It also is very harsh-sounding, being very distorted at times throughout the song. Whereas the distortion is very minor and only readily apparent with headphones on the Australian pressing, it jumps out of the speakers and grates on the listener's ears on this pressing. This is a record that should be avoided.

    Ranking:
        Japan
        Australia
        England
        US

COME TOGETHER

1. (Australia) **The Beatles Singles Collection Australian 20th Anniversary 1962-1982** Parlophone A8943 Master Number 7XAPA 1796-2 YEX749-2 S1B1_A8943.
2. (England) **The Beatles Singles Collection** Apple R5811 Master Number 7YCE 21370-1U.
3. (Japan) **The Beatles Singles Collection** Odeon EAS-17331 **Stereo** Master Number 7YCE-21370-U_1S_3.
4. (US) Rainbow Colorband Edition Capitol 2654 **Stereo** Master Number S45-X46991-H12#1_1-2654.

    Note: All above say mono or are assumed to be mono unless the label says stereo, in which case it is listed above.

    While not being so labelled, the English pressing of *Come Together* is in stereo. As the best of the four editions reviewed here (an honor it shares with the Japanese record), it will be discussed first.

    The English edition, depending upon your personal expectations of stereo imaging, may be considered faultness. For the listener who expects a

An Audiophile's Guide to the Sound of the Fab Four

stereo image to present the Beatles in concert formation in your listening room, this record will be slightly disappointing. The listener who only expects to hear instruments defined in space, but not necessarily in a concert-type space, will be absolutely ecstatic with this pressing.

The stereo image, at the song's beginning, has John's vocals and Paul's bass guitar centered between the speakers, Ringo's drums on the right, and John and George's guitars on the left. When the organ makes it appearance it is also on the right. This presentation seems sensible and solidly fixed in space, until the first instrumental break, where the guitars shift from the left to the center and the right. At the song's conclusion the guitars move once again, this time to the center. It is this wandering of the instruments that may be upsetting to some listeners.

As for frequency response, excellent is the word. Bass is full and deep, allowing the "whack" of Ringo's bass drum to be felt as well as heard. Treble is airy and extended, providing "shimmer" to the cymbals. Transient response is lightning quick, giving detail to the sound and the appropriate "bite" to the guitars. All in all, this is a great-sounding record!

In describing the Japanese pressing, nothing can be said that hasn't already been said about the English. The reader might just as well re-read the previous three paragraphs and substitute the word Japanese for the word English.

The Australian pressing, which follows the English and Japanese in the ranking, is in mono. It also presents a sound quality that is somewhat common among the Australian Beatles singles. The frequency response is slightly deficient at both ends of the spectrum. At the high end, extension is a trifle limited, removing the "air" and "sheen" from Ringo's cymbals. The low end is well extended but somewhat reduced in level. Paul's bass guitar and Ringo's bass drum are audibly present, but lack the weight and transient impact they possess on the English and Japanese records. These minor problems create a polite-sounding record, one that would be perfectly acceptable save for the outstanding records previously described.

The US pressing, in stereo, is the worst of the four reviewed here. It is not bad, however; in fact it is very similar in sound to the Australian edition. The only reason this edition is ranked last is the unevenness of the treble presentation. During the instrumental breaks the treble is airy and extended, but during the vocal portions it is restricted and closed down. This gives the listener the impression that Ringo's cymbals are constantly changing in sonic character throughout the song. This character change is actually very minor and only readily apparent through close scrutiny. It is enough, however, to force this pressing to the bottom of the barrel.

Ranking:
   England
      (Both of these are recommended.)
   Japan
      (Both of these are recommended.)
   Australia
   US

LET IT BE

1. (Australia) **The Beatles Singles Collection Australian 20th Anniversary 1962-1982** Parlophone A9083 Master Number 7YCE_21407-1U.
2. (England) **The Beatles Singles Collection** Apple R5833 Master Number 7YCE_21407-1U.
3. (Japan) **The Beatles Singles Collection** Odeon EAS-17332 **Stereo** Master Number 7YCE-21407-U_1S_1.
4. (US) Rainbow Colorband Edition Capitol 2764 **Stereo** Master Number S-45-47129_Z-16_2764_2_#1.

   Note: All above say mono or are assumed to be mono unless the label says stereo, in which case it is listed above.

It seems only fitting that *Let It Be*, the final single released by the Beatles as an active group, should prove to have the best-sounding pressings. Both the Australian and English editions are in stereo, despite the lack of label indications. This creates the unique situation where all pressings of an original single (not an after-the-fact release, such as *Sgt. Pepper* and the like) are in stereo.

The stereo presentation is the same among the four editions reviewed here. The image is as follows: organ in the far left, piano just left of center, Paul's lead vocal and Ringo's drums right of center, and guitars and bass guitar in the far left. The background vocals (sometimes referred to as "the angel chorus") start in the far left and move across the soundstage to the far right during their first appearance.

It is easiest to discuss these four pressings by starting in the middle and working from there. The English and American records are virtually identical and feature an extended frequency response. Bass is deep and treble is airy and extended. These pressings are very satisfying and enjoyable. It is hard to imagine any record sounding better than these.

The Australian edition is ever so slightly less attractive. This is due to the fact that the bass frequencies are reduced in level by a small amount. In comparison to the English and American pressings this sounds a trifle

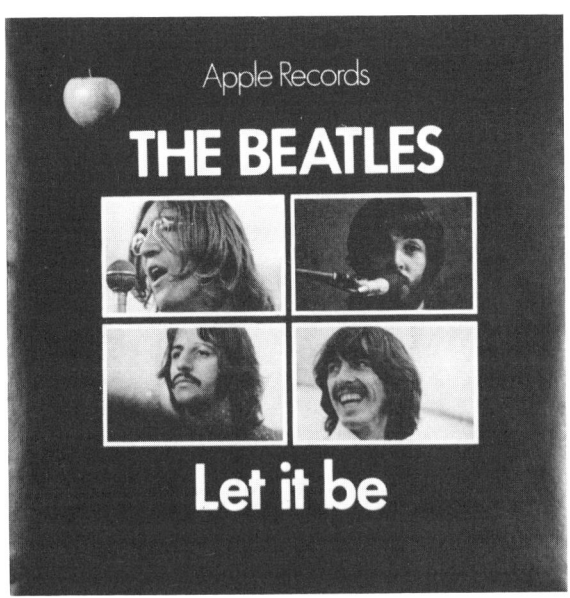

Let It Be (front)
(England)

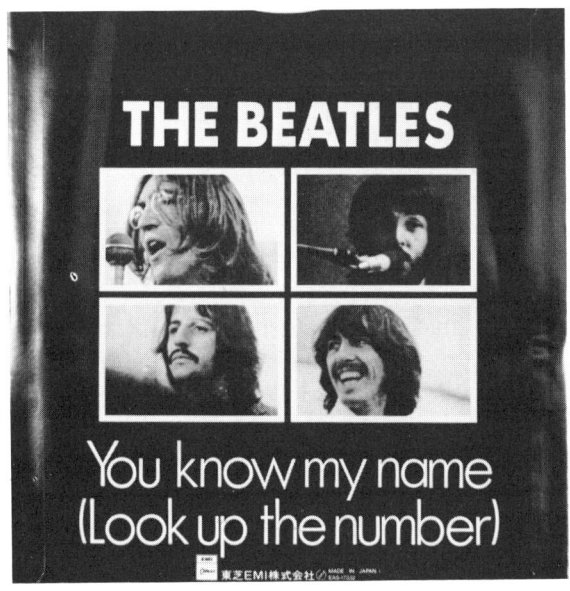

You Know My Name (Look Up The Number) (back)
(Japan)

"thin"; on its own it sounds excellent, with the thinness probably going unnoticed.

The Japanese pressing is unbelievably good. It starts with the excellent sound of the English and American editions and takes off into the realm of perfection. Treble is slightly "faster" and "airier." Paul's vocals float above the piano in their own well-presented space. Instrumentation has precise definition from top to bottom of the frequency spectrum. This is especially evident at the low end, where individual notes of the bass guitar are readily discernible, a feature not present on any of the other pressings.

In a word, a perfect record!

Ranking:
Japan
England
US
Australia

YOU KNOW MY NAME (LOOK UP THE NUMBER)

1. (Australia) **The Beatles Singles Collection Australian 20th Anniversary 1962-1982** Parlophone A9083 Master Number 7YCE 21408-1U.
2. (England) **The Beatles Singles Collection** Apple R5833 Master Number 7YCE-21408-2.
3. (Japan) **The Beatles Singles Collection** Odeon EAS-17332 **Stereo** Master Number 7YCE-21408-U_1S_3.
4. (US) Rainbow Colorband Edition Capitol 2764 **Stereo** Master Number S-45-47130Z14 2764 #2.

Note: All above say mono or are assumed to be mono.

As this is not a serious song by the Beatles, it does not merit a serious review of its sonic merit. Suffice it to say that all four editions are in mono and all are listenable, although the lower midrange/upper bass of the Australian disc is a little too full and seems overbearing at times.

By no means should the sonic quality of this song be used as consideration for a record's purchase. The listener should instead use the review of *Let It Be* as a guide.

Ranking:
No ranking given.

An Audiophile's Guide to the Sound of the Fab Four

BACK IN THE USSR

1. (England) **The Beatles Singles Collection** Parlophone R6016 Master Number 7YCE 21787-1.
2. (Japan) **The Beatles Singles Collection** Odeon EAS-17334 **Stereo** Master Number 7YCE-21787-U_1S_2.
Note: Both the above say mono or are assumed to be mono unless the label states stereo, in which case it is listed above.

Back In the USSR is not included in **The Beatles Singles Collection Australian 20th Anniversary 1962-1982**, and has never been released on a single in America; therefore only two editions are available for review. Both are in stereo even though the English pressing is not so labelled.
 These two pressings share a common stereo presentation. Lead vocals are centered between the speakers, one guitar is on each of the right and left sides of the soundstage, piano is on the right, drums are mostly on the right (although occasionally drums can be heard on the left as well), and the bass guitar is on the left. At the song's opening the jet plane sounds move from right to left across the image; at the conclusion just the opposite occurs.
 Sonically, both of these editions are outstanding. The Japanese pressing is slightly superior, however, as it surpasses the English in three areas that are familiar strengths of Japanese pressings: treble extension, detail of instrumentation, and weight and extension of the bass. The English record is definitely "lightweight" in sound - it is moderately lacking in bass presentation. This tilts the entire frequency response upward, robbing the piano of its fullness and almost totally removing the bass guitar from the mix. This upward tilt does effectively hide the lack of ultimate treble extension, since the overall thinness of sound is actually tempered by this high end problem. In total, the English edition is quite fine in the areas that it presents, only the lack of bass (which may well not be apparent on some audio systems) prevents it from being a real masterpiece.
 The Japanese pressing is better than the English in the low frequencies. The piano has some of its fullness and body, and the bass guitar is readily discernible. All is not roses, however, as this record is still deficient in this area and remains somewhat "lightweight" in sound. Ringo's cymbals possess more "shimmer" and "sparkle" than on the English record, "opening-up" the overall sound of the song. Instruments are more precisely defined in space, firming up the stereo image and providing additional detail to the sound. This is an outstanding pressing kept only from perfection by the somewhat reduced level of the low frequencies.

Back In The USSR (front)
(England)

Twist And Shout (front)
(U.S. Rainbow Swirl Edition)

Ranking:
Japan
England

TWIST AND SHOUT

1. (England) **The Beatles Singles Collection** Parlophone R6016 Master Number 7YCE 21788-1.
2. (Japan) **The Beatles Singles Collection** Odeon EAS-17334 **Stereo** Master Number 7YCE-21788-U_1S_2.
3. (US) Rainbow Colorband Edition Capitol B-5624 **Stereo** Master Number S-45-B-1-5624-X45018_G-2_R-16236-G2.

Note: All above say mono or are assumed to be mono unless the label states stereo, in which case it is listed above.

Until the 1986 release of this song in America (due to its inclusion in the soundtrack of two hit movies), there had been only two pressings available for review. The English pressing, while not indicating so on the label, is in stereo.

The stereo presentation of these records is the familiar words on one side, music on the other that characterized many early Beatles recordings. At the opening instrumental introduction the music appears in the left channel with minor leakage of Ringo's drums into the right. Vocals (lead and background) then enter in the right, overpowering and hiding the drum leakage. Since the vocals are isolated in one channel it is possible to detect the echo surrounding the voices. When John, Paul, and George join in the harmonious "Aahs" the fact that the vocals are confined to only the right channel causes a "bunching up" or "squashing together" of the voices. A more realistic presentation would have had the three singers spread across the soundstage in a left, center, and right configuration. Music is also "bunched-up due to this stereo imaging, preventing the listener from easily locating or focusing attention upon specific instruments.

In terms of frequency response these pressings are almost identical, although the Japanese edition is slightly better than the others. At the low end, all are lacking in definition and weight. Individual bass notes are not readily apparent. The overall sound resulting from this is a bit "light" or "thin." The remainder of the frequency spectrum is well balanced and extended, although the Japanese record presents a little more "air" and "shimmer" on Ringo's cymbals than the English and American discs. This difference is so minor as to go undetected without close scrutiny.

In summation, all of these records sound very fine. They are handicapped more by the stereo presentation than by anything else.

> Ranking:
> Japan
> US (tie)
> England (tie)

NOTE: An identical U.S. pressing (same master numbers as reviewed above) is available on the purple Capitol label.

SGT. PEPPER'S LONELY HEARTS CLUB BAND/ WITH A LITTLE HELP FROM MY FRIENDS

1. (Australia) **The Beatles Singles Collection Australian 20th Anniversary 1962-1982** Parlophone A12000 Master Number A12000A.
2. (England) **The Beatles Singles Collection** Parlophone R6022 Master Number 7YCE_21801-1U.
3. (Japan) **The Beatles Singles Collection** Odeon EAS-17335 **Stereo** Master Number 7YCE-21801-U_1S_3.
4. (US) Rainbow Colorband Edition Capitol 4612 **Stereo** Master Number S45X45964/X4596_F-2_4612_3.
   Note: All above say mono or are assumed to be mono unless the label says stereo, in which case it is listed above.

All four pressings reviewed here are in stereo, despite the absence of label indication on the Australian and English editions. These records are all very similar in sound and will be discussed by presenting the commonalities and then the differences.

The stereo presentation of these records is comprised of two distinct images, since this is actually two songs blended together. In *Sgt. Pepper's Lonely Hearts Club Band*, Ringo's drums are centered in the soundstage. Paul's lead vocals are on the right, and choral vocals are on the left. Horns appear on the left and the two guitars can be found one in the center and the other on the right. In *With A Little Help From My Friends*, Ringo's drums are to the right of center, with his lead vocals starting to the left of center and moving toward the far left as the song continues. Paul's bass guitar is joined on the right by a tambourine and one guitar. Background vocals can also be found on the left.

These two images are similar enough to make the transition between these two songs believable, although Ringo's part in *With A Little Help From My Friends* presents difficulties. At the song's beginning the

Sgt. Pepper's Lonely Hearts Club Band (front)
(England)

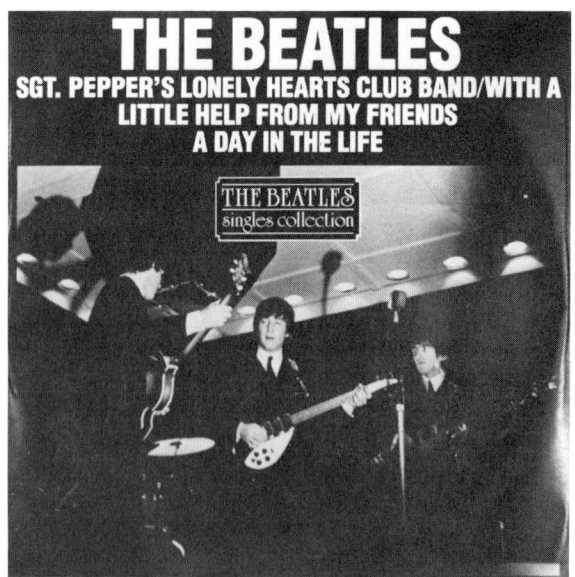

Sgt. Pepper's Lonely Hearts Club Band (front)
(Australia)

drums are distinctly to the right of the lead vocals, albeit only slightly. As unrealistic as this sounds (since obviously Ringo should be sitting behind the drum kit), by the song's conclusion the voice has moved to the far left, creating the situation where he seems totally separated (by half the soundstage width) from his instrument.

In terms of frequency response these pressings are very similar from the treble down to the lower midrange. Extension at the high end is very good, providing the metallic "shimmer" to the cymbals and "bite" to the guitars. Midrange is in balance with the top end, allowing instrument fundamentals and vocals to be clearly heard. It is in the bass region where these pressings are dissimilar.

The American and Japanese editions are the best in the bass, being well extended and in balance with the midrange and treble. Ringo's bass drum has resonant body and fullness that is easily felt during *With A Little Help From My Friends*, and Paul's bass guitar has transient impact and weight without ever being too prominent or overbearing. The English pressing suffers from unevenness at the low end, as if during mixdown or mastering the bass level or EQ was being constantly adjusted. The low end seems to drop out at times during *Sgt. Pepper*, and the bass drum is missing its expected fullness in *With A Little Help From My Friends*. The problem in the bass in the Australian pressing goes in the opposite direction as that in the English. While the low end is fine during *Sgt. Pepper*, during *With A Little Help From My Friends* it is too full. Paul's bass guitar is "fat" and ill-defined, clouding the midrange and obscuring the other instruments.

In trying to determine the ultimate rankings, personal preference comes into play. The deciding factor between the English and Australian editions is the bass. If "fat" bass is more tolerable than "thin," the Australian record is preferred. If the opposite is true, the English becomes the favorite. Top honors, however, must be shared by the American and Japanese pressings, which both border on perfection.

    Ranking:
    US
        (Both of these are recommended.)
    Japan
        (Both of these are recommended.)
    England
        (Personal preference will determine which of these is preferred; see review above.)
    Australia
        (Personal preference will determine which of these is preferred; see review above.)

A Day In The Life (back)
(Japan)

An Audiophile's Guide to the Sound of the Fab Four

A DAY IN THE LIFE

1. (Australia) **The Beatles Singles Collection Australian 20th Anniversary 1962-1982** Parlophone A12000 Master Number A12000B.
2. (England) **The Beatles Singles Collection** Parlophone R6022 Master Number 7YCE_21802-1U.
3. (Japan) **The Beatles Singles Collection** Odeon EAS-17335 **Stereo** Master Number 7YCE-21802-U_1S_2.
4. (US) Rainbow Colorband Edition Capitol 4612 **Stereo** Master Number S45-X45963_F-2_4612.

Note: All above say mono or are assumed to be mono unless the label says stereo, in which case it is listed above.

As with the flip side, *Sgt. Pepper's Lonely Hearts Club Band/With A Little Help From My Friends*, all of the pressings reviewed here are in stereo, even though the Australian and English records do not say so.

The stereo presentation of *A Day In The Life* is realistic at times, but in general rather gimmickly. At the song's beginning the piano is in the right channel and the acoustic guitar is in the left. Paul's bass guitar is right of center, Ringo's drums are centered, and the maracas are in the left. John's vocals appear in the far right. The gimmicks begin as John's voice starts to move across the soundstage. When he sings "House of Lords" his voice has obviously moved toward the center. By the time the words "having read the book" are sung the vocal is in the left.

When the song shifts to the middle section with Paul singing lead, vocals are back in the far right. Although the drums are still centered, the bass guitar is now also centered and the piano has been "ping-ponged" to the left. When John resumes singing duties he is in the left and the piano is once again in the right. Maracas have shifted to the right, as has the guitar.

Only Ringo's drums, firmly planted in the center, avoid the fate of being shuffled around the soundstage. At any one moment in time the image is believable and stable; however, the constantly moving and shifting voices and instruments serve to make the listener realize that much electronic manipulation has taken place in creating *A Day In The Life*.

As for sonics, these four editions are all outstanding! The differences among them are minor at best, the most noticeable being the fact that the English pressing begins with the clapping fade out from *Sgt. Pepper's Lonely Hearts Club Band Reprise* while the others do not. Frequency response is wide and well balanced in all versions, although the Japanese pressing is ever so slightly more extended at the top end, adding "air" to Ringo's cymbals.

285

The remaining differences can be found in the vocal presentation. The Australian edition has John's lead further back in the mix than the others. This makes the echo processing that was added to the vocals less noticeable. As a result John's voice sounds "smaller" and does not stand out as much as it does on the other editions. Paul's voice is presented in a very "dry" fashion on the Australian and English pressings. This dryness, or lack of air and space, makes the vocal sound flat and lifeless, almost muffled. In comparison to John's echoed, larger than life sound, Paul sounds flat and dull. The American and Japanese pressings do not suffer as greatly from this problem, however, as Paul's voice is more realistically presented.

In summation, the treble extension causes the Japanese pressing to be slightly preferred over the American. The lack of forward vocal presentation makes the Australian edition inferior to the English, which is not as good as the American or Japanese due to its dry presentation of Paul's vocals.

Ranking:
Japan
US
England
(This edition may be desirable because its introduction is unique.)
Australia

THE BEATLES' MOVIE MEDLEY

1. (Australia) **The Beatles Singles Collection Australian 20th Anniversary 1962-1982** Parlophone A689 Master Number A.689A.
2. (England) **The Beatles Singles Collection** Parlophone R6055 Master Number R_6055_A-1.
3. (Japan) **The Beatles Singles Collection** Odeon EAS-17336 **Stereo** Master Number R-6004-A_1S_2.
    Note: All above say mono or are assumed to be mono unless the label says stereo, in which case it is listed above.

Only three editions are reviewed here since the American pressing is no longer in print. This is a curious fact since *The Beatles' Movie Medley* was invented and created by Capitol Records in the USA. All three records are in stereo, even though, as usual, the Australian and English are not so labelled.

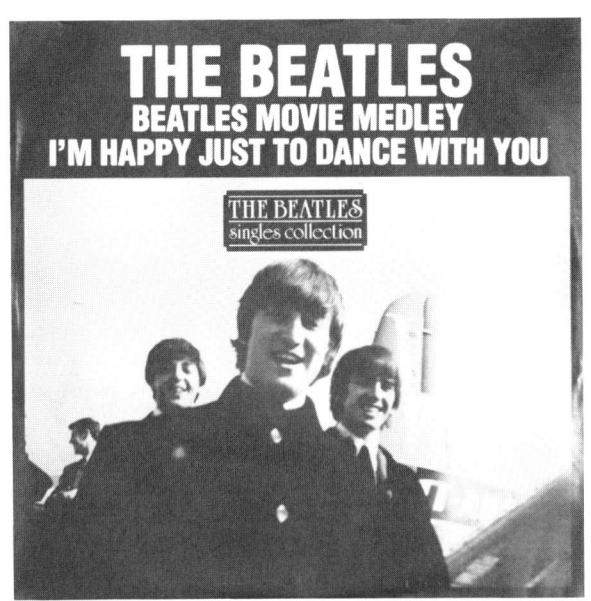

The Beatles' Movie Medley (front)
(Australia)

The Beatles' Movie Medley (front)
(England)

This medley consists of pieces of the following seven songs: 1) *Magical Mystery Tour*, 2) *All You Need Is Love*, 3) *You've Got To Hide Your Love Away*, 4) *I Should Have Known Better*, 5) *A Hard Day's Night*, 6) *Ticket To Ride*, and 7) *Get Back*. In discussing these discs the various parts of the medley will be referred to by number.

This song, not being a continuous piece of music, does not present a coherent stereo image. Each of the seven sections has its own soundstage, and this "song" is not worthy of the lengthy exposition that would be necessary to document them.

If the listener can get past the dreadful idea of Capitol Records bastardizing seven wonderful songs just for monetary gain, the Japanese pressing sounds quite fine. Each section is detailed in presentation and contains the entire frequency spectrum's material.

The English pressing is ranked second; sections 3, 6, and 7 match the Japanese in sonic quality. Each of the others suffers from a lack of treble extension and reduction in high frequency level. The Australian pressing, ranked third, only equals the Japanese record's quality in sections 6 and 7. Section 3 suffers from strained sounding vocals, and all others are plagued by the treble problems described for the English pressing.

Ranking:
Japan
England
Australia

I'M HAPPY JUST TO DANCE WITH YOU

1. (Australia) **The Beatles Singles Collection Australian 20th Anniversary 1962-1982** Parlophone A689 Master Number A.689B.
2. (England) **The Beatles Singles Collection** Parlophone R6055 Master Number R_6055_B-1.
3. (Japan) **The Beatles Singles Collection** Odeon EAS-17336 **Stereo** Master Number R-6055-B_1S_2.
4. (US) Rainbow Swirl Edition Capitol A-6282 **Stereo** Master Number A-6282_45050_H10#2.

Note: All above say mono or are assumed to be mono unless the label says stereo, in which case it is listed above.

While only three pressings of the flip side, *The Beatles' Movie Medley*, were available for review, four editions of this song are included due to the addition of the Blue Starline edition from Capitol Records in the US. Three of the four pressings are mislabelled, since both the Australian and English are in stereo and the American is not. The discussion of *I'm Happy Just To Dance With You* will be presented in order from worst to best.

The Australian pressing is in reprocessed stereo, with the high frequencies being boosted in the right channel. This seems to move George's vocals to the right of center and Ringo's cymbals slightly farther right than the vocals. This is not readily apparent, however, and headphones are required for verification. In general, this is a "thick" sounding song with all instruments bunched together. George's vocals are veiled and unclear, as if any space around them had been removed. Bass frequencies are lacking in weight, removing the body from Ringo's bass drum and leaving the song sounding lightweight at times.

The U.S. Blue Starline edition, in mono, is also somewhat thick-sounding, although not as bad as the Australian. The high frequencies are further extended into the uppermost octave, removing some of the thickness from the overall presentation. Low bass is also further extended, at least at the song's outset. In general, this pressing is more "powerful" sounding than the Australian.

The English pressing, in contrast to the Australian, is in true stereo. George's lead vocals are in the center between the speakers, with his guitar appearing in the right. Ringo's bass drum is to the right of center while the remainder of the drum set is in the left. Background vocals can be found behind George's lead, also in the center. This stereo presentation allows for separation of the instruments in space, removing any trace of thickness that was still evident in the American pressing. Ringo's bass drum possesses some of its characteristic body and "whack" due to the increased bass weight offered by this pressing.

The Japanese edition is everything the English one is and then some. It offers a more detailed soundstage with firmer stereo imaging. High-frequency response is further extended, providing additional "sparkle" to Ringo's cymbals. This is a very powerful song that reaches out and grabs the listener, demanding attention due to its exquisite sound. An almost perfect record!

Ranking:
Japan
England
US
Australia

NOTE: Two identical U.S. pressings (same master numbers as reviewed above) are available on the purple Starline and black-and-rainbow colorband Starline labels from Capitol.

THE LONG AND WINDING ROAD

1. (Australia) **The Beatles Singles Collection Australian 20th Anniversary 1962-1982** Parlophone A9163 Master Number 7XAPA1901.
2. (US) Rainbow Colorband Edition Capitol 2832 Master Number S-45-47181Z5 2832 #2.
    Note: Both the above say mono or are assumed to be mono.

Only two editions are available for review here, since *The Long And Winding Road* is not included as part of **The Beatles Singles Collection** from England or Japan. While both editions sound good, the American is slightly better.

The Australian pressing is in mono, with Paul's lead vocals mixed extremely far forward in relation to the music. Treble extension is slightly limited, although strict attention must be paid to the sound of the cymbals for this to become apparent. Because the music is so far in the background this treble problem is minor. This record is also restricted in extension at the low end, but because the song lacks heavy drums or electric bass the listener does not feel a void.

The American pressing, in stereo, does not present Paul's lead vocals as far forward as does the Australian. This brings the instruments out of the background and allows the listener to notice the extended high frequency response of Ringo's cymbals. The stereo imaging has Paul's vocals and Ringo's drums centered between the speakers with the orchestra spread across the soundstage. While not being spectacular, this does provide additional air and space to the song. As with the Australian, this edition is lacking in low frequency energy, so it is a good conclusion that it is the music, not the pressings, that causes this. All in all, this edition is slightly preferred over the Australian.

Ranking:
US
Australia

For You Blue (back)
(Australia)

FOR YOU BLUE

1. (Australia) **The Beatles Singles Collection Australian 20th Anniversary 1962-1982** Parlophone A9163 Master Number 7XAPA1902.
2. (US) Rainbow Swirl Edition Capitol 2832 Master Number S-45-47182 _Z8_2832_#2.
   Note: Both the above say mono or are assumed to be mono.

As with the flip side, *The Long and Winding Road*, only two editions of *For You Blue* are available for review. The American pressing, although not so labelled, is in stereo. In contrast to the flip side, both editions here do not sound equally good.

The Australian pressing, in mono, is difficult to tolerate. The entire song sounds clouded and veiled, as if a very heavy curtain were hanging between the music and the listener. All transient speed is gone, leaving the guitars lacking in "bite" and the drums missing their "snap." Vocals do not stand out over the music, helping to make this pressing sound crowded and bunched together.

The American edition, in contrast, is excellent. Frequency response is wide and well balanced from top to bottom. Vocals are forward and clear; the clouds and veils are gone. Transient speed is lightning fast, allowing the "bite" and impact of the guitars and drums to be faithfully reproduced. The stereo presentation features George's vocals and Ringo's drums centered between the speakers, opening acoustic guitar in the center, John's slide guitar left, and electric guitar in the right. This stable image provides air and space around each of the instruments. All in all, a great pressing!

Ranking:
US
Australia

ACT NATURALLY

1. (Australia) **The Beatles Singles Collection Australian 20th Anniversary 1962-1982** Parlophone A8173 Master Number A8173-B.
2. (US) **Blue Starline Edition** Capitol A-6291 (or X-6291) **Stereo** master Number A-6291_45-45316-_G11#2.
   Note: Both the above say mono or are assumed to be mono unless the label indicates stereo, in which case it is listed above.

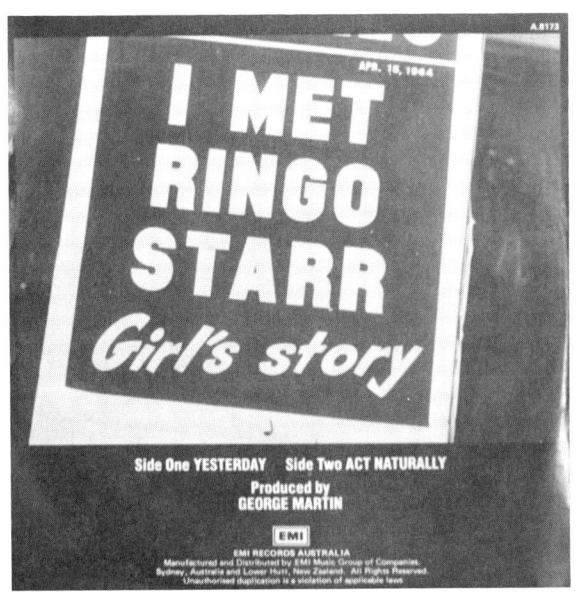

Act Naturally (back)
(Australia)

I Saw Her Standing There (back)
(U.S. 20th Anniversary Edition)

Act Naturally is not contained in **The Beatles Singles Collection** from England or Japan; hence this review is of pressings from Australia and the US only. The Australian edition, although not so labelled, is in true stereo, while the US Blue Starline edition, labelled as stereo, is actually mono.

The Australian edition presents most of the music in the left channel and Ringo's vocals centered between the speakers. The midrange and upper bass are slightly "fat" and ill-defined. The high frequencies are not extended into the uppermost octave. These problems are minor in scope, however, and this is a very listenable record.

The US Blue Starline edition, albeit in mono, is better than the Australian pressing. The midrange and upper bass are slightly leaner and not as "fat" sounding. The top end is further extended and more prominent, making this edition sound "airier" than the Australian. All in all, this is a fine sounding record, definitely the better of the two reviewed here.

Ranking:
US
Australian

I SAW HER STANDING THERE

1. (Australia) **The Beatles Singles Collection Australian 20th Anniversary 1962-1982** Parlophone A8105 Master Number A_8105_B.
2. (US) Blue Starline Edition Capitol X-6278 (or A-6278) Master Number A-6278_44772_H7#2.
3. (US) 20th Anniversary edition with yellow/orange swirl label Capitol 5112 Master Number 45-_5112-#44772_G-1.
   Note: All above say mono or are assumed to be mono.

I Saw Her Standing There is not contained in **The Beatles Singles Collection** from England or Japan, hence this review is of pressings from Australia and the US only. Although not so labelled, the Australian edition is in true stereo.

I Saw Her Standing There is unique in the fact that each of the versions reviewed here is a gem. The Australian pressing presents the vocals in the right channel, most of the music and hand clapping in the left channel, and Paul's bass guitar centered between the speakers. Vocals are clear and forward in the mix. Treble is extended into the highest frequencies, providing "air" and "shimmer" to the sound. Bass is deep and well controlled, allowing each note to be individually distinguished beneath the rest of the instrumentation.

The US 20th Anniversary edition is very similar to the Australian. Its only difference is in the vocal presentation. This pressing has the vocals slightly further forward in the mix. In combination with the monophonic presentation, the vocals seem to float above the music. This is a more realistic presentation than that offered by the "words on the right, music on the left" stereo pressing.

The US Blue Starline edition is also very fine-sounding. It is different from the 20th Anniversary edition in the upper bass and lower midrange. This record has a slightly stronger output in this part of the frequency range. This gives a fuller sound to the song. The presentation is not overbearingly full, just not as lean and tight as the other two editions reviewed here. Personal taste will be the determining factor as to whether this edition is the preferred edition.

Ranking:
US 20th Anniversary edition
Australian
US Blue Starline edition

NOTE: All three editions sound very fine. Those who favor stereo over mono will prefer the Australian pressing, those who favor full or "bassy" sound will prefer the US Blue Starline edition.

NOWHERE MAN

1. (Australia) **The Beatles Singles Collection Australian 20th Anniversary 1962-1982** Parlophone A8193 Master Number A8293A.
2. (US) Blue Starline Edition Capitol A-6294 (or X-6294) **Stereo** Master Number A-6294_45406_H6#2.
   Note: Both the above say mono or are assumed to be mono unless the label says stereo, in which case it is listed above.

Nowhere Man is not contained in **The Beatles Singles Collection** from England or Japan, therefore only two pressings are available for review.

The Australian pressing, although not so labelled, is in true stereo. This is the familiar "words on the right, music on the left" presentation. This record sounds very good, with a fairly wide frequency range and good

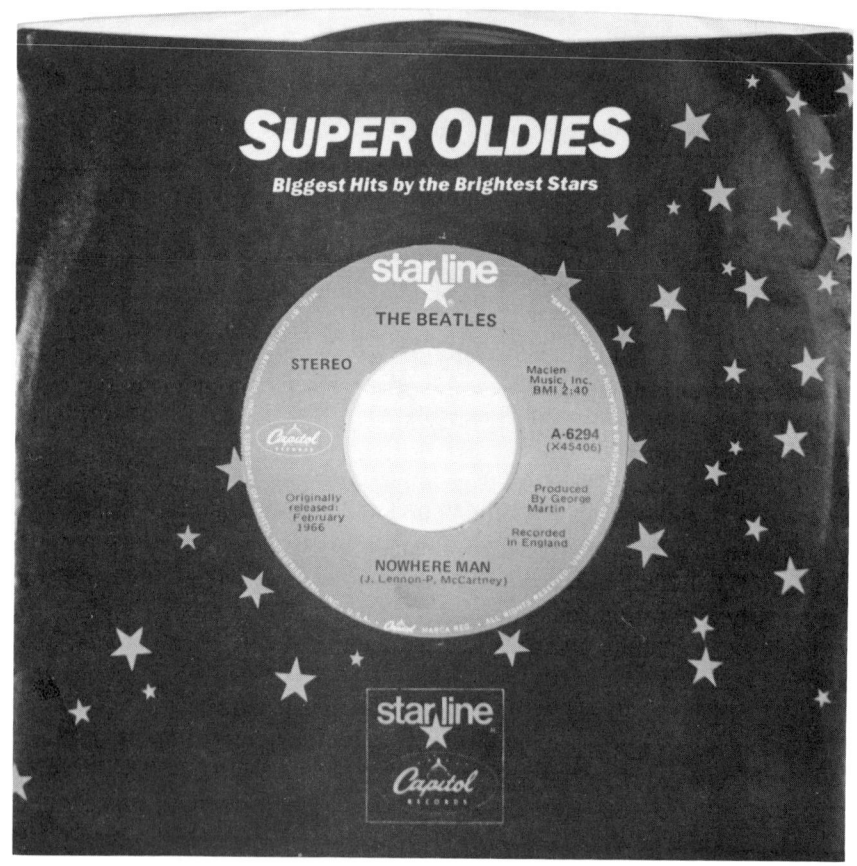

Nowhere Man (Side 1)
(U.S. Blue Starline Edition)

definition on vocals and instruments. Both ends of the frequency spectrum are slightly depressed in level, this being the pressing's only deviation from perfection. The reduction in bass level makes Paul's bass guitar sound distant in relation to the other instruments. The depression at the high end, rather than making the song sound dull, just robs the guitars of their transient "snap."

The US Blue Starline edition, though labelled as being in stereo, is actually mono. Potentially this could have surpassed the Australian in sonic quality, but a problem with distortion prevents that from happening. The slight depression of the frequency extremes found on the Australian disc is absent here. Guitars have their transient "snap" and Paul's bass is not distant-sounding in relation to the other instruments. The mono presentation makes this pressing slightly dense-sounding, however. The downfall in this pressing is in the fact that distortion is present in both the vocals and guitar parts. This distracts the listener from the positive aspects of the wide, balanced frequency response of the song.

Ranking:
Australian
US

NOTE: Two identical U.S. pressings (same master numbers as reviewed above) are available on the purple Starline and black-and-rainbow colorband Starline labels from Capitol.

YESTERDAY

1. (Australia) **The Beatles Singles Collection Australian 20th Anniversary 1962-1982** Parlophone A8173 Master Number A8173A.
2. (Australia) **The Beatles Singles Collection Australian 20th Anniversary 1962-1982** Parlophone A11115 Master Number 7YCE_21783.
3. (England) **The Beatles Singles Collection** Parlophone R6013 Master Number 7YCE_21783-1.
4. (Japan) **The Beatles Singles Collection** Odeon EAS-17333 **Stereo** Master Number 7YCE-21783-U_1S.
5. (US) Blue Starline Edition Capitol A-6291 **Stereo** Master Number (A-6291)_45-45319_J-7.

Note 1: All above say mono or are assumed to be mono unless the label indicates stereo, in which case it is listed above. Note 2: Record 1 above is from the *Yesterday/Act Naturally* pressing, Record

Yesterday (front)
(Australia)

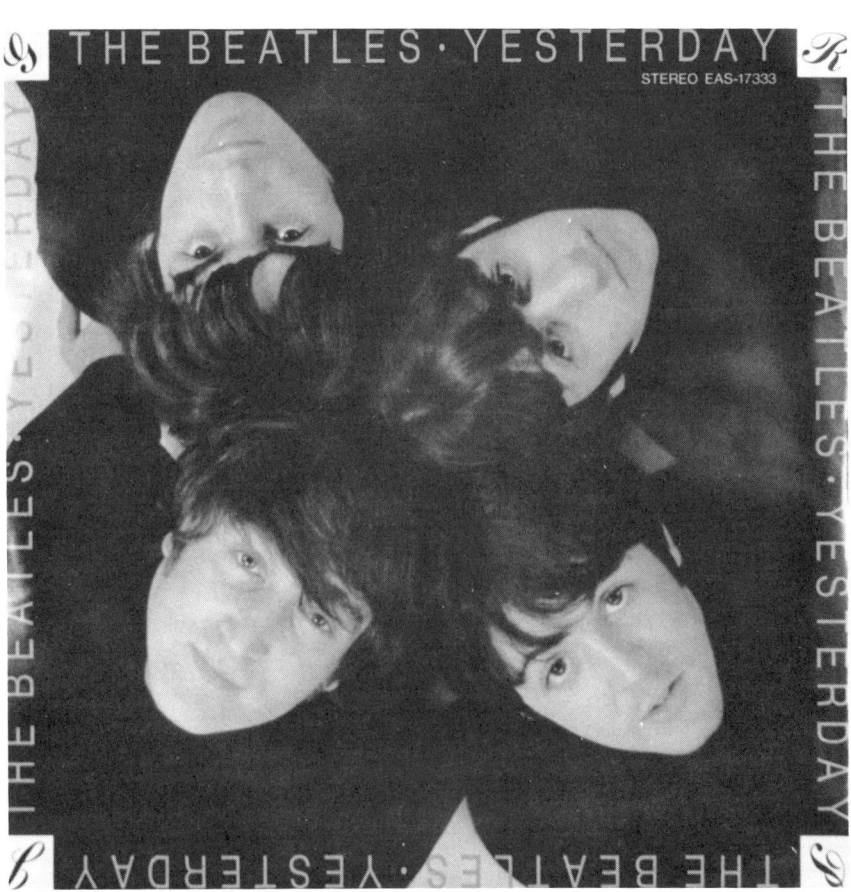
Yesterday (front)
(Japan)

2 is from the *Yesterday/I Should Have Known Better* pressing.

The US Blue Starline edition, labelled as being in stereo, is not. Each of the other four editions reviewed here is, in fact, in true stereo, even though the English and both Australian pressings are not so labelled.

Sonically, *Yesterday* is not a song that easily lends itself to analysis. It is rather simple instrumentally, consisting of an acoustic guitar and a string quartet. Because of this, these five editions sound rather similar. The US Blue Starline pressing is the best of the group; this review will discuss the five editions in the order listed above.

The first Australian pressing, in soundstage, is typical of all the stereo editions. The left channel presents the string quartet, the right channel presents the acoustic guitar, and Paul's voice is in the center. The frequency range is not very extended at either end of the spectrum - this song consists mostly of midrange information. Unfortunately, the midrange presentation is thick and overblown. Paul's voice is "echoey" and "fat" sounding, and at times this song is very overbearing. It is not possible to enjoy this edition at realistic listening levels, and that is a shame. This is one of the few "acoustic" Beatles songs, the kind that should present the "instruments in your listening room" type of sound. In order to enjoy this pressing, due to the extremely "fat" midrange, volume levels must be kept rather low.

The second Australian pressing is almost identical to the first. Only headphone listening reveals the fact that this is slightly less "fat" sounding. Through speakers this sounds every bit as "fat" and overbearing as the first Australian edition.

The English edition, also in stereo, is better than the Australian editions in the sense that it is not so "fat" in the midrange. It is still too prominent in this area, but definitely listenable at realistic levels.

The Japanese pressing, in comparison to the English, is both better and worse. It is better in the fact that definition and extension at the top end is superior. Paul's acoustic guitar sounds sharper and more realistic. It is worse in the fact that the midrange is once again "fat" and overblown. This version is also hard to tolerate at realistic listening levels.

As mentioned previously, the US Blue Starline edition is the best of those reviewed here. High-frequency presentation shares the positive qualities of the Japanese pressing, while the midrange is lean and controlled. Vocals are not "echoey" and are presented forward in the mix. This pressing sounds "lighter" than the others, and because of this it can be enjoyed at high volume levels. Even though this is in mono it is by far superior in sound to all of the other editions.

An Audiophile's Guide to the Sound of the Fab Four

Ranking:
US
Japanese
English
Australian #1
Australian #2

I SHOULD HAVE KNOWN BETTER

1. (Australia) **The Beatles Singles Collection Australian 20th Anniversary 1962-1982** Parlophone A11115 Master Number 7YCE_21784.
2. (England) **The Beatles Singles Collection Australian 20th Anniversary 1962-1982** Parlophone R6013 Master Number 7YCE_21784-1.
3. (Japan) **The Beatles Singles Collection** Odeon EAS-17333 **Stereo** Master Number 7YCE-21784-U_1S.
4. (US) Blue Starline Edition Capitol A-6281 (or X-6281) **Stereo** Master Number (A-6281)_S45-45036_H-7.
   Note: All above say mono or are assumed to be mono unless the label indicates stereo, in which case it is listed above.

The US Blue Starline edition, labelled as being in stereo, is actually mono. Each of the other three pressings reviewed here is in true stereo, although only the Japanese edition is so labelled.

The Australian pressing, typical of the three stereo editions reviewed here, presents most of the instrumentation in the left channel. Vocals are centered in the stereo spread, with the right channel featuring John's harmonica and the electric guitar solo. This is a fairly good-sounding record, with generally balanced sound throughout the entire frequency range. One small problem does exist, however, and that is in the uppermost highs. The very top end is slightly depressed in level, robbing the electric guitar and harmonica of their "bite." This makes these two instruments sound "softer" than would be expected if listening to a live performance. This is not a major problem, however, leaving this a very enjoyable record.

The Japanese edition is not as good as the Australian. It is significantly "lighter" in sound; instruments do not have their characteristic "fullness." What little low frequency information that is present in quite undefined. Paul's bass playing does not sound like individual notes, but more like waves of low-frequency energy. The top end is slightly more extended than the Australian pressing, but this, in conjunction with the reduced bass levels, produces a very "thin" sounding record.

301

The English record is very similar in sound to the Japanese, although the vocal are slightly more clear and up-front in the mix. In overall quality it falls between the Australian and Japanese pressings.

One thing that is troublesome about the stereo editions is the soundstage presentation. If the real goal of stereophonic sound is to more faithfully reproduce an original performance, *I Should Have Known Better* widely misses the mark. An unrealistic as "all words in one channel and all music in the other channel" is (typical of many early Beatles stereo discs), this stereo presentation, to someone familiar with the Beatles' instrumental talents, is incomprehensible. George's electric 12-string guitar is presented mostly in the right channel, with John's acoustic guitar being mostly in the left. Yet when John plays the harmonica, it appears in the right. How can John play instruments in both of the stereo channels? This type of stereo "game playing" is very upsetting and detracts from the overall realism of the song.

The US Blue Starline edition, although the only mono pressing in the group, sounds the best. Bass presentation is good, being very similar to the Australian edition. The top end is the most extended of all, making Ringo's drumming more prominent and restoring the "bite" to the harmonica. The electric guitar solo is visceral in its realism, and is quite ear-catching. Vocals are clear and further forward in the mix than on any of the other pressings.

>Ranking:
>US
>Australian
>English
>Japanese

NOTE: Two identical U.S. pressings (same master numbers as reviewed above) are available on the purple Starline and black-and-rainbow colorband Starline labels from Capitol.

Ratings Summaries

The two tables that follow summarize all of the reviews above by coverting the rankings assigned into numerical points. Lower average points result in a better score. Points were awarded on the following basis:

        First   = 1 point
        Second = 2 points
        Third   = 3 points
        Fourth = 4 points
        Fifth   = 5 points

In case of ties, the points for the tied positions are totalled and shared among the tied countries. For example, if two countries are tied for first, the points for first and second are totalled and shared: 1 plus 2 equals 3; each country is awarded 1.5 points.

Singles Package Comparisons

Song Title	\<Country of Origin\>					
	Aus.	Eng.	Fra.	Jap.	US	Can.
Love Me Do	3	2	-	1	4	-
P.S. I Love You	-	2	4	1	3	-
Please Please Me	3	2	-	1	1	-
Ask Me Why	2	3	-	1	-	-
From Me To You	2	3	-	1	-	-
Thank You Girl	2	1	-	3	-	-
She Loves You	4	1	3	2	-	-
I'll Get You	2	3	4	1	-	-
I Want To Hold Your Hand	2	5	-	1	3&4	-
This Boy	-	3	-	2	-	1
Can't Buy Me Love	3 (tie)	3 (tie)	-	1 (tie)	1 (tie)	-
You Can't Do That	1 (tie)	1 (tie)	-	3 (tie)	3 (tie)	-
A Hard Day's Night	3	2	-	1	4	-
Things We Said Today	3	1	-	2	-	-
I Feel Fine	2	4	-	1	3	-
She's A Woman	2	3	-	1	4	-
Ticket To Ride	4	1	-	2	3	-
Yes It Is	4	1	-	3	2	-
Help!	3	2	-	4	1	-
I'm Down	4	3	-	2	1	-
We Can Work It Out	4	1	-	2	3	-
Day Tripper	2	3	-	1	4	-
Paperback Writer	4	3	-	2	1	-
Rain	3	4	-	2	1	-
Yellow Submarine	4	3	-	2	1	-
Eleanor Rigby	3	4	-	2	1	-
Strawberry Fields Forever	4	3	-	1	2	-
Penny Lane	4	3	-	1	2	-
All You Need Is Love	4	3	-	1	2	-
Baby, You're A Rich Man	4	1	-	2	3	-
Hello Goodbye	4	3	-	1	2	-

An Audiophile's Guide to the Sound of the Fab Four

	Aus.	Eng.	Fra.	Jap.	US	Can.
I Am The Walrus	3	2	-	1	4	-
Lady Madonna	4	3	-	1	2	-
The Inner Light	4	1 (tie)	-	1 (tie)	3	-
Hey Jude	4	1 (tie)	-	3	1 (tie)	-
Revolution	4	1 (tie)	-	3	1 (tie)	-
Get Back	4	2	-	1	3	-
Don't Let Me Down	4	2	-	1	3	-
The Ballad of John & Yoko	4	1 (tie)	-	1 (tie)	3	-
Old Brown Shoe	4	2	-	1	3	-
Something	2	3	-	1	4	-
Come Together	4	1 (tie)	-	1 (tie)	4	-
Let It Be	4	2 (tie)	-	1	2 (tie)	-
You Know My Name	N/R	N/R	N/R	N/R	N/R	N/R*
Back In The USSR	-	2	-	1	-	-
Twist And Shout	-	2 (tie)	-	1	2 (tie)	-
Sgt. Pepper's Lonely Hearts Club Band/ With A Little Help From My Friends	4	3	-	1 (tie)	1 (tie)	-
A Day In The Life	4	3	-	1	2	-
The Beatles' Movie Medley	3	2	-	1	-	-
I'm Happy Just To Dance With You	4	2	-	1	3	-
The Long and Winding Road	2	-	-	-	1	-
For You Blue	2	-	-	-	1	-
Act Naturally	2	-	-	-	1	-
I Saw Her Standing There	2	-	-	-	1&3	-
Nowhere Man	1	-	-	-	2	-
Yesterday	4&5	3	-	2	1	-
I Should Have Known Better	2	3	-	4	1	-
Number of Records	53	51	3	51	49	1
Total Points	170	122.5	11	82	114.5	1
Average Per Record*	3.21	2.40	3.67	1.61	2.34	1.00

*N/R = No rating.
**Lower average denotes more highly rated records overall.

Individual Singles Comparisons

Song Title	1	2	3	4	5
Love Me Do	Jap.	Eng.	Aus.	US	-
P.S. I Love You	Jap.	Eng.	US	Fra.	-
Please Please Me	Jap.	Eng.	Aus.	-	-
Ask Me Why	Jap.	Aus.	Eng.	-	-
From Me To You	Jap.	Aus.	Eng.	-	-
Thank You Girl	Eng.	Aus.	Jap.	-	-
She Loves You	Eng.	Jap.	Fra.	Aus.	-
I'll Get You	Jap.	Aus.	Eng.	Fra.	-
I Want To Hold Your Hand	Jap.	Aus.	US	US	-
This Boy	Can.	Jap.	Eng.	-	-
Can't Buy Me Love	Jap.	-	Aus.	-	-
	US	-	Eng.	-	-
You Can't Do That	Aus.	-	Jap.	-	-
	Eng.	-	US	-	-
A Hard Day's Night	Jap.	Eng.	Aus.	US	-
Things We Said Today	Eng.	Jap.	Aus.	-	-
I Feel Fine	Jap.	Aus.	US	Eng.	-
She's A Woman	Jap.	Aus.	Eng.	US	-
Ticket To Ride	Eng.	Jap.	US	Aus.	-
Yes It Is	Eng.	US	Jap.	Aus.	-
Help!	US	Eng.	Aus.	Jap.	-
I'm Down	US	Jap.	Eng.	Aus.	-
We Can Work It Out	Eng.	Jap.	US	Aus.	-
Day Tripper	Jap.	Aus.	Eng.	US	-
Paperback Writer	US	Jap.	Eng.	Aus.	-
Rain	US	Jap.	Aus.	Eng.	-
Yellow Submarine	US	Jap.	Eng.	Aus.	-
Eleanor Rigby	US	Jap.	Aus.	Eng.	-
Strawberry Fields Forever	Jap.	US	Eng.	Aus.	-
Penny Lane	Jap.	US	Eng.	Aus.	-
All You Need Is Love	Jap.	US	Eng.	Aus.	-
Baby, You're A Rich Man	Eng.	Jap.	US	Aus.	-
Hello Goodbye	Jap.	US	Eng.	Aus.	-

An Audiophile's Guide to the Sound of the Fab Four

	1	2	3	4	5
I Am The Walrus	Jap.	Eng.	Aus.	US	-
Lady Madonna	Jap.	US	Eng.	Aus.	-
The Inner Light	Jap.(tie) - Eng.(tie) -	-	US -	Aus. -	- -
Hey Jude	Eng.(tie) - US (tie) -	-	Jap. -	Aus. -	- -
Revolution	Jap.(tie)US Eng.(tie) -		Aus. -	- -	- -
Get Back	Jap.	Eng.	US	Aus.	-
Don't Let Me Down	Jap.	Eng.	US	Aus.	-
The Ballad of John & Yoko	Eng.(tie) - Jap.(tie) -		US -	Aus. -	- -
Old Brown Shoe	Jap.	Eng.	US	Aus.	-
Something	Jap.	Aus.	Eng.	US	-
Come Together	Eng.(tie) - Jap.(tie) -		Aus. -	US -	- -
Let It Be	Jap. -	Eng.(tie) US (tie)	- -	Aus. -	- -
You Know My Name	N/R	N/R	N/R	N/R	N/R*
Back In The USSR	Jap.	Eng.	-	-	-
Twist And Shout	Jap. -	US (tie) Eng.(tie)-	-	-	-
Sgt. Pepper's Lonely Hearts Club Band/ With A Little Help From My Friends	US Jap.	- -	- Eng.	- Aus.	- -
A Day In The Life	Jap.	US	Eng.	Aus.	-
The Beatles' Movie Medley	Jap.	Eng.	Aus.	-	-
I'm Happy Just To Dance With You	Jap.	Eng.	US	Aus.	-
The Long and Winding Road	US	Aus.	-	-	-
For You Blue	US	Aus.	-	-	-
Act Naturally	US	Aus.	-	-	-
I Saw Her Standing There	US20th	Aus.	US	-	-
Nowhere Man	Aus.	US	-	-	-
Yesterday	US	Jap.	Eng.	Aus.	Aus.
I Should Have Known Better	US	Aus.	Eng.	Jap.	-

*N/R = No rating.

Summary Of Individual Single Comparisons

Number Of Singles Per Position

Country	First	Second	Third	Fourth	Fifth
Australia	2	14	12	24	1
England	13	14	20	3	0
France	0	0	1	2	0
Japan	33	12	4	2	0
US	15	11	14	8	0
Canada	1	0	0	0	0

About Record Care

It cannot be stressed strenuously enough the value and importance of keeping your vinyl records and phono stylus scrupulously clean. As well as allowing for proper high fidelity playback, good audio system hygiene will help preserve your valued Beatles collection.

The use of "rice paper" type sleeves for vinyl records, such as the V.R.P. by Discwasher and the Original Master Sleeve by Mobile Fidelity Sound Labs, are invaluable in protecting those fragile records surfaces from the ravages of the normal paper inner sleeve provided by your friendly local record company.

About The Equipment

The audio equipment used in the review process for this book consisted of the following:
Phase Linear Model 8000 Series II turntable
Orsonic AV-1 resonace-cancelling headshell
Micro-Acoustics 530 MP phono cartridge
Orsonic DS-250 disc stabilizer
Monitor Audio POD disc clamping device
Carver Corporation C-2 preamplifier
Carver Corporation M-400t power amplifier
Carver Corporation M-1.0t power amplifier
Ohm Acoustics Model F coherent sound loudspeakers
Stax, Inc. Model SRX III/SRD 7 electrostatic headphone system
Monster Cable speaker cables
Watts, Inc. and Discwasher, Inc. record and stylus cleaning products

Glossary

A Capella Singing without musical accompaniment.

Acetate An aluminum disc coated with acetate that is cut from tape for use as a reference record. Acetates are generally used by performers, producers, and publishers, and are not intended for general release. Acetates were sometimes cut for the Beatles when they wanted to take home copies of the day's studio work. (Remember, the cassette was not a true high fidelity recording medium in the sixties.)

Bass The low frequency portion of the audio spectrum, occupied by such instruments as the electric bass guitar, bass drum, upright acoustic bass, and others.

BBC An acronym for the British Broadcasting Corporation, the government-sponsored radio and television networks in the U.K.

Beatlefan A Beatles fanzine run by William King. It is published bi-monthly, and is currently in its twelfth year of existence. For information contact: The Goody Press, P.O. Box 33515, Decatur, Georgia 30033.

Bootleg An illegal record, tape, or CD that contains material never before, and/or not intended for commercial release by the artist. Bootleg recordings can take on many form, such as recordings of live concerts, radio or TV specials originally made for broadcast only and not for sale, or outtakes from studio sessions.

Bottom The lower or bass portion of the audio range.

CD This acronym of Compact Disc refers to the 4.72-inch or 3-inch disc containing digitized music stored in the industry-standard compact disc format as developed by Phillips of Holland. The music is digitally stored as 44,100 sixteen-bit words per channel per second. Playback is accomplished via laser beam reading of the depressions ("pits") in a metallized layer beneath the disc's polycarbonate outer surface.

Counterfeit An illegal record, tape, or CD that duplicates a legitimate release as closely as possible. Counterfeit records are analogous to counterfeit money; that is, designed to be indistinguishable from the real thing, although actually worthless.

Dark Sound that is lacking in high frequency extension.

Decibel (dB) A unit of intensity of sound, equal to twenty times the common logarithm of the ratio of the pressure produced by the sound wave to a reference pressure. In simple terms, if a sound seems twice as loud as another sound, its intensity is 10dB greater.

Definition Sonic precision; the ability for the listener to detect the details of a recording. A record with good definition allows the listener to distinguish each of the individual instruments and each note produced by those instruments.

DEMO Short for "demonstration." This refers to what is usually a rough or sparsely instrumented recording of a song performed by the writer to demonstrate how the song should be performed.

DISTORTION   Any unwanted sound in a recording.

DUB   A tape that is copied from another tape or disc. Because it doesn't originate from the master, sonic quality is usually compromised.

ECHO   The repetition of a sound usually produced by the reflection of sound waves from a surface. On records, echo can be added electronically or in an acoustic chamber with very reflective walls.

EP   This acronym of Extended Play refers to a seven-inch record with more material on it than a standard single. In America and England, this meant four songs pressed at 45 rpm. In Japan, this meant four songs pressed at 45 rpm or 33 1/3 rpm.

EXTENSION   In sound, extension refers to the upper and lower ends of the frequency spectrum - the low bass and the upper treble. A record with good extension at both ends possesses both firm, solid bass and light, airy treble.

FLEXI-DISC A record pressed on very thin flexible vinyl. The Beatles' Christmas messages were sent as flexi-discs to UK fan club members every Christmas from 1963 through 1969, and to US fan club members every Christmas from 1964 through 1969.

FREQUENCY BALANCE   The ratio of high to low frequencies in a recording. A well-balanced recording presents all frequencies in their proper proportions. A lightweight recording is balanced toward the treble (either because of too much treble or too little bass), and a heavyweight recording is balanced toward the bass (either because of too much bass or not enough treble).

FREQUENCY RESPONSE   The range of sounds produced, such as by a piece of audio equipment or by a record. The frequency response is expressed as a range of values with an accuracy tolerance, such as 20 Hz - 20000 Hz +/- 3dB (decibels).

FUNDAMENTAL   The main frequency of a note produced by a musical instrument. For example, pianos are tuned so that A above middle C has a fundamental frequency of 440 Hz.

GOOD DAY SUNSHINE   A Beatles fanzine run by Charles Rosenay!!! It is published bi-monthly and has been in existence for almost ten years. For information contact: Charles Rosenay!!! 397 Edgewood Avenue, New Haven, CT 06511

HARMONIC   See OVERTONE.

HERTZ (Hz) The term used for the unit by which frequency is measured. (Same as cycles per second.)

HISS An extraneous sound on a record, tape, or CD that sounds just as it (hiss) is produced. Hiss can occur due to worn-out records, bad radio reception, multiple-generation copying of tapes, etc.

LP This acronym of Long Playing refers to the twelve-inch album. It is a registered trademark.

MASTER LACQUER A lacquer-coated metal disc cut (on a cutting lathe) from the master tape. This is the first step in the creation of vinyl records.

MASTER NUMBER Sometimes referred to as MATRIX NUMBER, this is the number stamped or scratched in the flat area around the record's label. This number signifies both the code number of the tape (or copy of the tape) used as the record's source, and also the cutting number of the master lacquer that ultimately led to the pressed record.

MASTER TAPE The first generation of a final performance used for cutting the master lacquer or generating the digital master for CDs. The master tape is usually created by mixing together the tracks of a multi-track recording.

MATRIX NUMBER See MASTER NUMBER.

MIDRANGE The middle frequency range of the audio spectrum, containing the findamentals of most instruments.

MIX The blending of live and/or recorded tracks to produce a final version (final mix) of a song. The term thus applies both to a process, and the product of that process. See also OVERDUB, part of the process of mixing.

MONO Short for Monophonic, a recording technique utilizing only one channel of sound. A monophonic recording played on stereophonic equipment will present the same sounds from both the left and right speakers, creating an apparent image that is centered between the speakers.

OUTTAKE Literally, an out take. A take (the performance of all or part of a song) not used as part of the final recording that gets released. In many cases outtakes are thrown out or erased by recording studios; those outtakes that do survive are highly sought after by bootleggers.

OVERDUB An additional part to a song recorded separately from the basic track. Currently, most rock recordings are created by laying down a basic rhythm track, and then adding a dozen or more overdubs. See MIX above.

OVERTONE Also known as harmonics, overtones are multiples of a findamental frequency produced by a musical instrument. The overtones are what differentiate the sounds of musical instruments; two different instruments playing the same note (fundamental) will sound different because they produce different mixtures of overtones.

PICTURE DISC A seven- or twelve-inch record with a photograph or drawing beneath the grooves. The clear vinyl layer containing the grooves that overlays the picture is usually very thin and subject to wear. It is not recommended that picture discs be played very often.

PIRATE An illegal record, tape, or CD that contains commercially released material. Pirate recordings, although similar to counterfeits, are different in execution. Whereas a counterfeit tries to pass as the real thing, a pirate does not. Although the recorded material in a pirate is a direct copy (or "dub") of a legitimate commercial release, the album cover and packaging is not.

POP   An extraneous sound on a record that sounds just as it (pop) is pronounced. Pops usually occur due to excessive wear or mishandling, such as failure to clean a record before playing it.

PROMO   A promotional copy of a record, tape, or CD that is given away by record companies. In some cases, promo items contain versions of songs not available to the general public, such as special remixes or edits.

RE-MIX A tape created by mixing together the tracks of a multi-track recording. A re-mix is usually a mix that is different from one that was previously released.

REPROCESSED STEREO   Electronically created stereo from a monaural recording. This is usually accomplished by boosting the bass in one channel, and boosting the treble in the other.

SIBILANTS   Words characterized by a hissing sound, such as "this," "rose," "pressure," "pleasure," and certain similar uses of the letters "s," "sh," "z," "zh," etc.

SOUNDTRACK   Refers to the audio portion of television, film, or video tape. Originally, this referred specifically to the magnetic track on film where the accompanying sound was recorded.

STEREO   Short for Stereophonic, a recording technique utilizing two channels of sound. A stereophonic recording played on stereophonic equipment can present different sounds from the left and right speakers. A stereophonic recording is capable, when correctly done, of presenting a three-dimensional sonic image possessing width, height, and depth.

STRAWBERRY FIELDS FOREVER   A Beatles fanzine run by Joe Pope, it has been published somewhat erratically since the late seventies. For information contact: Joe Pope at 310 Franklin Street, #117, Boston, MA 02110.

TICK   An extraneous sound on a record that sounds just as it (tick) is pronounced. Ticks usually occur due to excessive wear or mishandling, such as failure to clean a record before playing it.

TOP   The upper or treble portion of the audio range.

TRACK   The path of recorded information on a record, tape, or CD, broken into separate, successive songs or other segments (hence, the "tracks" on an album, etc.).

TRANSIENT   The sharp leading edge of a sound wave, also known as the attack of a sound. Examples include the pluck of an acoustic guitar, the impact of a stick on a drum, etc.

TREBLE   The high frequency range of the audio spectrum, containing the overtones of most instruments.

UNDERGROUND Any illegal recording, be it bootleg, pirate, or counterfeit.

VEILED Sound that is not clear; analogous to looking through a veil. Details are lost and transients are softened.

Song & Record Title Index

Abbey

Abbey Road (CD)
111
Abbey Road (LP)
47, 51, 111, 112, 177
Abbey Road Show 1983 (CD)
41
Abilene (song)
117
Across The Universe (song)
37, 55, 92, 107, 109
Act Naturally (song)
83, 85, 87, 103, 292, 294, 297, 305, 307
Ain't Nothing Shakin (song)
89
All Along The Watchtower (song)
93
All I Have To Do Is Dream (song)
134
All I Want For Christmas Is A Bottle (song)
137
All I Want To Do (song)
94
All My Loving (song)
34, 47, 49, 55, 57, 61, 62, 81, 83, 137, 138, 139, 141
All Shook Up (song)
93
All Things Must Pass (song)
32, 93, 109
All You Need (song)
65
All You Need Is Love (song)
113, 114, 156, 157, 158, 180, 245, 288, 304, 306
Almost Grown (song)
94, 97
And I Love Her (song)
143, 145
Anna (song)
28, 71
Anna (Go To Him) (song)
125, 126
Ask Me Why (song)
28, 116, 117, 133, 179, 190, 193, 304, 306
Autumn Leaves (song)
134
Baby It's You (song)
123, 124

Beatles

Baby, You're A Rich Man (song)
55, 180, 246, 248, 304, 306
Baby's In Black (song)
64, 88, 103
Back In The USSR (song)
277, 305, 307
Back Seat Of My Car (song)
94, 97
Back To Commonwealth (song)
39
Back Track (CD)
152
Bad Boy (song)
94
Bad To Me (song)
74, 75, 77
Ballad (song)
65
The Ballad Of John And Yoko (song)
180, 265, 267, 269, 270, 305, 307
Band On The Run (LP)
47
Be Bop A Lula (song)
37, 92, 109
Beatle Chat (LP track)
137
The Beatles (EP)
217
The Beatles (2 LPs)
109
The Beatles At Shea (LP)
103, 168, 171
The Beatles At The BEEB (13-LP series)
116, 117, 121, 123, 124, 125, 126, 128, 130, 133, 135, 138, 139, 143, 146, 147
The Beatles At The BEEB Volume 1 (CD)
123
The Beatles At The BEEB Volume 1 (LP)
120, 169, 170
The Beatles At The BEEB Volume 2 (CD)
125
The Beatles At The BEEB Volume 2 (LP)
123, 169, 170
The Beatles At The BEEB Volume 3 (CD)
126

315

SONG & RECORD TITLE INDEX

Beatles

The Beatles At The BEEB Volume 3 (LP)
125, 169, 170
The Beatles At The BEEB Volume 4 (CD)
129
The Beatles At The BEEB Volume 4 (LP)
128, 129, 169, 170
The Beatles At The BEEB Volume 5 (CD)
132
The Beatles At The BEEB Volume 5 (LP)
130, 169, 170
The Beatles At The BEEB Volume 6 (CD)
134
The Beatles At The BEEB Volume 6 (LP)
132, 169, 170
The Beatles At The BEEB Volume 7 (CD)
135
The Beatles At The BEEB Volume 7 (LP)
134, 169, 171
The Beatles At The BEEB Volume 8 (CD)
138
The Beatles At The BEEB Volume 8 (LP)
137, 138, 169, 170
The Beatles At The BEEB Volume 9 (CD)
141
The Beatles At The BEEB Volume 9 (LP)
139, 141, 169, 171
The Beatles At The BEEB Volume 10 (CD)
143
The Beatles At The BEEB Volume 10 (LP)
141, 169, 171
The Beatles At The BEEB Volume 11 (CD)
145
The Beatles At The BEEB Volume 11 (LP)
143, 169, 170
The Beatles At The BEEB Volume 12 (CD)
146
The Beatles At The BEEB Volume 12 (LP)
145, 169, 170
The Beatles At The BEEB Volume 13 (CD)
149

Beatles

The Beatles At The BEEB Volume 13 (LP)
147, 149, 169, 171
The Beatles Broadcasts (LP)
54, 168, 170
The Beatles Budokan 1966 (LP)
87, 168, 171
The Beatles By Royal Command (EP)
21, 166, 167
The Beatles Christmas Album (LP)
3
The Beatles Collection (England - box set)
177
The Beatles Collector's Items (LP)
4, 55, 168, 170
The Beatles Conquer America (2 LPs)
81, 168, 170
The Beatles EP Collection (box set)
217
Beatles Farewell To Miami (LP track)
83
The Beatles Greatest Vol II (LP)
217
The Beatles Live At Abbey Road Studios (2 LPs)
39, 168, 170, 75
The Beatles Live At The Star Club In Hamburg, Germany, 1962 (LP)
89
The Beatles Mach Shau! (LP)
89, 168, 171
The Beatles Movie Medley (12-inch promo)
84
The Beatles' Movie Medley (45 rpm)
286, 288, 305, 307
Beatles: Not Guilty (LP)
168, 171
The Beatles On Stage In Japan - The 1966 Tour (LP)
64, 88, 168, 170
The Beatles Open-End Interview (LP track)
81
The Beatles Rarities (LP)
30, 47, 55, 57, 62, 114, 150
The Beatles Second Album (LP)
26
The Beatles Singles Collection (Australia - box set)
180, 183, 185, 187, 188, 190, 193, 195, 197, 198, 199, 203, 205, 208, 211, 212, 214, 215, 219, 221, 223, 225, 227, 229, 231, 233, 235, 237, 240, 242, 245, 246, 249, 251, 253, 255, 257, 259, 262, 264, 265, 267, 270, 272, 274, 276, 277, 281, 285, 286, 288, 290, 292, 294, 295, 297, 301

SONG & RECORD TITLE INDEX

The Beatles Singles Collection
(England - box set)
180, 183, 185, 188, 190, 193, 195,
197, 198, 199, 203, 205, 208, 211,
212, 214, 215, 219, 221, 223, 225,
227, 229, 231, 233, 235, 237, 240,
242, 245, 246, 249, 251, 253, 255,
257, 259, 262, 264, 265, 267, 270,
272, 274, 276, 277, 280, 281, 285,
286, 288, 290, 294, 295, 297, 301

The Beatles Singles Collection (Japan
- box set)
180, 183, 185, 188, 190, 193, 195,
197, 198, 199, 203, 205, 208, 211,
212, 214, 215, 219, 221, 223, 225,
227, 229, 231, 233, 235, 237, 240,
242, 245, 246, 249, 251, 253, 255,
257, 259, 262, 264, 265, 267, 270,
272, 274, 276, 277, 280, 281, 285,
286, 288, 290, 294, 295, 297, 301

The Beatles Stockholm & Blackpool
(LP)
85, 168, 170

The Beatles/The Collection (U.S. -
box set)
40

Beautiful Dreamer (LP)
49, 168, 171

Beautiful Dreamer (song)
50, 116

Because (song)
40, 111, 112, 156, 157, 159

Besame Mucho (song)
18, 67, 73, 102, 103, 116, 117, 149,
152, 166, 167

Birthday (song)
77, 79

The Black Album (3 LPs)
96, 108, 169, 170

Blackbird (song)
51

Blowin In The Wind (song)
93

Blue Jay Way (song)
47, 113

Blue Suede Shoes (song)
75, 93

Bound By Love (song)
58, 59

Boys (song)
36, 71, 83, 120, 120, 121, 123, 124,
125, 126, 133, 137, 138, 143

Bring It On Home (song)
93

Brown Shoes (song)
65

By Royal Command (EP)
21, 166, 167

Can You Dig It! (song)
95, 97

Can't Buy Me Love (song)
43, 49, 61, 103, 106, 107, 108, 139,
141, 142, 149, 152, 180, 205, 206,
208, 304, 306

Carol (song)
54, 55, 125, 126

Carry That Weight (song)
51, 111, 112

Casualties (LP)
45, 168, 170

Catswalk (song)
77

Cha Cha Cha (song)
67

Chains (song)
71, 123, 124, 125, 126, 133

Child Of Nature (song)
159, 160

Christmas Record 1963 (LP track)
57

Christmas Record 1964 (LP track)
57

Christmas Record 1965 (LP track)
57

Christmas Record 1966 (LP track)
57

Christmas Record 1967 (LP track)
58

Christmas Record 1968 (LP track)
58

Christmas Record 1969 (LP track)
58

Christmastime (Is Here Again) (song)
74, 99, 101, 102, 107, 113, 114

Clarabella (song)
54, 55, 125, 126

Come And Get It (song)
74, 75, 101, 102

Come Together (song)
180, 272, 305, 307

Commonwealth (song)
91, 108

The Continuing Story Of Bungalow
Bill (song)
159, 160

Copper Path (song)
67

Cry Baby Cry (song)
159, 160

Crying, Waiting, Hoping (song)
18, 43, 58, 59, 61, 73, 128, 129, 166,
167

A Day In The Life (song)
40, 77, 113, 113, 114, 157, 285, 305,
307

Day Tripper (song)
45, 64, 87, 88, 150, 152, 153, 154,
156, 180, 229, 304, 306

Dear Prudence (song)
159, 160

317

SONG & RECORD TITLE INDEX

The Decca Tapes (LP)
73, 79, 168, 170
Derrick Rudy Interviews the Beatles (LP track)
81
Devil In Her Heart (song)
130, 132, 133
Dig A Pony (song)
94
Dig It (CD)
108
Dig It (LP)
106, 114, 168, 170
Dig It (song)
57, 97, 107, 108
Dizzy Miss Lizzy (song)
68, 103
Dizzie Miss Lizzy (song)
147
Do You Want To Know A Secret (song)
54, 61, 62, 68, 77, 79, 120, 121, 123, 124, 128, 129, 153, 154
Domino (song)
92, 109
Don't Bother Me (song)
40
Don't Ever Change (song)
130, 132
Don't Let Me Down (song)
37, 67, 92, 93, 95, 96, 108, 109, 180, 264, 265, 305, 307
Don't Let Me Down (Reprise) (song)
37
Don't Pass Me By (2 LPs)
57, 168, 171
Down In Mississippi (song)
94
Dream Baby (song)
116, 117
Early In The Morning (song)
92, 109
Early In The Morning - Hi Ho Silver (song)
30
Eleanor Rigby (song)
180, 237, 304, 306
EMI Outtakes (LP)
47, 168, 171
Every Night (song)
94, 97
Everybody's Got Something To Hide Except Me And My Monkey (song)
160
Everybody's Trying To Be My Baby (song)
54, 89, 123, 124, 141, 142, 145, 146, 147
Everyone Loves Someone (song)
58

Everyone Wants Someone (song)
59
Exclusive! Beatles Interviews 1966 (EP)
24, 166, 167
The Fab Four On Film (LP track)
83
Fans in front of Plaza Hotel, Manhattan (LP track)
137
File Under: Beatles (LP)
74, 79, 114, 168, 170
A Fool Like Me (song)
32, 93, 109
The Fool On The Hill (song)
113, 114, 149, 152, 152
Fools Rush In (song)
134
For You Blue (song)
39, 92, 95, 108, 292, 305, 307
From Me To You (song)
21, 41, 49, 55, 61, 62, 71, 77, 80, 83, 85, 116, 120, 121, 123, 124, 133, 134, 135, 137, 149, 152, 179, 193, 304, 306
From Us To You (10-inch EP)
34, 166, 167
From Us To You (song)
137, 138, 139, 141, 142, 143
From Us To You (Version 1) (song)
34
From Us To You (Version 2) (song)
36
Futting Around (song)
30, 166, 167
George Harrison (LP)
80
Get Back (LP)
96, 97
Get Back (song)
37, 39, 75, 92, 94, 95, 97, 108, 180, 262, 264, 288, 305, 307
Get Back (Reprise) (song)
96
The Get Back Journals (11 LPs)
91, 96, 97, 111, 112, 168, 170
Gimme Some Truth (song)
93, 96
Glad All Over (song)
50, 58, 59, 130, 132
Golden Slumbers (song)
51, 111, 112
Good Rocking Tonight (song)
37, 92, 109
Goodbye (song)
75, 77, 160
The Guitar Bop (song)
161
Hahst Az Sun (2 LPs)
37, 168, 170

SONG & RECORD TITLE INDEX

Hallelujah

Hallelujah, I Love Her So (song)
 161
Happy Birthday (song)
 134
Happy Birthday Paul (song)
 125, 126
A Hard Day's Night (song)
 24, 36, 40, 45, 62, 103, 143, 145,
 150, 152, 180, 211, 212, 214, 288,
 304, 306
Hare Krishna (song)
 92, 109
Hare Krishna Mantra (song)
 30
Have You Heard The Word (LP)
 67, 168, 171
Have You Heard The Word (song)
 30, 67, 68, 166, 167
Heather (song)
 51
Hello Goodbye (song)
 40, 157, 158, 159, 180, 249, 251,
 304, 306
Hello Little Girl (song)
 10, 73, 161, 163, 166, 167
Help (song)
 55, 83, 85, 94, 106, 153, 156, 180,
 223, 224, 304, 306
Help (Instrumental) (song)
 40
Her Majesty (song)
 45, 51, 54, 111, 112
Here Comes The Sun (song)
 26
Hey Darling (song)
 161
Hey Jude (LP)
 81
Hey Jude (song)
 40, 62, 64, 67, 99, 101, 157, 158,
 159, 180, 257, 305, 307
Hi Ho Silver (song)
 39, 92, 108, 109
High Heeled Sneakers (song)
 37, 92, 94, 109
Hippy Hippy Shake (song)
 54, 59, 68, 93, 116, 117, 119, 128,
 129, 133, 134, 139
Hitchhike (song)
 93
Hold Me Tight (CD)
 156
Hold Me Tight (song)
 153, 154, 156
Homeward Bound (song)
 26
Honey Don't (song)
 71, 73, 130, 132, 142, 143, 145, 146,
 147

Honey Pie (song)
 160
The Honeymoon Song (song)
 50, 128, 129
House Of The Rising Sun (song)
 39, 91, 108
How Do You Do (song)
 51
How Do You Do It (song)
 7, 39, 77, 79, 102, 149, 150, 166,
 167
I Am The Walrus (song)
 45, 47, 55, 113, 150, 152, 180, 251,
 305, 307
I Call Your Name (song)
 141
I Dig A Pony (song)
 75, 94, 95
I Feel Fine (song)
 54, 55, 64, 83, 85, 88, 103, 145, 146,
 153, 156, 180, 214, 304, 306
I Forgot To Remember (song)
 59
I Forgot To Remember To Forget
 (song)
 68, 142
I Got A Woman (song)
 54, 58, 59, 130, 132, 141, 142
I Got To Find My Baby (song)
 49, 123, 124, 124
I Had A Dream (song)
 94
I Hate To See (song)
 157
I Just Don't Understand (song)
 58, 59, 59, 61, 130, 132
I Me Mine (song)
 37, 67, 74, 77, 92, 95, 109
I Saw Her Standing There (song)
 34, 39, 41, 71, 83, 84, 85, 87, 116,
 116, 120, 120, 121, 123, 125, 126,
 133, 134, 135, 137, 138, 141, 142,
 149, 150, 153, 154, 294, 305, 307
I Shall Be Released (song)
 93, 94
I Should Have Known Better (song)
 36, 143, 145, 231, 288, 300, 301,
 302, 305, 307
I Threw It All Away (song)
 92, 109
I Wanna Be Your Man (song)
 47, 64, 80, 88, 106, 107, 108, 139,
 141
I Wanna Hold Your Hand (song)
 137, 138, 139
I Want To Hold Your Hand (song)
 34, 45, 49, 61, 77, 80, 83, 84, 138,
 180, 199, 205, 304, 306
I Want You (She's So Heavy) (song)
 107

SONG & RECORD TITLE INDEX

If I Fell (song)
36, 143, 145
If I Needed Someone (song)
64, 65, 87, 88
If You've Got Troubles (song)
75, 77, 102, 149, 150
I'll Always Be In Love With You (song)
161
I'll Be On My Way (song)
106, 107, 120, 121, 123
I'll Cry Instead (song)
45
I'll Follow The Sun (song)
54, 145, 146, 161, 163
I'll Get You (song)
50, 61, 130, 133, 180, 198, 199, 304, 306
I'm A Loser (song)
40, 54, 83, 145, 146, 147, 149
I'm An Opulent Man (song)
65
I'm Down (song)
55, 57, 65, 83, 85, 87, 88, 103, 106, 180, 225, 304, 306
I'm Gonna Sit Right Down And Cry (song)
59
I'm Gonna Sit Right Down And Cry Over You (song)
50, 58, 128, 129
I'm Happy Just To Dance With You (song)
36, 143, 145, 288, 289, 305, 307
I'm Laid (song)
65
I'm Looking Through You (song)
40, 101, 102, 103, 149, 150
I'm Only Sleeping (song)
45, 99, 101
I'm So Tired (song)
74, 93, 159, 160
I'm Sure To Fall (song)
58, 59, 71
I'm Talking About You (song)
49, 116
I'm Walking (song)
62, 64
Imagine (LP)
96
Inert Lightnin' (song)
65, 67
The Inner Light (song)
55, 67, 180, 255, 305, 307
It's All Too Much (song)
113
It's Just For You (song)
94
I've Got A Feeling (song)
37, 37, 77, 92, 92, 94, 95, 108, 109

I've Got To Find My Baby (song)
123
Jealous Guy (song)
93, 95, 96, 97
Johnny & The Moondogs: Silver Days Air Time (LP)
41, 87, 168, 170
Johnny B. Goode (song)
49, 94, 139, 141
Judy! Judy! (song)
65, 67
Judy (LP)
65, 168, 171
Julia (song)
159, 160
Kansas City (song)
34, 71
Kansas City/Hey-Hey-Hey-Hey (song)
43, 83, 128, 129, 141, 142, 143, 146
Keep Your Hands Off My Baby (song)
49, 116
Kennedy Airport: Arrival Of Beatles Plane (LP track)
137
Kennedy Airport: Interview With Teenagers (LP track)
137
Kum Back (LP)
4
Lady Madonna (song)
40, 107, 156, 157, 160, 180, 253, 255, 305, 307
Lady Mother (song)
65
Lalena (song)
51
Land Of Gisch (song)
51
Leave My Kitten Alone (song)
40, 41, 74, 75, 77, 101, 102, 150, 152
Lend Me Your Comb (song)
54, 59, 89, 125, 126
Let It Be (LP)
39, 51, 68, 75, 97, 150, 177
Let It Be (song)
39, 45, 80, 81, 92, 95, 108, 109, 180, 274, 276, 305, 307
Let It Be (By The Numbers) (song)
37
Like Dreamers Do (song)
13, 15, 73, 74, 166, 167
Little Queenie (song)
89
Lonesome Tears In My Eyes (song)
43, 58, 59, 128, 129
The Long And Winding Road (song)
67, 95, 178, 290, 292, 305, 307
Long Tall Sally (song)
24, 34, 47, 54, 62, 68, 71, 80, 106, 107, 120, 121, 123, 124, 130, 132, 141, 143, 143, 145, 147, 149

SONG & RECORD TITLE INDEX

The Lost BEEBs (LP)
 116, 117, 169, 171
Love Me Do (song)
 39, 41, 49, 55, 57, 61, 62, 71, 77,
 80, 123, 124, 132, 133, 134, 137,
 179, 183, 187, 188, 304, 306
Love Of The Loved (song)
 13, 32, 59, 73, 166, 166, 167, 167
Lucille (song)
 59, 68, 71, 73, 93, 133, 134, 134
Mad Man A Comin' (song)
 94
Maggie Mae (song)
 95
Magical Mystery Tour (LP)
 178
Magical Mystery Tour (song)
 106, 107, 113, 114, 288
Mailman Bring Me No More Blues (song)
 102, 103
Matchbox (song)
 54, 89, 128, 129, 142, 161
Maxwell's Silver Hammer (song)
 51, 67, 95, 111, 112
McCartney (LP)
 97
Mean Mr. Mustard (song)
 92, 109, 111, 112
Medley (Love Me Do, Please Please Me, From Me To You, She Loves You, I Want To Hold Your Hand) (song)
 49, 77, 80
Meet The BEEB (LP)
 116, 119, 120, 169, 171
Memphis (song)
 13, 54, 73, 74, 166, 167
Memphis, Tennessee (song)
 116, 117, 119, 123, 124, 125, 126,
 128, 129, 134, 135
Midnight Special (song)
 93
Minneapolis Press Conference (LP track)
 83
Misery (song)
 28, 68, 116, 117, 119, 121, 133, 150,
 152, 153, 154
Momma You've Been On My Mind (song)
 37, 39, 92, 96, 109
Money (song)
 15, 41, 43, 45, 68, 71, 73, 85, 87,
 93, 119, 137, 138, 139, 166, 167
Money (That's What I Want) (song)
 117, 119, 120, 125, 126
Mr. Wind (song)
 51

Murray The K: Interview (LP track)
 137
My Bonnie (song)
 58
My Evelyne (song)
 116, 117
Negro In Reserve (song)
 75, 93
The Night Before (song)
 147
1967 (LP)
 113, 169, 170
No. 3 Abbey Road (LP)
 51, 111, 112, 168, 170
No. 9 Dream (song)
 40
No No Song (song)
 26
No Pakistanis (song)
 37, 92, 108
No Particular Place To Go (song)
 94, 97
Norwegian Wood (song)
 37, 40, 41, 150, 152, 156, 157, 158
Not Fade Away (song)
 74
Not For Sale (LP)
 77, 79, 84, 114, 168, 170
Not Guilty (song)
 79, 80, 99, 101, 102, 103, 156, 157,
 159
Not Guilty: The Beatles (LP)
 79
Nothin' Shakin' (But The Leaves On The Tree) (song)
 43, 58, 128, 129
Nothing Is Easy (song)
 57
Nothing Is Real (LP)
 99, 101, 114, 168, 170
Nowhere Man (song)
 65, 88, 295, 305, 307
Ob-La-Di, Ob-La-Da (song)
 93, 95, 106, 107
Octopus's Garden (song)
 51, 67, 94, 111, 112
Off White (CD)
 160
Off White (LP)
 159, 169, 171
Oh Carol (song)
 59
Oh Darling (song)
 51, 107, 108, 111, 112
Old Brown Shoe (song)
 180, 267, 269, 270, 305, 307
On Our Way Back Home (song)
 92, 108
On Our Way Home (song)
 95, 97

SONG & RECORD TITLE INDEX

One After 909 (song)
37, 40, 41, 75, 77, 79, 92, 93, 95, 102, 103, 109, 149, 150, 163
The One After 909 Ver. 1 (song)
161
The One After 909 Ver.2 (song)
161
One And One Is Two (song)
153, 156, 156
Only A Northern Song (song)
45, 113, 114
Ooh! My Soul (song)
50, 130, 132
Original Audition Tape - Circa 1962 (LP)
58, 59, 73, 168, 171
The Original Greatest Hits (LP)
61, 67, 168, 170
Outtakes Vol. 1 (LP)
68, 73, 168, 171
Outtakes Vol. 2 (LP)
71, 168, 171
Paperback Writer (song)
40, 57, 65, 77, 79, 80, 88, 149, 152, 157, 158, 159, 180, 231, 233, 304, 306
Paul & Rich Duet (song)
94
Penina (song)
92, 109
Penny Lane (song)
28, 30, 40, 47, 55, 57, 113, 114, 149, 150, 166, 167, 180, 242, 304, 306
People Say (song)
62, 64
Piano Boogie (song)
67
A Picture Of You (song)
116, 117
Please Don't Ever Change (song)
58, 59
Please Mr. Postman (song)
43, 61, 116, 117, 119, 128, 129, 139, 141
Please Please Me (LP)
124
Please Please Me (song)
45, 47, 49, 61, 62, 71, 77, 80, 83, 94, 116, 120, 121, 130, 134, 137, 179, 188, 190, 191, 304, 306
Polythene Pam (song)
95, 111, 112
Pop Go The Beatles (song)
54, 125, 126, 128, 128, 130
P.S. I Love You (song)
125, 126, 179, 185, 187, 304, 306
Quarrymen Rehearse With Stu Sutcliffe Spring 1960 (LP)
161, 169, 171

Rain (song)
40, 65, 79, 80, 81, 157, 180, 233, 304, 306
Raspberry Gardens (song)
67
The Really Big Shew (EP)
34, 166, 167
Return To Abbey Road (LP)
111, 169, 170
Revolution (song)
7, 45, 62, 64, 99, 101, 160, 166, 167, 180, 257, 259, 261, 305, 307
The Right String, But Wrong Yo Yo (song)
93
Rock And Roll Music (song)
43, 64, 87, 145, 146
Roll Over Beethoven (song)
41, 47, 61, 64, 68, 71, 80, 85, 87, 89, 94, 106, 107, 108, 123, 124, 130, 132, 137, 138, 139, 139, 141
Round & Round (song)
94
Rudolf The Red-Nosed Reindeer (song)
137
The Saints (song)
58
Sally Ann (song)
134
Save The Last Dance For Me (song)
95, 97
Searchin' (song)
13, 15, 73, 166, 167
September In The Rain (song)
10, 73, 166, 167
Sessions (CD)
103
Sessions (LP)
101, 107, 168, 170
Sexie Sadie (song)
159, 160
Sgt. Pepper Inner Groove (song)
55
Sgt. Pepper's Lonely Hearts Club Band (LP)
47, 113, 176, 177, 178
Sgt. Pepper's Lonely Hearts Club Band (picture disc)
177
Sgt. Pepper's Lonely Hearts Club Band (song)
274, 283, 285, 305, 307
Sgt. Pepper's Lonely Hearts Club Band Reprise (song)
285
Shake, Rattle & Roll (song)
74
Shaking In The Sixties (song)
37, 92, 109

She Came In Through The Bathroom
    Window (song)
    37, 92, 93, 94, 109, 109, 111, 112
She Loves You (song)
    21, 34, 41, 49, 61, 64, 71, 77, 80,
    83, 85, 130, 132, 133, 134, 135, 137,
    138, 147, 180, 197, 199, 221, 304,
    306
She Said, She Said (song)
    92, 109
Sheik Of Araby (song)
    10, 73, 166, 167
She's A Woman (song)
    40, 54, 55, 64, 87, 88, 106, 107, 108,
    145, 146, 147, 149, 149, 150, 153,
    154, 156, 180, 215, 304, 306
She's Got The Devil In Her Heart
    (song)
    71
Short Fat Fanny (song)
    93
A Shot Of Rhythm And Blues (song)
    58, 59, 116, 117, 119, 125, 126
A Shot Of Rhythm And Blues (Live)
    (song)
    59, 61
Shout (song)
    62, 64, 77
Side By Side (song)
    120, 121
Sie Liebt Dich (song)
    47, 49, 55
Singing The Blues (song)
    93
Slippin' And Sliddin' (song)
    26
Slow Down (song)
    58, 130
So How Come (No One Loves Me)
    (song)
    43, 128, 129
Soldier Of Love (song)
    54, 95, 125, 126
Some Days (song)
    161
Some Other Guy (song)
    49, 116, 120, 121, 123
Something (song)
    51, 111, 180, 270, 305, 307
Souvenir Of Their Visit To America
    (EP)
    28, 166, 167
Spoken (song)
    103
Stand By Me (song)
    30, 92, 109
Starting Over (song)
    178
Strawberry Fields Forever (song)
    28, 40, 41, 45, 64, 99, 101, 113, 114,
    149, 150, 157, 158, 159, 166, 167,
    180, 181, 240, 242, 304, 306

Sun King (song)
    93, 96, 111, 112
Sure To Fall (song)
    15, 54, 73, 125, 126, 133, 134, 166,
    167
Sure To Fall (In Love With You) (song)
    141, 142
Suzy Parker (song)
    92, 108
Sweet Apple Trax (LP)
    4
Sweet Little Sixteen (song)
    50, 94, 128, 129
Take Good Care Of My Baby (song)
    73, 134
Take This Hammer (song)
    94
Talkin' Bout You (song)
    89
A Taste Of Honey (song)
    28, 89, 120, 121, 123, 125, 126, 133,
    153, 154
Tea For Two (song)
    93
Teddy Boy (song)
    95, 97
Television Outtakes (EP)
    26, 166, 167
Tennessee (song)
    39, 91, 108
Thank You Girl (song)
    55, 120, 121, 123, 124, 179, 195,
    304, 306
That Means A Lot (song)
    75, 102, 150, 152
That'll Be The Day (song)
    161, 163
That's All Right (song)
    106, 107
That's All Right Mama (song)
    50, 125, 126
There's A Place (song)
    50, 71, 116, 125, 126, 130, 132, 149,
    152, 153, 154
There's Nothin' Shakin'
    59
Things We Said Today (song)
    24, 36, 62, 64, 143, 145, 180, 212,
    304, 306
Thinking Of Linking (song)
    161
Third Man Theme (song)
    74, 93
This Boy (song)
    43, 55, 83, 137, 138, 139, 141, 180,
    203, 304, 306
This Guy (song)
    65
Three Cool Cats (song)
    10, 73, 93, 166, 167

SONG & RECORD TITLE INDEX

Ticket To Ride (song)
  40, 43, 45, 83, 84, 85, 103, 106, 106,
  107, 147, 153, 154, 180, 219, 288,
  304, 306
Tie Me Kangaroo Down, Sport (song)
  137, 138
Till There Was You (song)
  18, 21, 34, 54, 68, 73, 74, 81, 89,
  117, 123, 124, 128, 129, 134, 137,
  138, 139, 141, 166, 167
To Know Her Is To Love Her (song)
  50, 58, 59, 61, 73, 89, 128, 129
To Know Him Is To Love Him (song)
  18, 166, 167
Too Bad About Sorrows (song)
  92, 94, 109
Too Much Monkey Business (song)
  49, 116, 120, 121, 123, 123, 124,
  132, 134
Top Of The Pops (EP)
  24, 145, 166, 167
Top Of The Pops (LP)
  62, 168, 171
True Love (song)
  93
12 Bar Original (song)
  153, 154
Twickenham Jams (EP)
  30, 166, 167
Twist And Shout (song)
  21, 40, 41, 47, 61, 62, 68, 80, 83,
  85, 103, 106, 106, 107, 108, 120,
  121, 125, 126, 128, 129, 130, 132,
  133, 134, 135, 147, 280, 305, 307
Two Of Us (song)
  37, 37, 92, 93, 93, 95, 96, 97, 109
Ultra Rare Trax (6-LP series)
  154, 156, 157, 158, 159
Ultra Rare Trax Vol. 1 (CD)
  152
Ultra Rare Trax Vol. 2 (CD)
  152
Ultra Rare Trax Vol. 1 & Vol. 2 (2 LPs)
  114, 149, 156, 169, 170
Ultra Rare Trax Vol. 3 & Vol. 4 (2 LPs)
  153, 169, 170
Ultra Rare Trax Vol. 5 & Vol. 6 (2 LPs)
  156, 169, 170
The Unicorn (song)
  51
The Walrus And The Carpenter (song)
  51
Watching Rainbows (song)
  93, 109
We Can Work It Out (song)
  150, 152, 153, 154, 179, 180, 227,
  228, 229, 304, 306

We Love You Beatles (song)
  80
What A Shame Mary Jane Had A Pain At The Party (song)
  47
What's The New Mary Jane (song)
  101, 102, 157, 158, 160
When I'm Sixty Four (song)
  95
When You Get To Suzy Parker Everybody Gets Well Done (song)
  37
When Your Heartaches Begin (song)
  161
Where Have You Been All My Life (song)
  89
While My Guitar Gently Weeps (song)
  40, 41, 99, 101, 102, 103, 160
Whit Monday To You (song)
  141
"The White Album" (2 LPs)
  80, 109, 160
White Power (song)
  91, 108
White Power Promenade (song)
  39
Whole Lotta Shakin (song)
  93
WINS Radio, New York: Beatles Sweatshirt Plug (LP track)
  137
Winston, Richard, And John (song)
  92, 108
With A Little Help From My Friends (song)
  281, 283, 285, 305, 307
Woman (song)
  94, 97
Words Of Love (song)
  50, 71, 130, 132
The WWDC Interview (LP track)
  83
Yellow Submarine (LP)
  114
Yellow Submarine (song)
  180, 235, 304, 306
Yer Blues (song)
  159, 160
Yes It Is (song)
  45, 77, 79, 106, 107, 153, 154, 180,
  221, 304, 306
Yesterday (song)
  64, 65, 83, 84, 85, 87, 88, 297, 300,
  305, 307
You Can't Do That (song)
  62, 93, 139, 141, 141, 142, 143, 145,
  147, 180, 208, 304, 306
You Got Me Thinking (song)
  94

SONG & RECORD TITLE INDEX

You

You Just Don't Understand (song)
 161
You Know My Name (Look Up The Number) (song)
 55, 180, 276, 305, 307
You Must Lie Everyday (song)
 161, 163
You Never Give Me Your Money (song)
 51, 111, 112
You Really Got A Hold On Me (song)
 41, 67, 68, 85, 123, 125, 130, 133
You Win Again (song)
 32, 93, 109

You've

You'll Be Mine (song)
 161
Youngblood (song)
 49, 123, 124
Your Feets Too Big (song)
 89
Your Mother Should Know (song)
 77, 79, 113
You're Going To Lose That Girl (song)
 79, 81
You've Got To Hide Your Love Away (song)
 288

People, Places & Things Index

Abbey Road Studios
40, 150, 154
Apple Records
176, 178, 179, 180, 264, 265, 267, 272, 274, 276
Around The Beatles (TV special)
49, 77, 80, 107, 108
Badfinger
75, 102
"Ban The Beatles" (radio campaign)
26
Barber, Adrian
89
Barber, Chris
77
BBC Radio
36, 50, 54, 58, 59, 68, 71, 73, 107, 108, 117, 119, 120, 124, 128, 129, 132, 133, 147
Beatlefan (magazine)
3
The Beatles Again (book)
85
The Beatles At Abbey Road Studios (multimedia show)
40
The Beatles At Shea (TV special)
106
The Beatles At The BEEB (radio special)
4, 50, 54
Beatles For Sale (recording sessions)
152
The Beatles (Invite You To Take A Ticket To Ride) (radio show)
147
The Beatles: Recording Sessions (book)
156, 57
The Bee Gees
179
BEEB Transcription Records
116, 120, 123, 125, 128, 130, 132, 134, 137, 139, 141, 145, 147, 153, 156
Berry, Chuck
121, 124
Best, Pete
13, 43, 74, 116, 117, 119, 151
Billboard (magazine)
179
Brown, Joe
134
Budokan Martial Arts Hall
65, 88, 91
"Butcher Cover"
47
Capitol Records
24, 28, 30, 45, 47, 55, 57, 62, 64, 84, 177, 178, 179, 181, 183, 187, 188, 199, 203, 206, 208, 211, 214, 215, 219, 221, 223, 224, 225, 227, 229, 231, 232, 233, 235, 237, 239, 240, 242, 243, 245, 246, 248, 249, 251, 253, 255, 257, 259, 262, 264, 265, 269, 270, 272, 274, 276, 280, 281, 285, 286, 288, 290, 292, 294, 295, 297, 301, 302
The Carefrees
80
Carver Corporation
308
Castleman, Harry
30, 85
Cavern Club
121
CBM Records
57
CBS Records
34
Chris Barber Band
77
Christ, Jesus
26, 49
Circuit Records
54, 73
Cleave, Maureen
26
Concerts for the People of Kampuchea
61
Condor Records
79, 103, 108, 156
Contra Band Music
67
Crudup, Big Boy
126
The David Frost Show (TV show)
7, 64
Davis, Malcolm
137
Decca Records
59, 74, 103, 124
Decca Tapes (recording sessions)
151, 163

327

PEOPLE, PLACES & THINGS INDEX

Deccagone

Deccagone Records
  10, 13, 15, 18, 21, 32, 61, 73, 79
Dexter, Dave, Jr.
  217
Discwasher
  308
Disques du Monde
  103
Do You Want To Know A Secret (book)
  4, 5, 21, 24, 34, 39, 41, 51, 54, 55, 67, 73, 74, 77, 81, 85, 91, 99, 101, 106, 123, 125, 128, 130, 132, 137
Dream Records
  49
Dylan, Bob
  39
Easy Beat (radio show)
  117, 120, 121, 135
Ed Sullivan Show (TV show)
  26, 34, 81, 83, 84
E.H.M.V. Records
  79
EMI Records
  3, 4, 40, 77, 103, 161, 175, 176, 177, 179
Empire Pool, Wembley
  85
Epstein, Brian
  26
Everly Brothers
  134
"Everything You Always Wanted To Know About Bootlegs, But Were Too Busy Collecting Them To Ask" (essay)
  6
Exclusive Beatles Interview Records
  24
Fixing A Hole (book)
  5, 47, 57, 62, 65, 113, 116, 117, 139, 141, 143, 153, 156, 159, 161
Freeman, Clive
  91
From Me To You (recording sessions)
  150
From Us To You (radio show)
  137, 138, 139, 141, 142, 143, 145
Frost, David
  7, 64
Fut Records
  30
Gnat Records
  74
Greatest Hits Records
  61
A Hard Day's Night (film)
  75
A Hard Day's Night (recording sessions) 152

Micro-Acoustics

Harris, Rolf
  138
Heathrow Airport
  141
Help (recording sessions)
  151
Here We Go Again (radio show)
  116, 119
Highway Records
  62
HMV Records
  111
Hollywood Bowl
  64, 65
Hopkin, Mary
  75
Horweite Stereophile Records
  51
Huebers, Bettina
  91
Indra Club
  68
James, Tommy
  26
Joe Brown and his Bruvers
  134
Kaiserkeller
  68
King, L.R.E.
  4, 5
Kramer, Billy J.
  121
Kustom Records
  65
Lemay, J.
  178
Let It Be (film)
  109
Let It Be (recording sessions)
  32, 102, 107, 108, 111, 112
Lewisohn, Mark
  156, 57
Little Richard
  132
Maclen Records
  159
Magical Mystery Tour (film)
  113, 114
Magical Mystery Tour (recording sessions)
  114, 151
Martin, George
  7, 41, 99, 152, 158, 159
Matthew, Brian
  141
McCartney, Mike
  163
Micro-Acoustics
  308

PEOPLE, PLACES & THINGS INDEX

Mobile Fidelity Sound Lab
  40, 178, 308
Monitor Audio
  308
Monster Cable
  308
Murray the K
  64, 106, 137, 138
Mystery Tour '76 (convention)
  7
Nelson, Rick
  134
NEMS Records
  77, 81, 106, 107
New Musical Express Awards Show
  107, 108
New Musical Express 1963-64 Annual Poll-Winners All Star Concert
  147, 149
New Musical Express 1964-65 Annual Poll-Winners All-Star Concert
  147, 149
Odeon Records
  176, 178, 183, 185, 188, 190, 193, 195, 197, 198, 199, 203, 205, 208, 211, 212, 214, 215, 219, 221, 223, 225, 227, 229, 231, 233, 235, 237, 240, 242, 245, 246, 249, 251, 253, 255, 257, 259, 262, 264, 265, 267, 270, 272, 274, 276, 277, 280, 281, 285, 286, 288, 297, 301
Ohm Acoustics
  308
"One World One People"
  178
Original Master (record sleeve)
  308
Orsonic
  308
Our World (TV special)
  113, 114, 158, 57
Parlophone Records
  101, 102, 113, 177, 178, 179, 180, 183, 185, 188, 190, 193, 195, 197, 198, 199, 203, 205, 208, 211, 212, 214, 215, 219, 221, 223, 225, 227, 229, 231, 233, 235, 237, 240, 242, 245, 246, 249, 251, 253, 255, 257, 259, 262, 264, 265, 267, 270, 272, 274, 276, 277, 280, 281, 285, 286, 288, 290, 292, 294, 295, 297, 301
People (magazine)
  91
Peter and Gordon
  97
Phase Linear
  308
"Phil + Ronnie"
  178
Plaza Hotel
  137
Please Please Me (recording sessions)
  150, 151
Podrazik, Wally
  30, 85
Polythene Pam
  112
Pop Go The Beatles (radio show)
  119, 124, 125, 126, 128, 129, 130, 133
Portrait Records
  178
Pre Beatle Records
  161
Presley, Elvis
  126
Preston, Billy
  262
Prince of Wales Theatre
  21
Proby, P.J.
  152
Pyramid Records
  123, 125, 126, 129, 132, 134, 135, 138, 141, 143, 145, 146, 149
The Quarrymen
  150, 161
Radio Luxembourg
  59
Rediffusion Television
  80
Reinhart, Charles
  4, 5, 68
Ricker, Stand
  178
Rockestra
  61
Royal Command Performance
  21
The Royal Variety Performance (radio show)
  135
Royal Variety Show
  21
Rubber Soul (recording sessions)
  150, 152
Rudy, Derrick
  81, 84
Ruthles Rhymes Records
  34
Saturday Club (radio show)
  116, 117, 119, 120, 121, 123, 124, 135, 137, 138, 139, 142, 146
Saturday Night Fever (film)
  179
Saturday Night Live (TV show)
  26
Savage Records
  85, 87, 89
Schultheiss, Tom
  6

329

Sgt. Pepper (recording sessions)
114
Shannon, Mike
156
Shindig (TV show)
83
Shirley
112
Side By Side (radio show)
120, 123, 124
Simon, Paul
26
Spector, Phil
97
Star Club
68, 89, 91
STASH Records
149
Stax, Inc.
308
Steppin' Out (radio show)
121, 121
The Strangers with Mike Shannon
156
Strawberry Fields Forever (fan magazine)
7, 10, 13, 15, 18, 21, 64
Sullivan, Ed
26, 34, 81, 83, 84, 106
Swingin' Pig Records
152, 153, 156
Swinging Sound '63 (radio show)
120, 121
TAKRL Records
37, 47, 64, 88
TMOQ Records
68, 71
Taylor, Ted "Kingsize"
89
Teenagers Turn (radio show)
116, 119
Tiger Beat Records
117

Tobe-Milo Records
26
Top Gear (radio show)
143, 146
Top of the Pops (radio show)
64
Top Ten Club
68
Trade Mark of Quality Records
91, 103
Twickenham Film Studios
39, 81, 96, 97
V.R.P. (record sleeve)
308
Vee, Bobby
134
Vee Jay Records
28
Vewy Queen Weccods
21
WINS (radio station)
137
WQAM (radio station)
83
WWDC (radio station)
83, 84
Wally
178
Warwick Records
41
Watts, Inc.
308
Webb, Bernard
97
Wizardo Records
58, 59
Wohlers, Erika
91
You Can't Do That (book)
4, 5, 6, 7, 10, 13, 15, 18, 21, 24, 26, 28, 30, 32, 34, 37, 39, 47, 51, 54, 55, 57, 59, 61, 62, 64, 65, 67, 68, 71, 73